Study Guide

Management Accounting

SEVENTH EDITION

Don R. Hansen
Oklahoma State University

Maryanne M. Mowen
Oklahoma State University

Prepared by

Donna K. Ulmer, MBA, Ph.D.
St. Louis Community College

THOMSON
SOUTH-WESTERN

Australia · Canada · Mexico · Singapore · Spain · United Kingdom · United States

THOMSON
SOUTH-WESTERN

Study Guide to accompany Management Accounting, 7e
By Don R. Hansen and Maryanne M. Mowen

Prepared by Donna K. Ulmer

Vice President/Editorial Director
Jack Calhoun

Vice President/Editor-in-Chief
George Werthman

Publisher
Rob Dewey

Acquisitions Editor
Jennifer Codner

Sr. Developmental Editor
Ken Martin

Sr. Production Editor
Tim Bailey

Manager of Technology Solutions
Jim Rice

Technology Project Editor
Sally Nieman

Media Editor
Kelly Reid

Editorial Assistant
Janice Hughes

Sr. Design Project Manager
Michelle Kunkler

Manufacturing Coordinator
Doug Wilke

Cover Design
Beckmeyer Design
Cincinnati, OH

Internal Design
Christy Carr

Photo Manager
Deanna Ettinger

Cover Images
© Terry Vine/The Image Bank,
© David Lees/Taxi,
© Getty Images, Inc.

Printer
Globus Printing

ISBN: 0-324-23488-0

Printed in the United States of America

1 2 3 4 5 08 07 06 05 04

For more information, contact South-Western, 5191 Natorp Boulevard, Mason, OH 45040; or find us on the World Wide Web at http://www.swlearning.com

Contents

To the Student

This study guide, a supplement to *Management Accounting, Seventh Edition,* by Don R. Hansen and Maryanne M. Mowen, is designed to assist you in reviewing important concepts and testing your understanding of the material. The study guide contains the following:

- **CHAPTER REVIEW.** A summary of the important points in each chapter.
- **KEY TERMS TEST.** A test of your understanding of the key terms in each chapter.
- **CHAPTER QUIZ.** Multiple choice, true-false, and completion questions to test your comprehension of the chapter material.
- **PRACTICE TEST.** A test of your ability to apply the concepts.
- **ANSWERS.** Suggested solutions, which appear at the end of each chapter.

The following 5-step sequence is recommended to make the most effective use of your study time:

1. Read the assigned chapter in the text.
2. Read the Chapter Review in the study guide. Add your notes or questions to the Chapter Review.
3. Complete the Key Terms Test, Chapter Quiz, and Practice Test in the study guide.
4. Review any difficult topics, if necessary.
5. Prepare text exercises and problems assigned by your instructor.

Additional suggestions to assist you in your course preparation are as follows:

- Try to understand the important concepts and how they are applied. Do not try to memorize formulas and plug in numbers without first understanding *why* the formulas work.
- Ask questions when you do not understand. If you do not understand something, write your questions down so that you can ask at a later time. Simply formulating the questions may help you clarify your thinking.
- Always attempt to answer questions and problems before looking at the solution. This tests your understanding of the material and indicates the areas that need further study.

Best wishes for your continued college success,
Donna Ulmer

CHAPTER 1

Introduction: The Role, History, and Direction of Management Accounting

CHAPTER REVIEW

MANAGEMENT ACCOUNTING INFORMATION SYSTEM

- The **management accounting information system** has three broad objectives:
  1. To provide information for costing services, products, and other objects of interest to management.
  2. To provide information for planning, controlling, evaluation, and continuous improvement.
  3. To provide information for decision making.

Information Needs of Managers and Other Users

- Accounting information can be used to:
  - identify problems
  - identify solutions to problems
  - evaluate the effectiveness of decisions, such as continuous improvement efforts
- **Continuous improvement** involves searching for ways to increase overall efficiency and productivity of activities by reducing waste, increasing quality, and reducing costs. Information is needed to:
  1. identify opportunities for improvement, and
  2. evaluate progress made in implementing actions to create improvement.
- The need for greater accuracy has produced an improved management accounting information system called an *activity-based cost management information system.*
- **Strategic decision making** is choosing among alternative strategies with the goal of selecting one or more strategies that provide a company with a reasonable assurance of long-term growth and survival.

The Management Process

- The management process includes three activities:
  - planning
  - controlling
  - decision making
- Managers and empowered workers participate in the management process. **Employee empowerment** authorizes operational personnel to plan, control, and make decisions without explicit authorization from middle- and higher-level management. It is based on the belief that the employee closest to the work can provide valuable input in ideas, plans, and problem solving.

❒ The management process is summarized below:

Management Process

Planning

- Setting objectives
- Identifying ways to achieve the objectives
- Example: budgets

Controlling

- Monitoring a plan's implementation
- **Feedback** is information used to evaluate or correct implementation of a plan.
- Based on feedback, a manager might:
  - continue the implementation as originally planned
  - take corrective action if needed, or
  - modify the plan.
- Example: **performance reports**, which are accounting reports that provide feedback by comparing actual results with plans

Decision Making

- Choosing among competing alternatives
- Example: deciding the selling price of products

MANAGEMENT ACCOUNTING AND FINANCIAL ACCOUNTING

❒ The accounting information system within an organization has two major subsystems:
- a management accounting system
- a financial accounting system

Accounting Information System

	Management Accounting Information System	**Financial Accounting Information System**
Targeted user:	internal users managers	external users stockholders and creditors
Restrictions:	no mandatory rules for preparing reports	must follow GAAP when preparing financial statements
Types of information:	financial and nonfinancial information	financial information
Time orientation:	emphasizes the future (planning and decision making)	historical orientation (reports what has already occurred)
Aggregation:	detailed information about product line, departments, etc.	information about overall firm performance

- The accounting system should be flexible enough to supply different information for different users and different purposes. Frequently the reports of both management accounting and financial accounting are derived from the same database, which was originally established to support the reporting requirements of financial accounting. Many organizations need to redesign this database in order to satisfy more fully the needs of internal users.

CURRENT FOCUS OF MANAGEMENT ACCOUNTING

- Changes in the competitive environment require innovative and relevant management accounting practices.
- Management accounting must provide information so that managers can focus on:
  - customer value
  - total quality management
  - time-based competition

Activity-Based Management

- **Activity-based management** is an approach where managers focus on *activities* with the objective of improving customer value and resulting profits.
- Activity-based management emphasizes:
  1. *activity-based costing (ABC)*, which improves the accuracy of cost information by tracing costs first to activities and then to products or customers that consume the activities.
  2. *process value analysis*, which focuses on:
     - eliminating activities that do not add customer value, and
     - performing necessary activities more efficiently.

Customer Orientation

- **Customer value** is the difference between what a customer receives (customer realization) and what the customer gives up (customer sacrifice). Increasing customer value means:
  - increasing what the customer receives (such as product features, service, quality, training) and/or
  - decreasing what the customer gives up (such as purchase cost, time to learn to use the product, postpurchase costs of using and maintaining the product).
- **Strategic cost management** uses cost data to identify and develop superior strategies to produce a sustainable competitive advantage. Two strategies are:
  1. cost leadership strategy—providing the same or better customer value for a *lower cost* than competitors.
  2. product differentiation strategy—providing *better customer value* for the same or lower cost than competitors.
- The **internal value chain** consists of activities required to design, develop, produce, market, and deliver products and services to customers. Emphasizing customer value forces managers to determine which activities add value to customers.
- The **industrial value chain** is the linked set of value-creating activities from basic raw materials to final disposal by end-use customers. One firm may not span the entire industrial value chain. Instead, different firms may participate in different segments of the industrial value chain.

- The *internal value chain* is a particular firm's portion of the *industrial value chain.*
- There are two types of activity linkages:
  1. **Internal linkages**—relationships of activities performed *within* a firm's portion of the industrial value chain (the internal value chain).
  2. **External linkages**—relationships of a firm's activities with activities of suppliers and customers (supplier linkages and customer linkages).
- The objective of successful strategic cost management is to manage these linkages better than competitors in order to create a competitive advantage.

Cross-Functional Perspective

- Emphasis on the value chain means that today's management accountant must understand many functions of the business, from manufacturing to marketing to distribution to customer service.

Total Quality Management

- The twin objectives of world-class firms are:
  1. producing products with little waste, and
  2. producing products that perform according to specifications.
- **Total quality management** is an environment that enables workers to manufacture zero-defect products. A management accounting system provides quality cost measurement and reporting.

Time as a Competitive Element

- Time is a crucial element in all phases of the value chain.
- Decreasing nonvalue-added time appears to go hand in hand with increasing quality.
- Managers need information that enables them to respond quickly and decisively to changing market conditions.

E-Business

- **Electronic business (e-business)** is any business transaction or information exchange that is executed using information and communication technology. E-business facilitates value (supply) chain management.
- **Electronic commerce (e-commerce)** is buying and selling products using information and communication technology.

THE ROLE OF THE MANAGEMENT ACCOUNTANT

- Management accountants are responsible for identifying, collecting, measuring, analyzing, preparing, interpreting, and communicating information used by management to achieve the organization's objectives.
- The **controller** is the chief accounting officer and has responsibility for both internal and external accounting requirements. The controller may have direct responsibility for:
  - internal auditing
  - cost accounting
  - financial accounting (including SEC reports and financial statements)

- systems accounting (including analysis, design, and internal controls)
- taxes

❒ The **treasurer** raises capital and manages cash and investments.

MANAGEMENT ACCOUNTING AND ETHICAL CONDUCT

❒ One of the major goals of management accounting is to help managers increase the profitability of their organization.

❒ However, the objective of profit maximization should be constrained by the requirement that profits be achieved through legal and ethical means.

❒ The performance evaluation and reward system should be designed so that incentives to pursue undesirable behavior are minimized.

❒ The Standards of Ethical Conduct for Management Accountants address competence, confidentiality, integrity, and objectivity.

CERTIFICATION

❒ The Certificate in Management Accounting (CMA) examination emphasizes four areas: (1) economics, finance, and management; (2) financial accounting and reporting; (3) management reporting, analysis, and behavioral issues; and (4) decision analysis and information systems.

❒ The Certificate in Public Accounting (CPA) is the minimal professional qualification for external auditors who provide assurance concerning the reliability of a firm's financial statements.

❒ The Certified Internal Auditor (CIA) is certification for internal auditors.

KEY TERMS TEST

Test your recall of the key terms as follows. Try to recall as many key terms as possible without assistance. If you need assistance, refer to the list of key terms at the end of this section.

1. A(n) ____________ ____________ ____________ or ________ is an accountant certified to possess the minimal professional qualifications for an external auditor. This type of accountant provides assurance concerning the reliability of a firm's financial statements.

2. ____________ ____________ is the process of choosing among a set of competing alternatives.

3. ____________ ____________ results in choices or actions that are right and proper and just.

4. ____________ ____________ ____________ is choosing among alternative strategies with the goal of selecting one or more strategies that provide a company with a reasonable assurance of long-term growth and survival.

5. ____________ involves setting objectives and identifying methods to achieve those objectives.

6. The chief accountant of an organization is called the ____________.

7. ____________ is monitoring a plan using feedback to ensure the plan is being implemented as expected.

8. Information that can be used to evaluate or correct steps being taken to implement a plan is called ____________.

9. A(n) ____________ ____________ ____________ ____________ is an accounting information subsystem primarily concerned with producing information for external users.

10. A(n) ____________ ____________ ____________ ____________ is an information system that produces information to satisfy specific management objectives.

11. ____________ ____________ are reports that provide feedback to managers by comparing planned data with actual data.

12. The ____________ is responsible for the finance functions of raising capital and managing cash and investments.

13. ____________-____________ ____________ is a system-wide integrated approach that focuses management's attention on activities with the objective of improving customer value and the profit achieved by providing this value.

14. ____________ ____________ is the process of searching for ways of increasing the overall efficiency and productivity of activities by reducing waste, increasing quality, and reducing costs.

15. ____________ ____________ is the difference between what a customer receives and what a customer gives up.

16. The ____________ ____________ ____________ is the set of activities required to design, develop, produce, market, and deliver products and services to customers.

17. __________ ______________ ___________________ is an approach in which manufacturers strive to create an environment that will enable workers to manufacture perfect (zero-defect) products.

18. The costs of using, maintaining, and disposing of the product are ___________________ __________.

19. _______________ ___________________ involves authorizing operational personnel to plan, control, and make decisions without explicit authorization from middle- and higher-level management.

20. The _____________ __________ __________ is the linked set of value-creating activities from basic raw materials to end-use customers.

21. ____________ ____________ are the relationships of activities performed within a firm's portion of the industrial value chain.

22. The relationship of a firm's activities within its segment of the value chain with those activities of its suppliers and customers are ____________ ____________.

23. _________________ ______________ is buying and selling products using information and communication technology.

24. _________________ ______________ is any business transaction or information exchange that is executed using information and communication technology.

25. _____________ ___________ __________________ is the management of material flows beginning with suppliers and their upstream suppliers, moving to the transformation of materials into finished goods, and finishing with the distribution of finished goods to customers and their downstream customers.

KEY TERMS:

activity-based management
certified public accountant (CPA)
continuous improvement
controller
controlling
customer value
decision making
electronic business (e-business)
electronic commerce (e-commerce)
employee empowerment
ethical behavior
external linkages
feedback
financial accounting information system
industrial value chain
internal linkages
internal value chain
management accounting information system
performance reports
planning
postpurchase costs
strategic decision making
supply chain management
total quality management
treasurer

→ **Compare your answers with those at the end of the chapter. Review any key terms missed. If you missed several key terms, retake the Key Terms Test after reviewing.**

CHAPTER QUIZ

Write your answers in the spaces provided.

1. Complete the following:

Accounting Information System

	Management Accounting Information System	**Financial Accounting Information System**
Targeted user:		
Restrictions:		
Types of information:		
Time orientation:		
Aggregation:		

2. Managers need accounting information in order to be effective in fulfilling the management functions of:

   a. ______________________________

   b. ______________________________

   c. ______________________________

3. Control is the process of comparing ____________ ____________ with ____________.

4. Feedback is information that can be used to evaluate implementation of a plan. Based on feedback, a manager might take one of the following actions:

a. ____________________

b. ____________________

c. ____________________

5. A philosophy of total quality management is replacing the conventional philosophy of acceptable quality. Total quality management emphasizes:

a. ____________________

b. ____________________

6. The objective of maximizing profits should be constrained by ____________ and ____________ considerations.

Circle the single best answer.

7. Developing a cash budget for next year is an example of the management function of: (a) planning; (b) control; (c) decision making; (d) none of the above

8. Determining whether to buy new production equipment is an example of: (a) planning; (b) control; (c) decision making; (d) none of the above

9. Management accountants are considered: (a) line positions; (b) staff positions

10. Marketing is considered a: (a) line position; (b) staff position

→ **Compare your answers with those at the end of the chapter. Review any questions missed.**

ANSWERS

KEY TERMS TEST

1. certified public accountant, CPA
2. Decision making
3. Ethical behavior
4. Strategic decision making
5. Planning
6. controller
7. Controlling
8. feedback
9. financial accounting information system
10. management accounting information system
11. Performance reports
12. treasurer
13. Activity-based management
14. Continuous improvement
15. Customer value
16. internal value chain
17. Total quality management
18. postpurchase costs
19. Employee empowerment
20. industrial value chain
21. Internal linkages
22. external linkages
23. Electronic commerce
24. Electronic business
25. Supply chain management

CHAPTER QUIZ

1. See page 2.
2. **a.** planning
   b. controlling
   c. decision making
3. actual results, plans
4. **a.** continue the implementation as originally planned
   b. take corrective action
   c. modify the original plan
5. **a.** continual improvement
   b. elimination of waste
6. legal, ethical
7. a
8. c
9. b
10. a

CHAPTER 2
Basic Management Accounting Concepts

CHAPTER REVIEW

COST ASSIGNMENT: DIRECT TRACING, DRIVER TRACING, AND ALLOCATION

- ❒ An objective of a management accounting information system is to assign costs to products, services, and customers. Increasing the accuracy of cost assignment produces higher-quality information for decision making.

Cost

- ❒ A **cost** is the cash (or cash equivalent) value sacrificed for goods or services that are expected to produce current or future benefits.
- ❒ Firms achieve a competitive advantage by providing the same or greater customer value for lower cost than their competitors.
- ❒ An **opportunity cost** is the benefit given up when one alternative is chosen over another. Opportunity costs are not usually recorded in the accounting system; however, opportunity costs should be considered when evaluating alternatives for decision making.
- ❒ **Expenses** are *expired* costs. Expenses are costs that are used up when generating revenue.
- ❒ The selling price charged must exceed the cost so that sufficient income is earned for a firm to remain in business. Therefore, managers need to know the cost of products.

Cost Objects

- ❒ A **cost object** is any item such as products, departments, customers, and activities for which costs are measured and assigned.
- ❒ An **activity** is a basic unit of work performed within an organization. Activities are cost objects. Examples of activities include equipment setup, materials handling, and product inspection.

Accuracy of Assignments

- ❒ Distorted cost assignments can produce erroneous decisions.

Traceability

- ❒ **Traceability** is the ability to assign a cost to a cost object in an economically feasible way by means of a cause-and-effect relationship.
- ❒ The more costs that can be traced to a cost object, the greater the accuracy of the cost assignments.
- ❒ **Direct costs** can be easily and accurately traced to a cost object.
- ❒ **Indirect costs** cannot be easily and accurately traced to a cost object.

Methods of Tracing

- Tracing costs to cost objects can be done using:
  1. **direct tracing**, which identifies and assigns costs exclusively and physically associated with a cost object. (For example, wheels on a bicycle can be traced directly to the bicycle.)
  2. **driver tracing**, which uses drivers to assign costs to cost objects. **Drivers** are factors that cause changes in resource usage; there is a cause-and-effect relationship between the driver and cost.
- **Allocation** is used to assign indirect costs that cannot be traced to cost objects using direct tracing or driver tracing.
- Methods of cost assignment are summarized below:

Methods of Cost Assignment

	Direct Tracing	**Driver Tracing**	**Allocation**
Description:	identifying and assigning costs to a cost object that are specifically or physically associated with the cost object relies on physical observation	use of drivers to assign costs to cost objects	assignment of indirect costs to cost objects based on convenience or an assumed linkage
Cost assignment accuracy:	most precise	depends on the quality of the cause-and-effect relationship of the driver and cost	least accurate

PRODUCT AND SERVICE COSTS

- Two types of output of organizations are summarized below:

Output of Organizations

	Goods (tangible products)	**Services**
Definition:	goods produced by converting raw materials using labor and capital (plant, land, and machinery)	(1) activities performed for a customer or (2) activity performed by a customer using the organization's products or facilities
Examples:	laundry detergent television bicycles	accounting services dry cleaning services video rental
Organization:	Manufacturing organizations produce tangible products.	Service organizations produce intangible products.

Different Costs for Different Purposes

- **Product costs** consist of costs assigned to a product that satisfies a particular managerial objective. Since managerial objectives can differ, product cost definitions can differ—each depending on the managerial objective being served.
- Different cost information might be needed for internal managerial use than for external reporting.
- The **internal value chain** is the set of activities required to design, develop, produce, market, distribute, and service a product.
- A value-chain product cost consists of costs of the activities in the value chain that are assigned to the product.

Product Costs and External Financial Reporting

- For external product costing, costs are classified by the function they serve, as summarized below:

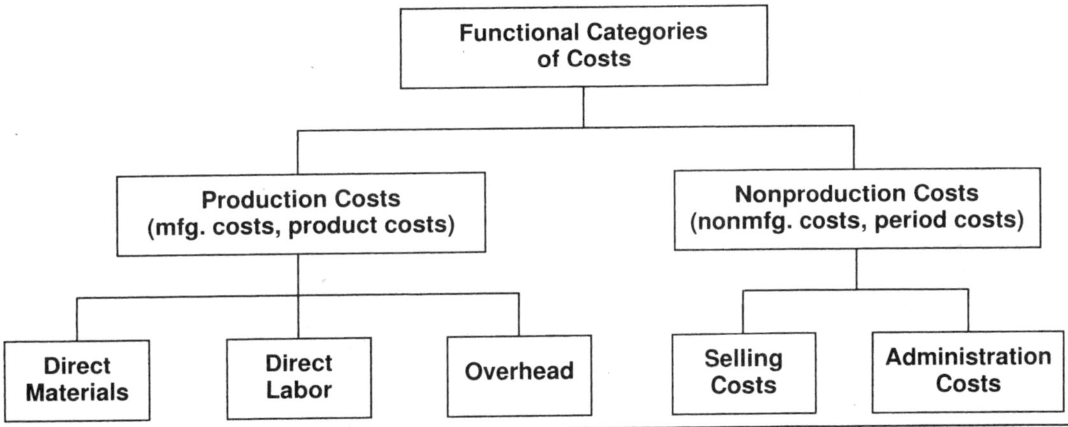

	Direct Materials	Direct Labor	Overhead	Selling Costs	Administration Costs
Definition:	materials traceable to goods or services produced become part of product	labor traceable to goods or services produced	all product costs other than direct materials and direct labor	costs to market, distribute, and service a product order-getting and order-filling costs	costs of research, development, and general administration
Examples:	wood in furniture	chef in restaurant, machine operator on assembly line	supervision, utilities, indirect materials, indirect labor	advertising, customer service	executive salaries, accounting, research and development

- Product costs, for external financial reporting, are manufacturing costs (direct materials, direct labor, and manufacturing overhead) that attach to the product and are first inventoried and then expensed when the product is sold.
- Period costs are nonproduction costs (selling and administrative) and are expensed when incurred.

Prime Costs and Conversion Costs

- **Prime costs** are direct materials costs and direct labor costs.
- **Conversion costs** are the costs of converting raw materials into a final product (direct labor costs and overhead costs).

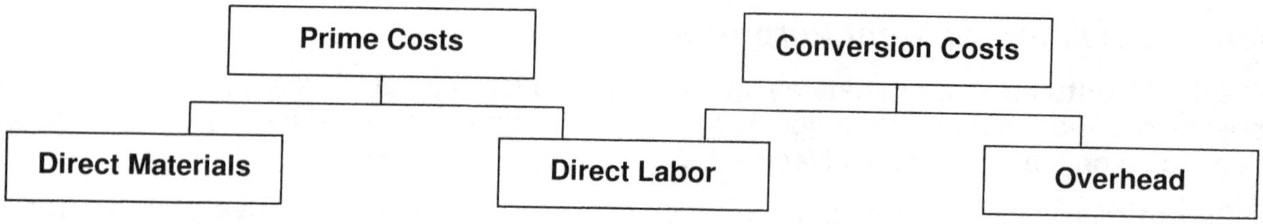

EXTERNAL FINANCIAL STATEMENTS

- The functional classification of costs is required for external reporting.
- Under absorption costing the two major functional categories of expenses are:
  1. cost of goods sold (production costs), and
  2. operating expenses (nonproduction costs).
- Production costs (direct materials, direct labor, and overhead) are product costs because these costs attach to the product.
- If the product is in inventory, the product cost is reported as inventory on the balance sheet.
- If the product has been sold, the product costs are recognized as an expense (cost of goods sold) on the income statement.
- Nonproduction costs (selling and administrative costs) are period costs that are expensed each period.

Income Statement: Manufacturing Firm

- Income computed using a functional classification frequently is referred to as **absorption-costing income** or **full-costing income** because all manufacturing costs are fully assigned or absorbed by the product.
- **Cost of goods sold** consists of the cost of direct materials, direct labor, and overhead attached to the units sold during a period.
- The **cost of goods manufactured** is the cost of direct materials, direct labor, and overhead attached to the units produced during a period.
- **Work in process** consists of all partially completed units in production.
- **Finished goods** are goods that are complete and ready for sale.
- Cost flows for a manufacturer are diagramed below:

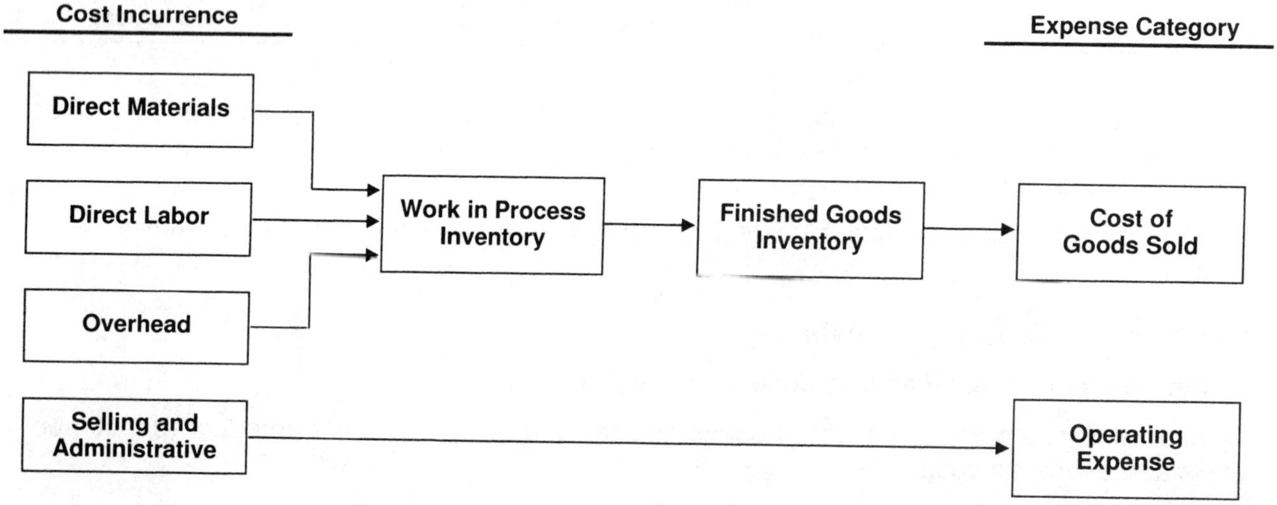

- As direct materials, direct labor, and manufacturing overhead are used in the production process, the associated costs are transferred to the Work-in-Process inventory account.
- As the goods in process are completed, the associated costs are transferred to the Finished Goods inventory account.
- As the goods are sold, the associated costs are transferred to the Cost of Goods Sold account. Thus, the product costs of direct materials, direct labor, and manufacturing overhead are not expensed until the goods are sold.
- A manufacturing firm might have three inventory accounts on the balance sheet:
    1. Raw Materials
    2. Work in Process
    3. Finished Goods

Income Statement: Service Organization

- Cost flows for a service firm are diagramed below:

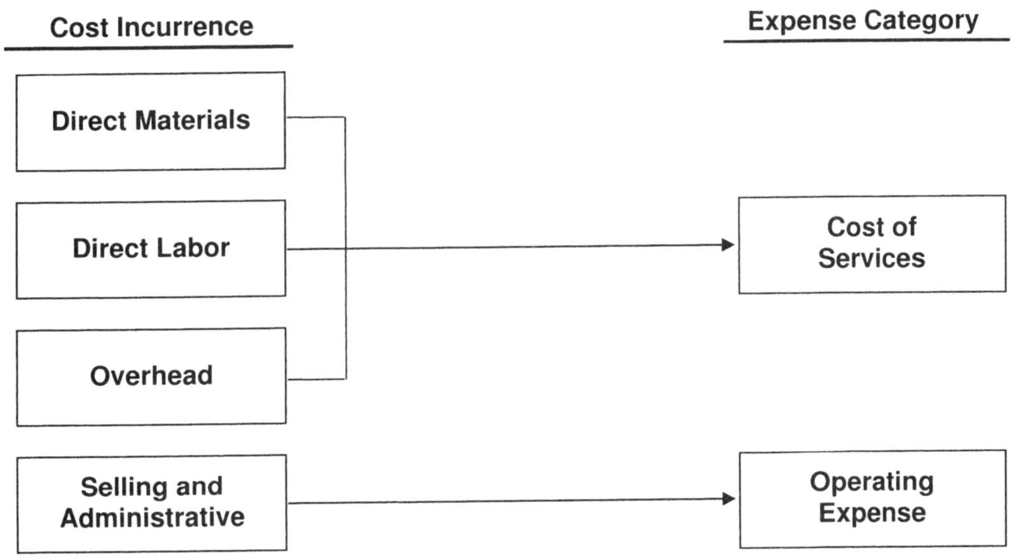

TYPES OF MANAGEMENT ACCOUNTING SYSTEMS

- Management accountings systems can be classified as follows:
    1. **Functional-based management (FBM) accounting system** is an accounting information system that emphasizes the use of functional organizational units to assign and manage costs. Functions, such as engineering and quality control, are grouped into functional units (e.g., departments or plants). When assigning costs, costs are assigned to functional units, such as departments, and then assigned to products.
        - **Functional-based costing (FBC)** assigns costs of shared resources to products and other cost objects using only **production** or **unit-level drivers** (drivers that are highly correlated with production output volume, such as direct hours or machine hours).
        - **Functional-based management (FBM)** attempts to manage costs by focusing on the efficiency of functional organizational subunits, such as departments.
    2. **Activity-based management (ABM) accounting system** is an accounting information system that emphasizes the use of activities for assigning and managing costs.

- **Activity-based costing (ABC)** traces costs to activities and then to products.
- **Activity-based management (ABM)** focuses on managing activities with an objective of increasing customer value and resulting profit.

❐ Functional-based and activity-based management accounting systems are compared below:

Functional-Based versus Activity-Based Management Accounting Systems

	Functional-Based Management Accounting System	**Activity-Based Management Accounting System**
Activity drivers:	unit-level drivers	unit- and nonunit-level drivers
Product cost assignment emphasis:	allocation	tracing
Product costing objective:	assign production costs to inventories and cost of goods sold for external reporting	external reporting and internal managerial use for planning, control, and decision making
Control:	focus on managing costs, emphasis on financial measures of performance	focus on managing activities, use both financial and nonfinancial measures of performance
Performance maximization emphasis:	maximization of individual unit performance	maximization of systemwide performance

KEY TERMS TEST

There are many new terms introduced in this chapter. The following is provided to assist you in reviewing the new terminology. Indicate which of the following terms best matches the statements listed below by placing the appropriate letter(s) in the blank preceding the statement.

KEY TERMS

A. activity
B. activity-based management
C. allocation
D. conversion cost
E. cost of goods manufactured
F. cost of goods sold
G. direct costs
H. direct labor
I. direct materials
J. direct tracing
K. driver tracing
L. expense
M. indirect costs
N. internal value chain
O. opportunity cost
P. overhead
Q. prime cost
R. product costs
S. service
T. work in process

DEFINITIONS

_____ **1.** Materials that can be traced to the good or service being produced.

_____ **2.** A cost assignment method that satisfies a well-specified managerial objective.

_____ **3.** Costs that are easily traceable to a cost object.

_____ **4.** Labor that is traceable to the goods or services being produced.

_____ **5.** Direct labor cost plus overhead cost.

_____ **6.** Direct materials cost plus direct labor cost.

_____ **7.** All production costs other than direct materials and direct labor.

_____ **8.** The cost of direct materials, direct labor, and overhead attached to the units sold.

_____ **9.** The cost of goods completed during the current period.

_____ **10.** The benefit sacrificed or foregone when one alternative is chosen instead of another.

_____ **11.** An expired cost.

_____ **12.** Costs that cannot be traced to a cost object.

_____ **13.** A basic unit of work performed within an organization.

_____ **14.** Assignment of indirect costs to cost objects.

_____ **15.** Process of identifying costs that are specifically or physically associated with a cost object.

_____ **16.** Use of drivers to assign costs to cost objects.

_____ **17.** Set of activities required to design, develop, produce, market, distribute, and service a product.

_____ **18.** A task or activity performed for a customer or an activity performed by a customer using an organization's products or facilities.

_____ **19.** A contemporary control system that focuses on the management of activities.

_____ **20.** All partially completed units in production.

Test your recall of the remaining key terms as follows. Try to recall as many key terms as possible without assistance. If you need assistance, refer to the list of key terms at the end of this section.

21. Costs which cannot be reasonably assigned to marketing or production categories are ________________ __________.

22. A(n) __________ is the cash or cash equivalent value sacrificed for goods and services expected to produce current or future benefits.

23. ______________-___________ income is computed using a functional classification.

24. Any item such as products, projects, or activities for which costs are measured and assigned is a(n) __________ ____________.

25. ________________ __________ are costs associated with selling and general administration.

26. ________________ is the ability to assign a cost directly to a cost object in an economically feasible way using a causal relationship.

27. ________________ or _______-_________ __________ are drivers that are highly correlated with production output.

28. ____________ are factors that cause changes in resource usage, activity usage, costs, and revenues.

29. ________________ __________ are costs necessary to market and distribute a product or service.

30. ________________ __________ are costs associated with the manufacture of goods or the provision of services.

31. ___________ is assigning costs to a cost object using an observable measure of the cost object's resource consumption.

32. A(n) ______________-_________ _________________ _______________ ____________ emphasizes the use of functional organizational units to assign and manage costs.

33. ______________-_________ _________________ assigns costs of shared resources to products and other cost objects using only production or unit-level drivers.

34. ______________-_________ _________________ is a managerial approach that attempts to control costs by focusing on the efficiency of organizational subunits.

35. A(n) ______________-_________ _________________ _______________ ____________ emphasizes the use of activities for assigning and managing costs.

36. ______________-_________ _________________ traces costs to activities and then to products.

37. ______________-_________ ____________ are drivers other than production drivers that describe cause-and-effect relationships.

KEY TERMS:

absorption costing
activity-based costing (ABC)
activity-based management accounting system
administrative costs
cost
cost object
drivers
functional-based costing (FBC)
functional-based management
functional-based management accounting system
marketing costs
nonproduction costs
nonunit-level drivers
production costs
production (unit-level) drivers
traceability
tracing

→ **Compare your answers with those at the end of the chapter. Review any key terms missed.**

CHAPTER QUIZ

Circle the single best answer.

1. Maytag is an example of a: (a) manufacturer; (b) merchandiser; (c) service company; (d) none of the above
2. Federal Express is an example of a: (a) manufacturer; (b) merchandiser; (c) service company; (d) none of the above
3. Cost of goods sold consists of the following costs: (a) direct materials only; (b) direct materials and direct labor only; (c) direct materials, direct labor, and variable overhead; (d) direct materials, direct labor, variable overhead, and fixed overhead
4. When absorption costing is used: (a) all manufacturing costs are viewed as product costs; (b) only variable manufacturing costs are viewed as product costs; (c) manufacturing and nonmanufacturing costs are viewed as product costs; (d) only direct materials and direct labor are viewed as product costs

Use the following information to answer Questions 5 through 8:

The Flowers Company costs at 50,000 units of production are:

Direct materials	$ 75,000
Direct labor	150,000
Overhead	140,000
Selling and administrative costs	90,000

Sales for the year totaled $700,000.

5. Total production costs equal: (a) $225,000; (b) $365,000; (c) $455,000; (d) $230,000; (e) $90,000
6. Total nonproduction costs equal: (a) $225,000; (b) $365,000; (c) $455,000; (d) $230,000; (e) $90,000
7. Gross margin is: (a) $610,000; (b) $475,000; (c) $470,000; (d) $335,000; (e) $245,000
8. The unit product cost is: (a) $4.50; (b) $7.30; (c) $9.10; (d) $4.60; (e) $1.80

9. The number of setups is a: (a) production or unit-level driver; (b) nonunit-level driver
10. Direct labor hours is a: (a) production or unit-level driver; (b) nonunit-level driver
11. Number of material moves is a: (a) production or unit-level driver; (b) nonunit-level driver
12. Machine hours is a: (a) production or unit-level driver; (b) nonunit-level driver
13. Complete the following:

Functional-Based versus Activity-Based Management Accounting Systems

	Functional-Based Management Accounting System	**Activity-Based Management Accounting System**
Activity drivers:		
Product cost assignment emphasis:		
Product costing objective:		
Control:		
Performance maximization emphasis:		

14. Complete the following:

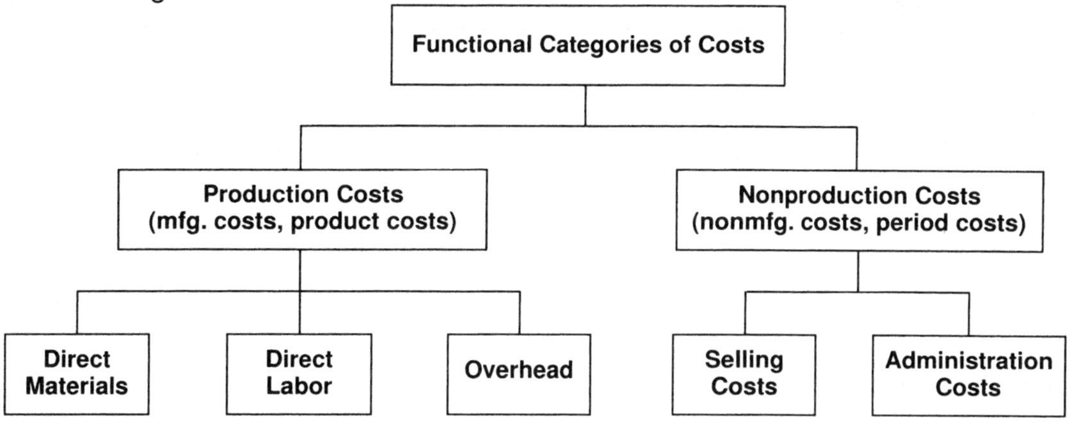

Definition:					
Examples:					

→ **Compare your answers with those at the end of the chapter. Review any questions missed.**

PRACTICE TEST

PROBLEM 1

Brigette & Company had the following beginning and ending inventories for the year 2004:

	Beginning	Ending
Raw materials	$80,000	$104,000
Work in process	40,000	57,200
Finished goods	30,000	54,000

During 2004, the following costs were incurred:

Purchase of raw materials	$520,000
Direct labor	400,000
Manufacturing overhead	840,000

Instructions:

Prepare a statement of cost of goods manufactured.

PROBLEM 2

The following information pertains to the York Company for the year ending December 31, 2004:

Sales	$840,000
Purchases of raw materials	220,000
Indirect labor	14,000
Indirect materials	9,000
Depreciation of factory equipment	50,000
Depreciation of factory buildings	29,000
Depreciation of administrative building	15,000
Marketing costs	130,000
Direct labor	110,000
Raw materials inventory, 12/31/04	22,000
Work in process, 1/1/04	54,000
Sales returns and allowances	17,000
Raw materials inventory, 1/1/04	33,000
Work in process 12/31/04	45,000
Sales discounts	12,000
Finished goods inventory, 1/1/04	124,000
Finished goods inventory, 12/31/04	115,000

Instructions:

Prepare a statement of cost of goods manufactured and an absorption-costing income statement in good form for the York Company for the year ending December 31, 2004.

PROBLEM 2 *(Continued)*

Use this page to continue your answer.

PROBLEM 3

The Jones Company currently produces one product, a cordless phone. The cost formula for the product is as follows:

Total manufacturing cost = $400,000 + 10X$

where X is direct labor hours.

The Jones Company is considering production of another version of the cordless phone. The new version would be similar to the existing version except the new version would have a ten-number memory. The same cost formula would be used to estimate costs.

Estimates of activity for each product are as follows:

	Cordless Phone	**Cordless Phone with Memory**
Units of product	12,000	3,000
Direct labor hours	30,000	8,000

Instructions:

1. Estimate total manufacturing costs if only the original cordless phone is produced.

2. Estimate total manufacturing costs if both models of the cordless phone are produced.

3. Does Jones Company use a unit-level driver or a nonunit-level driver?

ANSWERS

KEY TERMS TEST

1. I. direct materials
2. R. product costs
3. G. direct costs
4. H. direct labor
5. D. conversion cost
6. Q. prime cost
7. P. overhead
8. F. cost of goods sold
9. E. cost of goods manufactured
10. O. opportunity cost
11. L. expense
12. M. indirect costs
13. A. activity
14. C. allocation
15. J. direct tracing
16. K. driver tracing
17. N. internal value chain
18. S. service
19. B. activity-based management
20. T. work in process
21. administrative costs
22. cost
23. Absorption-costing
24. cost object
25. Nonproduction costs
26. Traceability
27. Production, unit-level drivers
28. Drivers
29. Marketing costs
30. Production costs
31. Tracing
32. functional-based management accounting system
33. Functional-based costing (FBC)
34. Functional-based management
35. activity-based management accounting system
36. Activity-based costing (ABC)
37. Nonunit-level drivers

CHAPTER QUIZ

1. a
2. c
3. d
4. a
5. b $75,000 + $150,000 + $140,000 = $365,000
6. e
7. d $700,000 – $365,000 = $335,000
8. b $365,000/50,000 units = $7.30 per unit
9. b
10. a
11. b
12. a
13. See page 16.
14. See page 13.

PRACTICE TEST

PROBLEM 1

Brigette & Company
Statement of Cost of Goods Manufactured
For the Year 2004

Direct materials:		
Beginning inventory of raw materials	$ 80,000	
Add: Purchases of raw materials	520,000	
Cost of raw materials available for use	$600,000	
Less: Ending inventory of raw materials	104,000	
Direct materials used		$ 496,000
Direct labor		400,000
Manufacturing overhead		840,000
Total manufacturing costs added		$1,736,000
Add: Beginning work-in-process inventory		40,000
Total manufacturing costs		$1,776,000
Less: Ending work-in-process inventory		57,200
Cost of goods manufactured		$1,718,800

PROBLEM 2

York Company
Statement of Cost of Goods Manufactured
For the Year Ended December 31, 2004

Direct materials:		
Beginning inventory of raw materials	$ 33,000	
Add: Purchases of raw materials	220,000	
Cost of raw materials available for use	$253,000	
Less: Ending inventory of raw materials	22,000	
Direct materials used		$231,000
Direct labor		110,000
Manufacturing overhead:		
Indirect materials	$ 9,000	
Indirect labor	14,000	
Depreciation of factory equipment	50,000	
Depreciation of factory buildings	29,000	102,000
Total manufacturing costs added		$443,000
Add: Beginning work-in-process inventory		54,000
Total manufacturing costs		$497,000
Less: Ending work-in-process inventory		45,000
Cost of goods manufactured		$452,000

York Company
Income Statement
For the Year Ended December 31, 2004

Sales		$840,000
Less: Sales returns and allowances		17,000
Sales discounts		12,000
Net sales		$811,000
Cost of goods sold:		
Beginning finished goods inventory	$124,000	
Add: Cost of goods manufactured	452,000	
Cost of goods available for sale	$576,000	
Less: Ending finished goods inventory	115,000	461,000
Gross profit		$350,000
Less operating expenses:		
Selling expenses	$130,000	
General and administrative expenses	15,000	145,000
Income		$205,000

PROBLEM 3

1. Total manufacturing costs = $400,000 + ($10 × 30,000)
   = $700,000
2. Total manufacturing costs = $400,000 + $10(30,000 + 8,000)
   = $780,000
3. Direct labor hours is a unit-level driver.

CHAPTER 3
Activity Cost Behavior

CHAPTER REVIEW

THE BASICS OF COST BEHAVIOR

- **Cost behavior** describes how a cost behaves or changes as output changes.
- Understanding cost behavior is vital to providing cost information for budgeting, cost control, and decision making.
- Three cost behavior patterns are:
  1. **fixed costs**—*in total, are constant* within a relevant range as activity output changes. **Relevant range** is the range over which the fixed costs are expected to remain the same.
  2. **variable costs**—*in total, vary* in direct proportion to changes in activity output.
  3. **mixed costs**—have both a fixed and a variable component.

Cost Behavior

	Fixed Costs	Variable Costs	Mixed Costs
Description:	*in total, are constant* within the relevant range as activity output changes	*in total, vary* in direct proportion to changes in activity output	have both a fixed and a variable component
Examples:	factory rent	direct materials	lease payment of $1,000 per month plus $10 per machine hour used
Per unit:	changes as activity level changes	remains constant per unit of activity	
Formula:		**Total variable cost = Variable cost per unit × Units of activity**	**Total mixed cost = Fixed costs + Variable costs**

- The following two graphs illustrate how variable costs increase with activity while fixed costs remain the same.

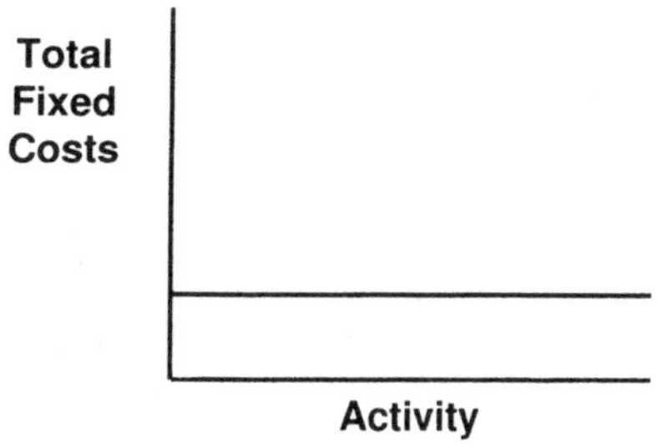

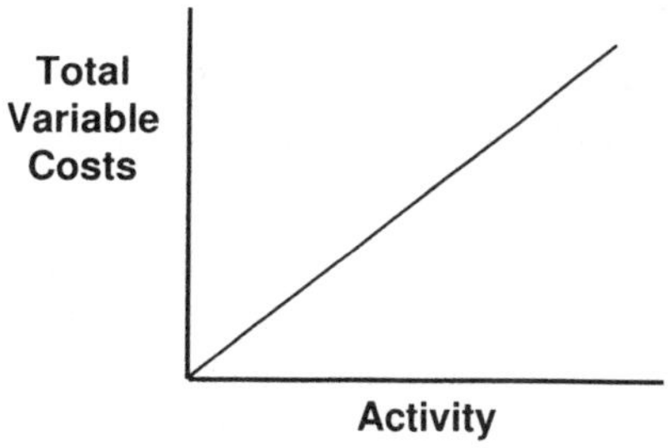

- Example: Assume Racing, Inc., manufactures racing bicycles. Each bicycle requires 1 handlebar costing $10 each. The handlebars are a direct material since they become part of the finished product, and they are a variable cost because the total handlebar cost varies with the number of bicycles produced. If Racing produces 1 bicycle, the total cost for handlebars would be $10; if it manufactures 100 bicycles, the total cost for handlebars would be $1,000. See below:

Bicycles	Handlebars	Cost per Handlebar Variable Cost per Unit	Total Handlebar Cost Total Variable Cost
1	1	$10	$ 10
10	10	10	100
100	100	10	1,000
1,000	1,000	10	10,000

If Racing pays $5,000 per month to rent factory space large enough to produce up to 10,000 bicycles a month, the $5,000 rent would be classified as manufacturing overhead because it is a manufacturing cost other than direct materials or direct labor. In addition, the rent is a fixed cost because the cost will be $5,000 a month if Racing produces between 0 and 10,000 bicycles.

Bicycles	Factory Rent Total Fixed Cost	Fixed Cost per Unit
1	$5,000	$5,000
10	5,000	500
100	5,000	50
1,000	5,000	5

- Note that *total* variable costs vary with changes in activity while the variable cost *per unit* remains constant with changes in activity. *Total* fixed costs remain constant while fixed costs *per unit* change with changes in activity.

Classifying Costs According to Behavior

- Whether a cost is fixed or variable depends upon the time horizon. For example, in the long run all costs are variable.
- In order to understand the behavior of costs, it is necessary to determine the underlying activities and associated activity drivers.
- *Activity drivers* are causal factors that measure the amount of resources a cost object uses. Activity drivers explain changes in activity costs by measuring changes in activity use or output. For example, the activity driver for material handling costs might be the number of material moves.
- Two categories of activity drivers:
  1. Production (or unit-level) drivers explain changes in cost as units produced change. Direct labor hours is an example of a production driver. As direct labor hours increase, output increases.
  2. Nonunit-level drivers explain changes in cost as factors other than units change. For example, the cost to set up a production run might be the same for a run of 50 units or 500 units. Thus, setup time and cost are not related to the number of units. Other examples of nonunit level costs are factory depreciation and factory manager salary.
- In a functional-based cost system, only unit-level drivers are used to describe cost behavior.

❒ In an activity-based cost system, both unit- and nonunit-level drivers are used to describe cost behavior.

ACTIVITIES, RESOURCES USAGE, AND COST BEHAVIOR

❒ Capacity is the amount of activity a company can perform.

❒ **Practical capacity** is an efficient level of activity performance.

❒ Resources are economic inputs consumed in performing activities. Resources include materials, labor, and capital.

❒ **Flexible resources** are supplied as used and needed.

❒ **Committed resources** are resources supplied in advance of usage.

❒ Characteristics of flexible and committed resources are summarized below:

	Flexible Resources	Committed Resources
Definition:	Resources are acquired from outside sources, and the organization is free to buy only the quantity of the resource needed.	Resources are acquired by either explicit or implicit contract to obtain a given quantity of resources, regardless of whether the quantity of the resource available is fully used or not.
Unused capacity:	No; Resource supplied = Resource usage and demand	Yes; Resource supplied ≥ Resource usage
Examples:	materials	equipment
Cost behavior:	usually variable	Cautiously treated as fixed expenses. **Discretionary fixed expenses** are incurred for short-term capacity.

Step-Cost Behavior

❒ A **step cost** has a constant level of cost for a range of output, then jumps to a higher level of cost where it remains for a range of output.

❒ Step costs with narrow ranges of activity are usually treated as a variable cost.

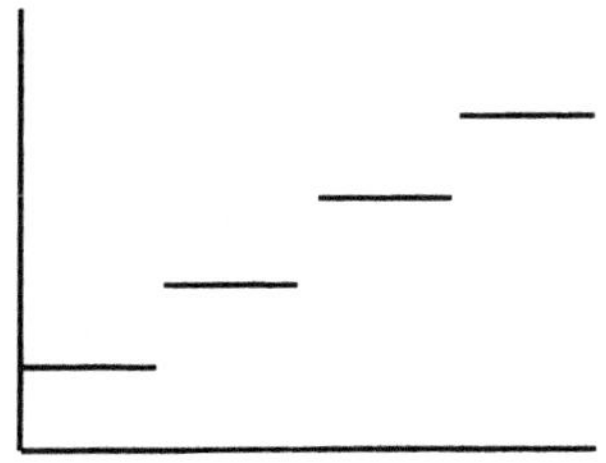

❒ Steps costs with steps that cover wide ranges of activity can be treated as fixed costs.

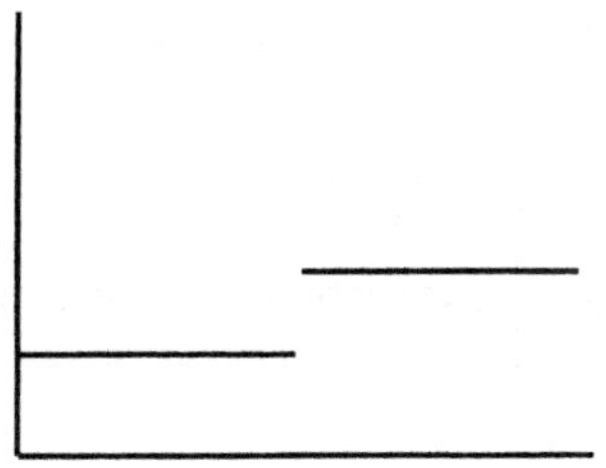

- Many committed resources follow a step-cost function.
- **Fixed activity rate** is based on committed resources so it is calculated as follows using capacity available:

Fixed activity rate = Total committed cost/Total capacity

- **Variable activity rate** is based on the actual capacity used because flexible resources are purchased as necessary.

Variable activity rate = Total cost of flexible resources/Capacity used

- A functional-based costing system provides information only about the cost of resources purchased, whereas an activity-based management system provides information about the amount of activity used and the cost of its usage.

Resources available = Resources used + Unused capacity

METHODS FOR SEPARATING MIXED COSTS INTO FIXED AND VARIABLE COMPONENTS

- Three widely used methods for separating a mixed cost into fixed and variable components are:
  1. the high-low method
  2. the scatterplot method, and
  3. the method of least squares.
- Each method assumes a linear cost relationship.
- Mixed costs can be estimated using the following equation for a straight line:

$$Y = F + VX$$

where Y = total activity cost (the dependent variable)
F = fixed cost (the intercept parameter)
V = variable cost per unit of activity (the slope parameter)
X = activity level (the independent variable)

- Y (total cost) is called the **dependent variable** because it is dependent on the value of another variable, the activity level.
- The **intercept** of the line (where the line intersects the vertical or cost axis) is an estimate of the fixed activity cost (F).
- The **slope** of the line is an estimate of the variable cost per unit of activity (V).
- A major goal of cost behavior analysis is to develop cost functions so costs can be estimated at various levels of activity.

The High-Low Method

- The **high-low method** uses two points (the high activity level and the low activity level) to determine the cost formula.
- The slope or variable cost per unit of activity is calculated as:

$$\textbf{Variable rate} = \frac{\textbf{Change in cost between high point and low point}}{\textbf{Change in output between high point and low point}}$$

- Total variable costs can be calculated for different activity levels as follows:

Total variable costs = Variable rate × Output

- The fixed cost component can be calculated using total cost at either the high point or the low point:

Fixed costs = Total (mixed) cost at high point – (Variable rate × High output)

or

Fixed costs = Total (mixed) cost at low point – (Variable rate × Low output)

- The cost formula for total costs is:

Total cost = Total fixed cost + (Variable rate × Output)

- A weakness of the high-low method is that it uses only two observations to develop the cost formula and the two points could be outliers (points that do not represent typical cost-activity relationships). It is important that the high and low levels of activity used are representative of the general cost-activity pattern.
- The scatterplot method assists in determining if the high-low method produces acceptable results.

The Scatterplot Method

- A **scattergraph** contains a vertical axis indicating the mixed cost being analyzed (the dependent variable) and a horizontal axis indicating the activity level (the independent variable). Past cost observations are plotted on the scattergraph.
- The **scatterplot method** involves visually fitting a line to the points on the scattergraph by selecting two points on the scattergraph that seem to best represent the relationship between cost and activity.
- The slope or variable cost per unit of activity is calculated as:

$$\textbf{Variable rate} = \frac{\textbf{Change in cost between Point 1 and Point 2}}{\textbf{Change in output between Point 1 and Point 2}}$$

- Total variable costs can be calculated for different activity levels as follows:

Total variable costs = Variable rate × Output

- The fixed cost component is calculated as:

Fixed costs = Total (mixed) cost at Point 1 – Total variable costs at Point 1

or

Fixed costs = Total (mixed) cost at Point 2 – Total variable costs at Point 2

- The cost formula for total costs is:

Total cost = Total fixed cost + (Variable rate × Output)

- The difference between the high-low method and the scatterplot method is the way the two points used are selected.
- One purpose of the scattergraph is to see if there is a linear relationship. Also, the scattergraph may reveal points (observations) that do not seem to fit the general pattern of behavior (outliers) and perhaps should be eliminated.

The Method of Least Squares

- The method of least squares is a statistical method for mathematically deriving a line that best fits a set of data.
- The **best-fitting line** is one that minimizes the differences between the cost predicted by the cost formula (the line) and actual cost observations.
- Deviation is the difference between the cost predicted by a cost formula and the actual cost. It measures the distance of a data point (actual cost) from the cost line (predicted cost).
- The formula used to predict costs is the formula for a straight-line:

$$Y = F + VX$$

- The **method of least squares** arrives at values for *F* (fixed costs) and *V* (variable cost per unit of activity) that result in a line that fits the points (cost observations) better than any other line.
- Electronic spreadsheets, such as Microsoft Excel® and Lotus 1-2-3®, have features to perform regression calculations.

RELIABILITY OF COST FORMULAS

- **Goodness of fit** measures the degree of association between activity cost and activity output.
- The coefficient of determination is a measure of the goodness of fit.
- The **coefficient of determination** (R^2) measures the percentage of change in the dependent variable (cost) that is explained by the change in the independent variable (activity usage).
- A coefficient of determination of .92 indicates that 92 percent of the change in cost is explained by changes in activity usage. The coefficient of determination is an indication of the usefulness of the regression line. The higher the percentage of variability explained, the better the fit.
- The **coefficient of correlation** is the square root of the coefficient of determination. (If the correlation coefficient is known, the coefficient of determination can be calculated by squaring the correlation coefficient.)
- The correlation coefficient can range from –1 to +1. A correlation coefficient of +1 would indicate perfect positive correlation, while a correlation coefficient close to 0 would mean the movement of the two variables is unrelated.
- Positive correlation is indicated by a positive value for *V*. If costs decrease as activity increases, then *V* would be negative (indicating a downward sloping line) and the coefficient of correlation would be negative.

MULTIPLE REGRESSION

- **Multiple regression** uses the method of least squares and involves one dependent variable (cost) and more than one independent variable (activity). For example, multiple regression can be used when there are two variables that are related to changes in costs.

  For example, multiple regression could be used to predict total factory overhead costs (the dependent variable) based on facility-level activity (the intercept) and three independent variables of unit-level activity, batch-level activity, and product-level activity.
- The equation used when there are two explanatory variables is:

$$Y = F + V_1X_1 + V_2X_2$$

where X_1 = activity level of the first independent variable
X_2 = activity level of the second independent variable
V_1 = variable rate for the first independent variable
V_2 = variable rate for the second independent variable

MANAGERIAL JUDGMENT

❒ Managerial judgment can be used alone or in conjunction with the high-low, scatterplot, or least squares methods to estimate fixed and variable costs.

SUMMARY

❒ Four methods can be used to estimated the variable and fixed cost components of a mixed cost:
1. High-low method
2. Scatterplot method
3. Method of least squares
4. Managerial judgment

❒ Although the scatterplot method, the high-low method, and managerial judgment involve simpler calculations, the method of least squares produces a line which best fits the points (cost observations) on a scattergraph.

KEY TERMS TEST

Test your recall of the key terms as follows. Try to recall as many key terms as possible without assistance. If you need assistance, refer to the list of key terms at the end of this section.

1. __________ _______________ describes how costs change as output changes.
2. The ____________________ _____________ depends on the value of another variable.
3. The ________-_________ _____________ is a method of fitting a line to a set of data points using the high and low points in the data set. For a cost formula, the high and low points represent the high and low activity levels. This method is used to estimate the fixed and variable components of a mixed cost.
4. The ____________________ _____________ does not depend on the value of another variable.
5. The ____________________ _____________ is a method for fitting a line to a set of data using two points that are selected by judgment. This method is used to estimate the fixed and variable components of a mixed cost.
6. _______________ _______________ uses least squares analysis to determine the parameters in a linear equation involving two or more explanatory variables.
7. _______________ _______________ are purchased in advance of usage. These resources may or may not have unused (excess) capacity.
8. _______________ _______________ are purchased as used and needed. There is no unused or excess capacity for these resources.
9. The line that minimizes the differences between the cost predicted by the cost formula (the line) and actual cost observations is called the ________-____________ ________.
10. The _________________ _______ _________________ is the square root of the coefficient of determination, which is used to express not only the degree of correlation between two variables, but also the direction of the relationship.
11. The _________________ _______ _________________ is the percentage of change in a dependent variable (cost) that is explained by the change in an independent variable (activity).
12. ____________________ __________ _____________ are costs incurred for the acquisition of short-term capacity or services.
13. _________________ _______ __________ is the degree of association between *Y* and *X* (cost and activity). It is measured by how much of the total variability in *Y* is explained by *X*.
14. The ______________ _______________ is the point where the cost formula intercepts the vertical axis.
15. The _____________ ______ __________ _____________ is a statistical method for finding a line that best fits a set of data. It is used to break out the fixed and variable components of a mixed cost.
16. A(n) ____________________ is a plot of past cost observations at different activity levels.
17. The ______________ _______________ is the variable cost per unit of activity, represented by *V* in the cost formula $Y = F + VX$.
18. A(n) __________ _____________ is a linear function, $Y = F + VX$.

19. The _______________ _______________ _________ is calculated as fixed activity cost divided by the total capacity of the activity driver.

20. The _______________ _______________ _________ is calculated as the total variable activity cost divided by the amount of the activity driver used.

21. The _______________ ___________ is the range of output over which the assumed cost/output relationship is valid.

22. _______________ _______________ is an efficient level of activity performance.

23. _______________-___________ _______________ explain changes in cost as factors other than units change.

24. A(n) _________ _________ displays a constant level of cost for a range of output and then jumps to a higher level of cost at some point, where it remains for a similar range of output.

KEY TERMS:

best-fitting line
coefficient of correlation
coefficient of determination
committed resources
cost behavior
cost formula
dependent variable
discretionary fixed expenses
fixed activity rate
flexible resources
goodness of fit
high-low method
independent variable
intercept parameter
method of least squares
multiple regression
nonunit-level drivers
practical capacity
relevant range
scattergraph
scatterplot method
slope parameter
step cost
variable activity rate

→ **Compare your answers with those at the end of the chapter. Review any key terms missed.**

CHAPTER QUIZ

Circle the single best answer.

1. Cost behavior patterns include: (a) variable costs; (b) fixed costs; (c) step costs; (d) mixed costs; (e) all of the above
2. Fixed costs: (a) remain the same in total; (b) vary per unit of activity; (c) remain constant per unit of activity; (d) vary in total; (e) a and b; (f) c and d
3. Variable costs: (a) remain the same in total; (b) vary per unit of activity; (c) remain constant per unit of activity; (d) vary in total; (e) a and b; (f) c and d
4. A car lease that specifies a $100 fee per month plus $0.30 per mile would be an example of a: (a) fixed cost; (b) variable cost; (c) mixed cost; (d) step cost
5. Supervisors' salaries of $3,000 per month would be an example of a: (a) committed resource; (b) flexible resource
6. Direct materials is an example of a: (a) committed resource; (b) flexible resource

7. The coefficient of determination indicates: (a) the percentage of change in the dependent variable explained by changes in the independent variable; (b) the percentage of change in the dependent variable caused by changes in the independent variable; (c) the percentage of change in the independent variable explained by changes in the dependent variable; (d) the percentage of change in the independent variable caused by changes in the dependent variable

8. The independent variable (activity) selected should have a high degree of correlation with the dependent variable (cost), as indicated by a coefficient of determination: (a) close to –1; (b) close to +1; (c) equal to 0; (d) none of the above

Use the following information to answer Questions 9 through 11:

The following information was collected regarding maintenance costs at different activity levels measured in machine hours:

Number of Machine Hours	Total Maintenance Costs
8,000	$600,000
10,000	640,000
11,000	800,000
9,000	700,000
14,000	900,000
12,000	870,000

9. Using the high-low method, an estimate of the variable component for maintenance costs is: (a) $50.00; (b) $52.50; (c) $64.28; (d) $75.00

10. Using the high-low method, an estimate of the fixed component for maintenance costs is: (a) $165,000; (b) $200,000; (c) $224,000; (d) $300,000

11. Using the cost formula developed using the high-low method, the estimate of maintenance costs if 13,000 machine hours are scheduled for next month would be: (a) $650,000; (b) $950,000; (c) $850,000; (d) $882,000

Use the following information to answer Questions 12 through 15:

The method of least squares produced the following computer printout using direct labor hours as the activity:

```
INTERCEPT                              20,318.00
SLOPE                                      42.00
CORRELATION COEFFICIENT                      .90
```

12. The estimate of the variable component for maintenance costs is: (a) $37.80; (b) $42.00; (c) $46.67; (d) $47.00

13. The estimate of the fixed component for maintenance costs is: (a) $18,286; (b) $20,276; (c) $20,318; (d) $20,360

14. If 5,000 machine hours are scheduled, an estimate of maintenance costs is: (a) $253,318; (b) $230,726; (c) $230,360; (d) $230,318

15. The coefficient of determination is: (a) 0.73; (b) 0.81; (c) 0.90; (d) 1.0

→ **Compare your answers with those at the end of the chapter. Review any questions missed.**

PRACTICE TEST

PROBLEM 1

AMK, Inc., believes its electricity costs are affected by the number of machine hours worked. Machine hours and electricity costs for 2004 were as follows:

Month	Machine Hours	Electricity Cost
January	1,500	$18,400
February	1,400	18,300
March	1,300	17,800
April	1,900	22,000
May	1,700	20,200
June	1,550	18,700
July	1,200	17,600
August	1,600	19,000
September	1,100	17,510
October	2,000	22,500
November	2,100	23,000
December	2,200	24,000

Instructions:

1. Using the high-low method, develop the cost function for monthly electricity cost.

2. Estimate total electricity cost for a month in which 1,800 machine hours are worked.

3. What are the weaknesses of the high-low method?

PROBLEM 2

The Koch Company incurred the following maintenance costs during the past six months:

Month	Machine Hours	Maintenance Cost
January	120,000	$456,000
February	100,000	420,000
March	140,000	492,000
April	160,000	528,000
May	130,000	474,000
June	90,000	402,000

Instructions:

1. Using the scatterplot method, the two points that seem to best represent the relationship between cost and activity are the activity levels of 100,000 and 140,000 machine hours. Using these two points, estimate the variable and fixed components of maintenance costs.

2. Develop a cost function that the Koch Company can use to estimate maintenance cost at different volume levels.

3. Estimate maintenance costs for July if the company expects to use 110,000 machine hours.

PROBLEM 3

Max Manufacturing has five salaried accounts payable clerks responsible for processing purchase invoices. Each clerk is paid a salary of $25,000 and is capable of processing 4,000 invoices per year. When 20,000 payments are processed, Max spends $8,000 per year for forms and supplies. During the year, 18,000 invoices were processed.

Instructions:

1. **a.** Calculate the fixed activity rate.

   b. Calculate the variable activity rate.

   c. Calculate the activity rate for the purchase order activity.

2. Complete the following:

   Resources available (supplied) = Resources used + Unused capacity

   ____________________ = ____________________ + ____________________

3. Complete the following:

   Cost of resources supplied = Cost of resources used + Cost of unused capacity

   ____________________ = ____________________ + ____________________

PROBLEM 4

Hentze Dental Center currently charges $20 per dental exam. A new company that recently located near the dental center asked if the dental center would be interested in providing dental services to their employees at a special rate of $15 per dental exam.

The dentists have agreed to offer the dental exams at the reduced fee if the $15 would cover the variable costs of the dental exam.

The dental center's accountant provided the following information about dental exams during the first six months of the year:

Month	Number of Exams	Total Cost of Exams
January	120	$1,850
February	150	2,020
March	110	1,600
April	140	1,960
May	100	1,450
June	80	1,200

The regression results are as follows:

REGRESSION OUTPUT	
CONSTANT (INTERCEPT)	266
R SQUARED	.955224
X COEFFICIENT(S)	12.12
STANDARD ERROR	75.74959
OBSERVATIONS	6

Instructions:

1. Using the regression results, determine the variable cost per dental exam.

2. Will the $15 reduced fee cover the dental center's variable cost of providing the dental exam?

3. Develop a cost function that can be used to estimate total exam costs at different activity levels.

PROBLEM 4 *(Continued)*

4. If a total of 200 exams are expected to be performed in July, what would be the total expected cost of performing the 200 exams?

5. If 50 additional exams are performed each month at the special rate:

a. What would be the incremental revenue resulting from the 50 exams?

b. What would be the incremental cost of providing the 50 exams?

c. What would be the incremental profit that would result from providing the 50 exams at the reduced rate?

6. Explain the significance of R^2.

PROBLEM 5

In order to better predict setup costs, the plant manager has asked the computer center to use the least squares method to generate a printout for use in estimating setup costs.

The following computer printout was generated and given to the plant manager:

INTERCEPT (CONSTANT)	150.00
SLOPE (X COEFFICIENT)	10.00
CORRELATION COEFFICIENT	.98
ACTIVITY	NUMBER OF SETUPS

The plant manager brought the printout to you and said, "How am I supposed to use this to estimate setup costs? This printout is worthless!"

Instructions:

1. Explain how the printout information can be used to estimate setup costs.

2. Estimate setup costs if 30 setups are expected next month.

3. What percentage change in setup costs can be explained by changes in the number of setups?

PROBLEM 6

The following information is the result of regression analysis for Felix, Inc., using factory overhead cost observations gathered during the past 18 months:

INTERCEPT	6,490
REGRESSION COEFFICIENTS:	
UNITS	23
INSPECTIONS	15
ENGINEERING HOURS	3
R^2	.94

Instructions:

1. Develop a function that can be used by Felix to estimate total factory overhead costs per month.

2. How useful is this function as a predictor of factory overhead costs?

3. Estimate total factory overhead for the month, given the following budgeted activity levels for next month:

Units	450
Inspections	30
Engineering hours	120

4. Which of the activities listed in Requirement 3 above would be considered unit-level drivers? Nonunit-level drivers?

   Unit-level drivers: ______________________

   Nonunit-level drivers: ______________________

ANSWERS

KEY TERMS TEST

1. Cost behavior
2. dependent variable
3. high-low method
4. independent variable
5. scatterplot method
6. Multiple regression
7. Committed resources
8. Flexible resources
9. best-fitting line
10. coefficient of correlation
11. coefficient of determination
12. Discretionary fixed expenses
13. Goodness of fit
14. intercept parameter
15. method of least squares
16. scattergraph
17. slope parameter
18. cost formula
19. fixed activity rate
20. variable activity rate
21. relevant range
22. Practical capacity
23. Nonunit-level drivers
24. step cost

CHAPTER QUIZ

1. e
2. e
3. f
4. c
5. a
6. b
7. a
8. b
9. a ($900,000 – $600,000)/(14,000 – 8,000) = $50
10. b $900,000 – ($50 × 14,000) = $200,000
11. c $200,000 + ($50 × 13,000) = $850,000
12. b
13. c
14. d $20,318 + ($42 × 5,000) = $230,318
15. b $.9^2 = 0.81$

PRACTICE TEST

PROBLEM 1

1. $$\text{Variable cost per machine hour} = \frac{\text{Difference in total cost}}{\text{Difference in high and low levels of activity}} = \frac{\$24{,}000 - \$17{,}510}{2{,}200 - 1{,}100} = \frac{\$6{,}490}{1{,}100} = \$5.90$$

   Total cost at high activity – Variable cost at high activity = Fixed cost
   $24,000 – ($5.90 × 2,200) = $11,020

   Cost function for electricity cost = $11,020 + $5.90*X*
   where *X* = machine hours

2. Total electricity cost at 1,800 machine hours = $11,020 + ($5.90 × 1,800 machine hours)
   = $11,020 + $10,620
   = $21,640

3. Weaknesses of the high-low method include:

   (1) The method uses only two points to develop the cost function, and the two points used must be representative of normal operations.

   (2) The method does not detect if the cost behavior is curvilinear.

PROBLEM 2

1. Variable cost per machine hour $= \dfrac{\text{Difference in total cost}}{\text{Difference in levels of activity}}$

$$= \frac{\$492{,}000 - \$420{,}000}{140{,}000 - 100{,}000}$$

$$= \frac{\$72{,}000}{40{,}000}$$

$$= \$1.80 \text{ per machine hour}$$

Total cost at 140,000 machine hours – Variable cost at 140,000 machine hours = Fixed cost
$492,000 – ($1.80 × 140,000) = $240,000

2. Cost function for maintenance cost = $240,000 + $1.80*X*
where *X* = machine hours

3. Maintenance cost at 110,000 machine hours = $240,000 + $1.80*X*
= $240,000 + ($1.80 × 110,000)
= $438,000

PROBLEM 3

1. **a.** Fixed activity rate = (5 × $25,000)/20,000 = $6.25 per invoice
   b. Variable activity rate = $8,000/20,000 = $0.40 per invoice
   c. Activity rate = [(5 × $25,000) + $8,000]/20,000 = $6.65 per invoice

2. Resources available (supplied) = Resources used + Unused capacity
20,000 invoices = 18,000 invoices + 2,000 invoices

3.

Cost of resources supplied		Cost of resources used		Cost of unused capacity
[Total fixed cost + (Variable rate × Activity usage)]	=	[Activity rate × Activity usage]	+	[Fixed rate × Unused capacity]
$125,000 + ($0.40 × 18,000)	=	$6.65 × 18,000	+	$6.25 × 2,000
$125,000 + $7,200	=	$119,700	+	$12,500
$132,200	=	$132,200		

PROBLEM 4

1. The slope of the regression line and an estimate of the variable cost per dental exam is $12.12.

2. Yes, the $15 reduced fee would cover the center's variable cost of $12.12 per exam.

3. The estimate of total fixed costs is $266.
The regression line equation is: *Y* = $266 + $12.12*X*

4. An estimate of costs for 200 dental exams would be:
Y = $266 + ($12.12 × 200)
= $2,690

5. **a.** Incremental revenue = Special rate × Additional exams
= $15 × 50
= $750

   b. Incremental cost = Variable cost per exam × Additional exams
= $12.12 × 50
= $606

   c. Incremental profit = Incremental revenue – Incremental cost
= $750 – $606
= $144

6. R^2 (the coefficient of determination) indicates the percentage change in cost that can be explained by changes in output or activity. In this case, approximately 95 percent of the change in dental exam costs can be explained by the number of dental exams.

PROBLEM 5

1. If the intercept is within the relevant range, it is an estimate of total fixed costs.
   The slope is an estimate of variable costs.
   The printout information can be used to develop the following cost function to estimate setup costs at different activity levels.

   Total setup costs = \$150 + \$10*X*
   where *X* = the number of setups

2. Total setup costs = \$150 + (\$10 × 30)
   = \$450

3. 96% ($.98^2$) of the change in setup costs can be explained by changes in the number of setups. This indicates that the cost function appears to be useful in estimating setup costs.

PROBLEM 6

1. Factory overhead = \$6,490 + \$23(Units) + \$15(Inspections) + \$3(Engineering hours)

2. R^2 of .94 indicates that this formula explains 94% of the variability of factory overhead costs.

3.

	Budgeted Activity	×	Regression Coefficient	=	Budgeted Overhead
Units	450		\$ 23		\$10,350
Inspections	30		15		450
Engineering hours	120		3		360
Fixed overhead			6,490		6,490
Total					\$17,650

4. Unit-level drivers: units
   Nonunit-level drivers: inspections, engineering hours

CHAPTER 4
Activity-Based Costing

CHAPTER REVIEW

UNIT COSTS

- Functional-based and activity-based costing assigns costs to cost objects such as products and customers. Once costs are assigned to the cost object, the **unit cost** is calculated by dividing the total cost assigned to the units produced by the number of units produced.
- Unit cost information is used to:
  - value inventory
  - determine cost of goods sold, which affects income
  - determine bids to give to potential customers
  - decide whether to make or buy a product
  - decide whether to accept or reject a special order
  - decide whether to keep or drop a product line
  - decide whether to introduce a new product
- Different cost information is needed for different purposes.
- For external reporting, product costs include direct materials, direct labor, and overhead.
- **Cost measurement** involves determining the dollar amount of direct materials, direct labor, and overhead used in production.
- Two cost measurement systems are:
  - actual costing
  - normal costing
- **Cost assignment** involves associating costs with units produced.
- Two cost assignment systems are:
  - functional-based costing
  - activity-based costing

Production of Unit Cost Information

- **Actual costing** assigns *actual* costs of direct materials, direct labor, and overhead to products.
- Actual cost systems are rarely used because they cannot provide accurate unit cost information on a timely basis.
- **Normal costing** uses:
  - actual costs for direct materials
  - actual costs for direct labor
  - a predetermined rate for manufacturing overhead

- A normal costing system can supply unit cost information on a timely basis.
- The predetermined overhead rate is calculated as:

$$\textbf{Predetermined overhead rate} = \frac{\textbf{Budgeted (estimated) overhead cost}}{\textbf{Estimated activity usage}}$$

- Overhead is assigned to products using the predetermined overhead rate.

FUNCTIONAL-BASED PRODUCT COSTING

- When functional-based costing is used, direct materials and direct labor are assigned to products using direct tracing.
- Overhead costs are assigned using driver tracing and allocations with unit-level activity drivers.
- **Unit-level activity drivers** are factors that cause changes in cost as the units produced change.
- Examples of unit-level drivers include:
  - units produced
  - direct labor hours
  - direct labor dollars
  - machine hours
  - direct material dollars
- An estimate for activity level can be based on:
  - **expected activity capacity**, the *expected* production level of activity for the *next* year.
  - **normal activity capacity**, the *average* activity that the firm *expects* in the *long term* (for example, average activity for the next three to five years).
  - **theoretical activity capacity**, the *maximum output* possible under perfect operating conditions.
  - **practical activity capacity**, the *output* a firm can achieve if it operates *efficiently.* Efficient operations allow for equipment breakdowns, material shortages, etc.
- Using practical or theoretical capacity avoids assigning unused capacity costs to products.
- Unit-level activity drivers assign overhead using either:
  - plantwide rates, or
  - departmental rates.

Plantwide Rates

- A plantwide overhead rate is calculated as:

$$\textbf{Plantwide rate} = \frac{\textbf{Budgeted plantwide overhead cost}}{\textbf{Estimated activity of unit-level driver}}$$

- Overhead cost assigned to product is calculated as:

$$\textbf{Applied overhead} = \textbf{Plantwide rate} \times \textbf{Actual activity used on product}$$

- The **overhead variance** is the difference between actual overhead and applied overhead.
- **Underapplied overhead** occurs when applied overhead is less than actual overhead for the period.
- **Overapplied overhead** occurs when applied overhead exceeds actual overhead for the period.

- The following T account for overhead illustrates the relationships:

Overhead

Actual overhead costs	Applied overhead (Plantwide rate × Actual activity)
Underapplied overhead	Overapplied overhead

- If the overhead variance is relatively small, underapplied or overapplied overhead may be treated as an adjustment to cost of goods sold. Underapplied overhead is added to cost of goods sold, and overapplied overhead is subtracted from cost of goods sold.

Departmental Rates

- Departmental rates are calculated as:

$$\textbf{Departmental rate} = \frac{\textbf{Budgeted departmental overhead cost}}{\textbf{Estimated departmental activity}}$$

- Overhead cost assigned to product is calculated as:

Applied overhead = Departmental rate × Actual departmental activity used on product

- See the summary below:

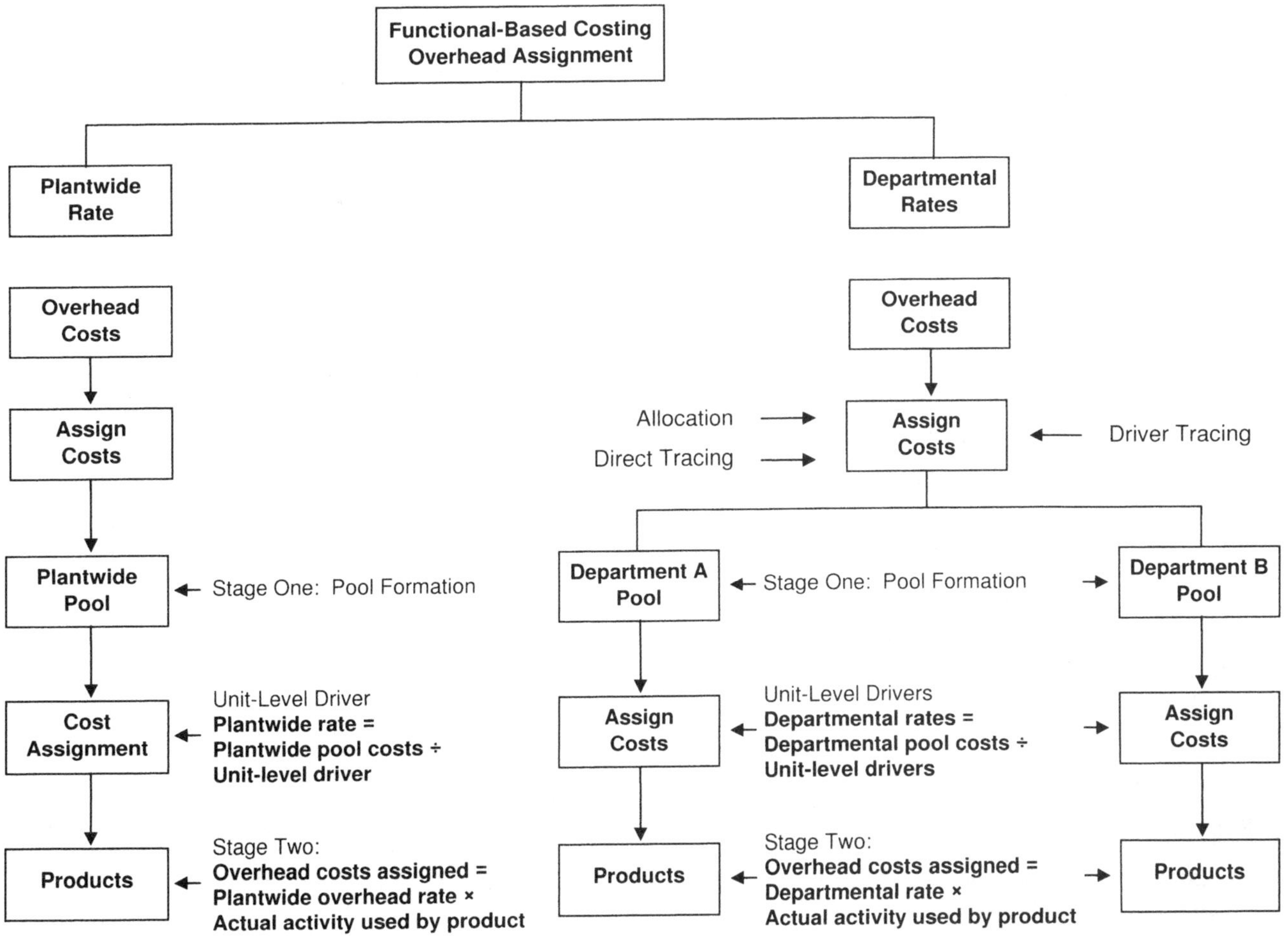

LIMITATIONS OF FUNCTIONAL-BASED COST ACCOUNTING SYSTEMS

- Plantwide and departmental rates may cause product cost distortions, which can be damaging for companies operating in an environment characterized by:
  - firms engaged in intense competition
  - continuous improvement
  - total quality management
  - total customer satisfaction
  - sophisticated technology
- As firms adopt new strategies to remain competitive, the cost accounting system must change to produce more accurate product costs.
- Symptoms of an outdated cost system include the following:
  - The outcome of bids is difficult to explain.
  - Competitors' prices appear unrealistically low.
  - Products that are difficult to produce show high profits.
  - Operational managers want to drop products that appear profitable.
  - Profit margins are hard to explain.
  - The company has a highly profitable niche all to itself.
  - Customers do not complain about price increases.
  - The accounting department spends a lot of time on special projects.
  - Some departments are using their own cost accounting system.
  - Product costs change because of changes in financial reporting regulations.
- Plantwide and departmental rates using unit-level drivers may not assign overhead costs accurately if:
  - the proportion of nonunit-level overhead costs to total overhead costs is large, and
  - the degree of product diversity is great.

Nonunit-Related Overhead Costs

- The main problem with the traditional approach of using plantwide and departmental overhead rates is that a product's consumption of overhead resources may not be strictly related to units produced. For example, *setup costs are related to the number of setups*.
- **Nonunit-level activity drivers** are factors, other than the number of units produced, that measure use of overhead resources. For example, setup costs are not driven by the number of units, but by the number of setups, a nonunit-level activity driver.
- Using only unit-level activity drivers to assign nonunit-related overhead costs can create distorted product costs. If nonunit-level overhead costs are only a small percentage of total overhead costs, the distortion of product costs would be small and the use of unit-level cost drivers might be acceptable.

Product Diversity

- **Product diversity** occurs when products consume overhead activities in different proportions.
- Reasons why products might consume overhead in different proportions include:
  - differences in product size
  - product complexity

- setup time
- size of batches

❒ **Consumption ratio** is the proportion of each activity consumed by a product.

❒ Product costs can be distorted if a unit-level cost driver is used and
- nonunit-level overhead costs are a significant proportion of total overhead, and
- the consumption ratios differ between unit-level and nonunit-level input categories.

ACTIVITY-BASED PRODUCT COSTING

❒ An **activity-based costing (ABC) system** traces:
1. overhead costs to activities, and
2. then traces costs to products.

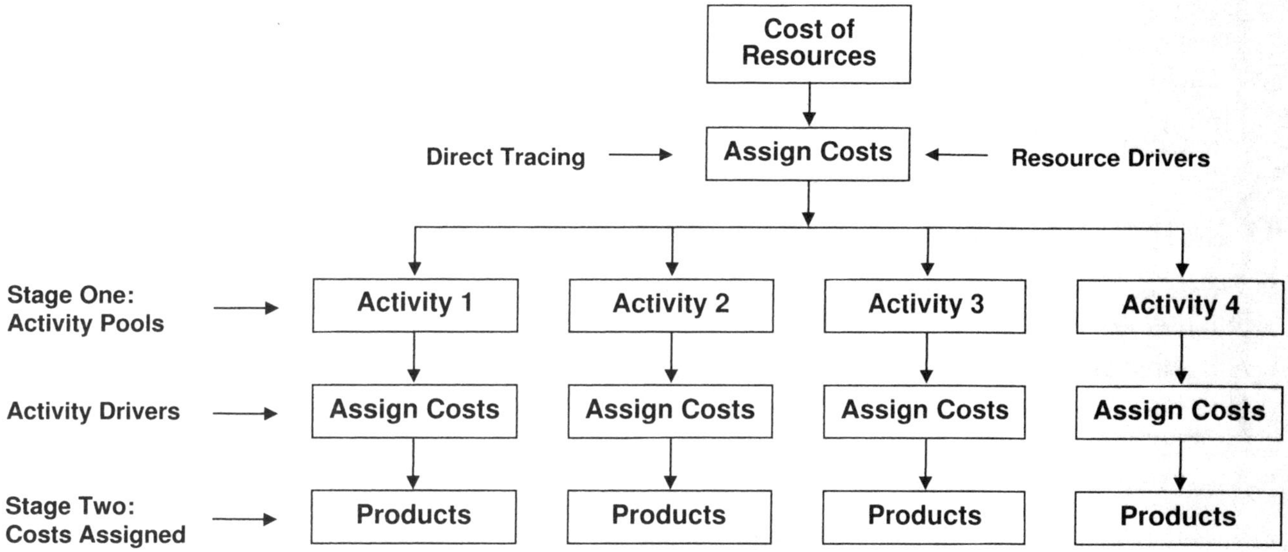

❒ Functional-based costing also involves two stages; however, overhead costs are traced to departments (instead of activities), and then traced to products.

❒ Functional-based costing and activity-based costing are compared below:

	Functional-Based Costing	**Activity-Based Costing**
First stage:	traces costs to plant or department	traces costs to activities
Second stage:	assigns costs to products	assigns costs to products
Cost tracing:	usually allocation-intensive	emphasizes direct tracing and driver tracing
Activity drivers:	unit-level	unit-level and nonunit-level

❒ Activity-based cost assignment consists of the following steps:
1. *Identify and define activities using interviews and surveys, then build an activity dictionary.* An **activity dictionary** lists activities and **activity attributes**—financial and nonfinancial information that describes the activities. Information includes:
   - activity name—usually consists of an action verb and an object

- a description of the tasks that make up the activity
- classification as a **primary activity** (activity consumed by a product or customer) or a **secondary activity** (activity consumed by other primary or secondary activities)
- activity driver—a measure of activity output

2. *Assign costs to activities.* Determine the cost of resources (such as materials, labor, and capital) consumed by each activity.
   - If the resource is exclusive to the activity (such as materials), use direct tracing.
   - If the resource is shared by several activities, use driver tracing to assign costs to the activities. **Resource drivers** are factors that measure the consumption of resources by activities.
   - The costs of secondary activities are ultimately assigned to primary activities using activity drivers.
3. *Assign costs to products.* After the cost of primary activities is calculated, assign the cost of these activities to products based on usage of the activity as measured by activity drivers. Costs assigned to products are calculated as follows:

   Cost assigned to product = Predetermined activity rate × Actual usage of activity

HOMOGENEOUS POOLS OF ACTIVITIES

- To reduce the number of predetermined overhead activity rates, activities can be grouped into homogeneous pools.
- A **homogeneous cost pool** is a collection of overhead costs associated with each set of activities. Only one activity driver need be used to assign the pool's costs, thus the number of rates required can be reduced.
- A **pool rate** is calculated as follows:

  Pool rate = Pool costs/Practical capacity of activity driver

- To build homogeneous sets of related activities, activities are classified into one of four general activity categories:
  - **Unit-level activities** are activities performed each time a unit is produced. For example, power is used each time a unit is produced.
  - **Batch-level activities** are activities performed each time a batch of products is produced. The costs of batch-level activities vary with the number of batches but are fixed with respect to the number of units in each batch. Examples include setups, inspections, production scheduling, and materials handling.
  - **Product-level (sustaining) activities** are activities performed as needed to support the products. Examples include engineering changes and equipment maintenance.
  - **Facility-level activities** are activities that support a factory's general manufacturing process. Examples include plant management and security.
- All unit-level activities that have the same cost driver would be grouped into homogeneous cost pools. For example, the unit-level category might have the following cost pools:
  - labor-related overhead cost pool
  - machine-related overhead cost pool
  - material-related overhead cost pool

- All batch-level activities that use the same cost driver would be grouped into homogeneous cost pools, and all product-level activities that use the same cost driver would be grouped into homogeneous cost pools.
- Unit-level costs vary as the number of units change; therefore, a unit-level cost driver can be used.
- Batch-level and product-level costs vary in proportion to factors other than changes in the number of units; therefore, they are assigned using nonunit-level cost drivers.
- Facility-level activities and costs are common to several products, and it is impossible to identify individual products that consume these activities. A pure ABC system would treat facility-level costs as period costs and would not assign them to products. In practice, facility-level costs might be allocated to individual products using unit-level, batch-level, or product-level cost drivers.

Comparison with Functional-Based Costing

- In a functional-based cost system, the demand for overhead is assumed to be explained only by unit-level cost drivers.
- ABC produces more accurate product costs by more accurately tracing the consumption of overhead resources to products.

Activity-Based Customer Costing

- Activity-based costing can be used to trace costs to specific customers. The cost of serving different customers can affect pricing decisions and profitability.

Customer Costing versus Product Costing

- Customer costing involves three steps:
  1. Activities, such as order entry, shipping, and sales calls, are listed in an activity dictionary. Different levels include order level, customer level, and channel level.
  2. Cost of resources used are assigned to activities.
  3. Cost of the activities are assigned to customers.
- See the cost assignment summary below:

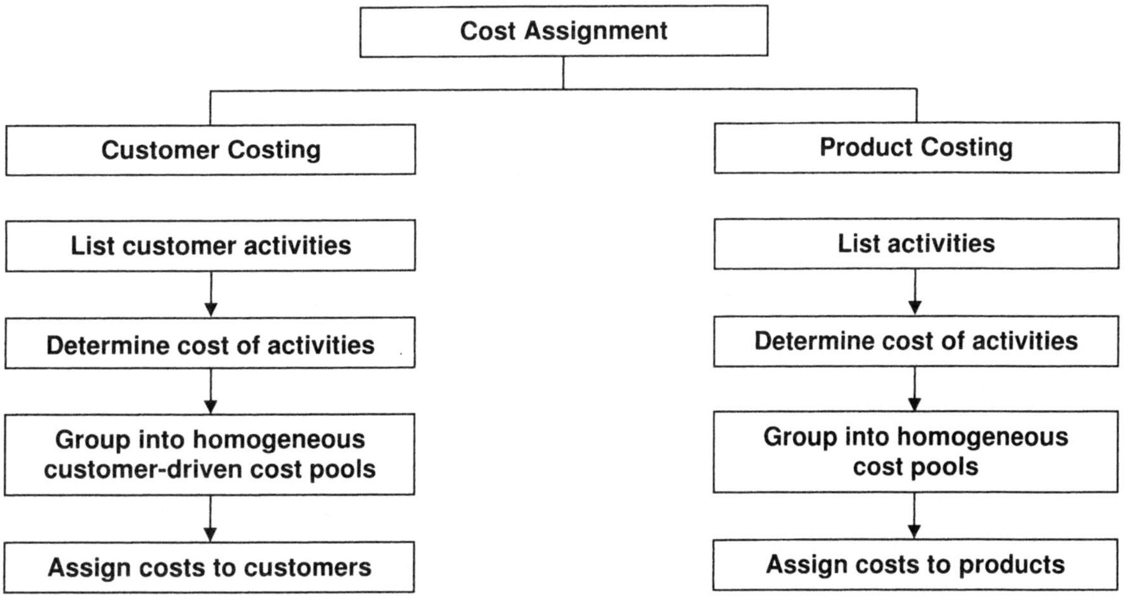

Activity-Based Supplier Costing

- Activity-based supplier costing uses activity-based costing to identify the true costs of suppliers. Activity-based costing traces costs related to purchase, quality, reliability, and delivery performance to specific suppliers.

KEY TERMS TEST

Test your recall of the key terms as follows. Try to recall as many key terms as possible without assistance. If you need assistance, refer to the list of key terms at the end of this section.

1. Activities that are performed each time a batch is produced are __________-__________ __________.

2. A(n) __________ __________ is a list of activities described by specific attributes such as name, definition, classification as primary or secondary, and activity driver.

3. The proportion of an overhead activity consumed by a product is the __________ __________.

4. __________ __________ assigns actual costs of direct materials, direct labor, and overhead to products.

5. __________ __________ assigns actual costs of direct materials and direct labor to products and uses a predetermined overhead rate to assign overhead costs.

6. A(n) __________ __________ __________ is a collection of overhead costs associated with activities that have the same level and use the same cost driver to assign costs to products.

7. A(n) __________ __________ __________ is an overhead rate computed using estimated data.

8. __________-__________ __________ __________ are factors, other than the number of units produced, that measure the demands that cost objects place on activities.

9. Activities performed to enable the production of each different type of product are __________-__________ __________.

10. __________ __________ occurs when products consume overhead in different proportions.

11. A cost system that first traces costs to activities and then traces costs from activities to products is a(n) __________-__________ __________ __________.

12. __________ __________ is overhead assigned to production using predetermined rates.

13. __________ __________ is the amount by which applied overhead exceeds actual overhead.

14. __________ __________ is the amount by which actual overhead exceeds applied overhead.

15. __________ __________ is the difference between actual overhead and applied overhead.

16. Activities that sustain a facility's general manufacturing process are __________-__________ __________.

17. __________-__________ __________ __________ are factors that cause changes in cost as the number of units produced change.

18. _____________ _____________ are nonfinancial and financial information items that describe individual activities.

19. _____________ _____________ measure the consumption of activities by products and other cost objects.

20. ________-__________ ____________ are performed each time a unit is produced.

21. The ________ ________ equals overhead costs for a homogeneous cost pool divided by the activity driver for the pool.

22. _______________ _____________ are activities consumed by products or customers.

23. _______________ _____________ are activities consumed by primary activities and/or other secondary activities.

KEY TERMS:

activity attributes
activity-based costing system
activity dictionary
activity drivers
actual costing
applied overhead
batch-level activities
consumption ratio
facility-level activities
homogeneous cost pool
nonunit-level activity drivers
normal costing
overapplied overhead
overhead variance
pool rate
predetermined overhead rate
primary activities
product diversity
product-level activities
secondary activities
underapplied overhead
unit-level activities
unit-level activity drivers

→ **Compare your answers with those at the end of the chapter. Review any key terms missed.**

CHAPTER QUIZ

Write your answers in the spaces provided.

1. Complete the following:

Costing Systems

Functional-Based Costing | **Activity-Based Costing**

First stage:		
Second stage:		
Cost tracing:		
Activity drivers:		

2. The two types of overhead rates used in functional-based costing are:

a. ______________________________

b. ______________________________

3. The overhead rates of functional-based product costing use __________-________ activity drivers.

4. Activity-based cost systems use __________-________ cost drivers.

5. When activity-based costing is used, activities are classified into one of four categories:

a. ____________________ activities

b. ____________________ activities

c. ____________________ activities

d. ____________________ activities

6. When activity-based costing is used, the first-stage procedure involves identifying cost pools and calculating a pool rate for each cost pool. The pool rate is calculated as follows:

Pool rate = ____________________ / ____________________

7. The second stage of activity-based costing involves tracing the costs of each overhead cost pool to products. The overhead assigned to each product is calculated as follows:

Applied overhead = ______________ × ____________________

Circle the single best answer.

8. Unit-level costs are assigned using: (a) unit-level activity drivers; (b) nonunit-level activity drivers

9. Batch-level costs are assigned using: (a) unit-level activity drivers; (b) nonunit-level activity drivers

10. Product-level costs are assigned using: (a) unit-level activity drivers; (b) nonunit-level activity drivers

11. A functional-based product costing system uses a two-stage procedure of (1) tracing overhead to activities, and (2) then tracing the costs to products: (a) true; (b) false

12. The use of unit-level activity drivers, such as direct labor hours or machine hours, can produce distorted product costs: (a) true; (b) false

13. A product's consumption of overhead always increases in proportion to increases in production volume: (a) true; (b) false

14. When customer costing is used, both manufacturing and nonmanufacturing costs are traced to customers to produce more accurate cost information for decision making: (a) true; (b) false

Use the following information to answer Questions 15 through 23:

The following data is available for the two products, Model E and Model Z, that Pack, Inc., manufactures:

Item	Quantity	Prime Costs	Machine Hours	Material Moves	Setups
Model E	350,000	$900,000	60,000	600,000	175
Model Z	100,000	$250,000	15,000	400,000	75
Dollar value		$1,150,000	$400,000*	$500,000	$600,000

*The cost of maintenance

Pack currently uses a functional-based costing system that assigns the costs of maintenance, material handling, and setups to the models based on machine hours, a unit-level driver. (Round numbers to two decimal places.)

15. The plantwide overhead rate is: (a) $12.00; (b) $14.67; (c) $20.00; (d) $25.00

16. Overhead assigned to Model E is: (a) $1,500,000; (b) $1,200,000; (c) $880,200; (d) $720,000

17. Overhead assigned to Model Z is: (a) $300,000; (b) $375,000; (c) $220,050; (d) $320,000

18. The unit cost of Model E is: (a) $5.40; (b) $6.00; (c) $5.50; (d) $6.86

19. The unit cost of Model Z is: (a) $4.58; (b) $5.40; (c) $6.00; (d) $5.50

20. If activity-based costing is used, overhead assigned to Model E is: (a) $1,039,800; (b) $939,800; (c) $799,800; (d) $739,800

21. If activity-based costing is used, overhead assigned to Model Z is: (a) $359,950; (b) $279,950; (c) $380,000; (d) $459,950

22. If activity-based costing is used, the unit cost of Model E is: (a) $5.26; (b) $5.54; (c) $4.31; (d) $4.86

23. If activity-based costing is used, the unit cost of Model Z is: (a) $6.30; (b) $4.28; (c) $7.10; (d) $4.60

Write your answers in the spaces provided.

Use the following information to answer Questions 24 through 29:

Classify each of the following activities as a:

- unit-level activity
- batch-level activity
- product-level activity
- facility-level activity

24. Setups: ______________________________

25. Electricity: ______________________________

26. Plant management: ______________________________

27. Engineering changes: ______________________________

28. Inspections: ______________________________

29. Plant security: ______________________________

→ **Compare your answers with those at the end of the chapter. Review any questions missed.**

PRACTICE TEST

PROBLEM 1

Paul's Plastics uses an activity-based cost system. The company produces Product X and Product Z. Information concerning the two products is given below:

	Product X	Product Z
Units produced	50,000	75,000
Machine hours	22,000	18,000
Direct labor hours	40,000	40,000
Material handling (number of moves)	10,000	15,000
Engineering labor (hours)	6,000	4,000
Setups	40	20
Maintenance (hours used)	1,500	1,000
Kilowatt hours	16,000	14,000
Inspections	18,000	12,000

The following overhead costs are reported:

Material handling	$ 70,000
Maintenance	50,000
Power	24,000
Engineering	60,000
Setups	75,000
Labor-related overhead	60,000
Machine-related overhead	120,000
Inspection	108,000

PROBLEM 1 *(Continued)*

Instructions:

1. Using the format below, classify the overhead activities as unit-level activities, batch-level activities, or product-level activities.

   Unit-level activities:

   ____

   ____

   ____

   Batch-level activities:

   ____

   ____

   ____

   Product-level activities:

   ____

   ____

   ____

2. Group all overhead costs into homogeneous cost pools. Select an activity driver for each cost pool and compute a pool rate.

Homogeneous Cost Pool		Activity Driver		Pool Rate
	/		=	
	/		=	
	/		=	
	/		=	
	/		=	
	/		=	
	/		=	
	/		=	

PROBLEM 1 *(Continued)*

3. Using the pool rates, assign overhead costs to the two products and compute the overhead cost per unit for each. Round answers to two decimal places.

	Product X	Product Z
Unit-level activities:		
______________________	__________	
______________________		__________
______________________	__________	
______________________		__________
______________________	__________	
______________________		__________
Batch-level activities:		
______________________	__________	
______________________		__________
______________________	__________	
______________________		__________
______________________	__________	
______________________		__________
Product-level activities:		
______________________	__________	
______________________		__________
______________________	__________	
______________________		__________
Overhead cost per unit	$ __________	$ __________

PROBLEM 2

Peach, Inc., has identified the following overhead costs and cost drivers for next year:

Overhead Item	Expected Cost	Cost Driver	Expected Actual Transactions
Setup costs	$ 90,000	Number of setups	400
Ordering costs	50,000	Number of orders	4,000
Maintenance costs	150,000	Machine hours	25,000
Power	30,000	Kilowatt hours	75,000

The following are two of the jobs completed during the year:

	Job 700	Job 701
Direct materials	$1,200	$600
Direct labor	$900	$400
Units completed	250	100
Direct labor hours	40	20
Number of setups	2	1
Number of orders	10	4
Machine hours	50	40
Kilowatt hours	60	25

The company's practical activity is 5,000 direct labor hours.

Instructions:

1. Determine the unit cost for each job using direct labor hours to apply overhead. Round answers to two decimal places.

PROBLEM 2 *(Continued)*

2. Determine the unit cost for each job using the four activity drivers. Round answers to two decimal places.

3. Which method produces the more accurate cost assignment? Why?

PROBLEM 3

Hanover Manufacturing has four categories of overhead. The four categories and expected overhead costs for each category for next year are listed below:

Maintenance	$200,000
Materials handling	32,000
Setups	100,000
Inspection	120,000

Currently, overhead is applied using a predetermined overhead rate based upon budgeted direct labor hours. For next year, 50,000 direct labor hours are budgeted.

The company has been asked to submit a bid for a proposed job. The plant manager thinks getting this job would result in new business in future years. Usually bids are based upon full manufacturing cost plus 20 percent.

Estimates for the proposed job (Job No. P902) are as follows:

Direct materials	$6,000
Direct labor (1,000 hours)	$10,000
Machine hours	500
Number of material moves	12
Number of setups	2
Number of inspections	10

In the past, full manufacturing cost has been calculated by allocating overhead using a volume-based cost driver (direct labor hours). The plant manager has heard of a new way of applying overhead that uses cost pools and cost drivers.

Expected activity for the four activity-based cost drivers that would be used are:

Machine hours	20,000
Material moves	1,600
Setups	2,500
Quality inspections	4,000

Instructions:

1. **a.** Determine the amount of overhead that would be allocated to the proposed job if a plant-wide rate with direct labor hours used the unit-level driver.

PROBLEM 3 *(Continued)*

b. Determine the total cost of the proposed job.

c. Determine the company's bid if the bid is based upon full manufacturing cost plus 20 percent.

2. a. Determine the amount of overhead that would be applied to the proposed project if activity-based drivers are used.

b. Determine the total cost of the proposed job if activity-based costing is used.

c. Determine the company's bid if activity-based costing is used and the bid is based upon full manufacturing cost plus 20 percent.

PROBLEM 3 *(Continued)*

3. Prepare a memorandum to the plant manager with your recommendation regarding the bid the company should submit. Include the reasons for your recommendation as well as any supporting calculations.

MEMORANDUM

DATE:

TO:

FROM:

SUBJECT:

PROBLEM 4

Ortegren, Inc., has two producing departments: Assembly and Finishing. The company has been using a plantwide predetermined overhead rate based on direct labor cost. The following amounts are for the current year:

	Assembly	Finishing
Actual overhead	$220,000	$215,000
Budgeted overhead	$240,000	$180,000
Budgeted direct labor hours	30,000	12,000
Budgeted machine hours	8,000	10,000
Actual activity in direct labor hours	31,000	13,000
Actual activity in machine hours	9,000	11,000

Instructions:

1. **a.** Calculate a plantwide predetermined overhead rate using direct labor hours.

   b. Calculate applied overhead.

   c. Calculate the amount of underapplied or overapplied overhead.

2. **a.** Calculate separate departmental overhead rates using direct labor hours for Assembly and machine hours for Finishing.

   b. Calculate the total amount of applied overhead for each department.

   c. Calculate the amount of underapplied or overapplied overhead for each department.

ANSWERS

KEY TERMS TEST

1. batch-level activities
2. activity dictionary
3. consumption ratio
4. Actual costing
5. Normal costing
6. homogeneous cost pool
7. predetermined overhead rate
8. Nonunit-level activity drivers
9. product-level activities
10. Product diversity
11. activity-based costing system
12. Applied overhead
13. Overapplied overhead
14. Underapplied overhead
15. Overhead variance
16. facility-level activities
17. Unit-level activity drivers
18. Activity attributes
19. Activity drivers
20. Unit-level activities
21. pool rate
22. Primary activities
23. Secondary activities

CHAPTER QUIZ

1. See page 53.
2. **a.** a plantwide overhead rate
   b. departmental overhead rates
3. unit-level
4. nonunit-level
5. **a.** unit-level
   b. batch-level
   c. product-level
   d. facility-level
6. Cost pool/Activity driver
7. Pool rate × Activity driver consumed by product
8. a
9. b
10. b
11. b False Functional-based product costing uses a two-stage procedure: (1) costs are traced to the plant or departments (instead of activities), and then (2) costs are traced to products.
12. a True
13. b False A product's consumption of overhead does NOT always increase in proportion to increases in production volume. For example, setup costs are related to the number of setups instead of production volume.
14. a True
15. c ($400,000 + $500,000 + $600,000)/75,000 machine hours = $20.00
16. b ($20 × 60,000 machine hours) = $1,200,000
17. a ($20 × 15,000 machine hours) = $300,000
18. b ($900,000 + $1,200,000)/350,000 units = $6.00
19. d ($250,000 + $300,000)/100,000 units = $5.50
20. a Maintenance: $400,000/75,000 machine hours = $5.33/machine hour
    Materials handling: $500,000/1,000,000 moves = $0.50/move
    Setups: $600,000/250 setups = $2,400/setup

Model E:		
$5.33 × 60,000	=	$ 319,800
$0.50 × 600,000	=	$ 300,000
$2,400 × 175	=	$ 420,000
Total		$1,039,800

21. d

Model Z:		
$5.33 × 15,000	=	$ 79,950
$0.50 × 400,000	=	$200,000
$2,400 × 75	=	$180,000
Total		$459,950

22. b ($900,000 + $1,039,800)/350,000 units = $5.54
23. c ($250,000 + $459,950)/100,000 units = $7.10
24. batch-level activity
25. unit-level activity
26. facility-level activity
27. product-level activity
28. batch-level activity
29. facility-level activity

PRACTICE TEST

PROBLEM 1

1. **Unit-level activities:**
   Labor-related overhead
   Machine-related overhead
   Power

   Batch-level activities:
   Material handling
   Setups
   Inspection

   Product-level activities:
   Engineering
   Maintenance

2.

Homogeneous Cost Pool		Activity Driver		Pool Rate
Labor-related overhead—$60,000	/	Direct labor hours—80,000	=	$0.75
Machine-related overhead—$120,000	/	Machine hours—40,000	=	$3.00
Power—$24,000	/	Kilowatt hours—30,000	=	$0.80
Material handling—$70,000	/	Number of moves—25,000	=	$2.80
Setups—$75,000	/	Number of setups—60	=	$1,250.00
Inspection—$108,000	/	Number of inspections—30,000	=	$3.60
Engineering—$60,000	/	Engineering labor hours—10,000	=	$6.00
Maintenance—$50,000	/	Maintenance hours used—2,500	=	$20.00

3.

	Product X	Product Z
Unit-level activities:		
Labor-related overhead:		
($0.75 × 40,000)/50,000 units	$0.60	
($0.75 × 40,000)/75,000 units		$0.40
Machine-related overhead:		
($3.00 × 22,000)/50,000 units	$1.32	
($3.00 × 18,000)/75,000 units		$0.72
Power:		
($0.80 × 16,000)/50,000 units	$0.26	
($0.80 × 14,000)/75,000 units		$0.15
Batch-level activities:		
Material handling:		
($2.80 × 10,000)/50,000 units	$0.56	
($2.80 × 15,000)/75,000 units		$0.56
Setups:		
($1,250 × 40)/50,000 units	$1.00	
($1,250 × 20)/75,000 units		$0.33
Inspections:		
($3.60 × 18,000)/50,000 units	$1.30	
($3.60 × 12,000)/75,000 units		$0.58
Product-level activities:		
Engineering:		
($6.00 × 6,000)/50,000 units	$0.72	
($6.00 × 4,000)/75,000 units		$0.32
Maintenance:		
($20.00 × 1,500)/50,000 units	$0.60	
($20.00 × 1,000)/75,000 units		$0.27
Overhead cost per unit	$6.36	$3.33

PROBLEM 2

1. Total overhead costs = $90,000 + $50,000 + $150,000 + $30,000
   = $320,000

   Plantwide overhead rate = $320,000/5,000
   = $64 per direct labor hour

	Job 700	Job 701
Direct materials	$1,200	$ 600
Direct labor	900	400
Overhead assigned:		
($64 × 40 direct labor hours)	2,560	
($64 × 20 direct labor hours)		1,280
Total cost	$4,660	$2,280
Cost per unit:		
($4,660/250 units)	$18.64	
($2,280/100 units)		$22.80

2. Activity-based overhead rates:

   Setup costs: $90,000/400 setups = $225 per setup
   Ordering costs: $50,000/4,000 orders = $12.50 per order
   Maintenance costs: $150,000/25,000 machine hours = $6 per machine hour
   Power: $30,000/75,000 kilowatt hours = $0.40 per kilowatt hour

	Job 700	Job 701
Direct materials	$1,200	$ 600
Direct labor	900	400
Overhead applied:		
($225 × 2 setups)	450	
($12.50 × 10 orders)	125	
($6.00 × 50 machine hours)	300	
($0.40 × 60 kilowatt hours)	24	
($225 × 1 setup)		225
($12.50 × 4 orders)		50
($6.00 × 40 machine hours)		240
($0.40 × 25 kilowatt hours)		10
Total cost	$2,999	$1,525
Cost per unit:		
($2,999/250 units)	$12.00	
($1,525/100 units)		$15.25

3. Activity-based costing produces the more accurate cost assignment because it uses multiple drivers that are related to overhead consumption. A product or job's consumption of overhead does not always increase in proportion to a single volume-based cost driver, such as direct labor hours.

   Setup costs are related to the number of setups, ordering costs are related to the number of orders, maintenance costs are related to the number of machine hours, and power costs are related to the number of kilowatt hours.

PROBLEM 3

1. **a.** Total overhead = $200,000 + $32,000 + $100,000 + $120,000
   = $452,000

   Overhead rate = $452,000/50,000 direct labor hours
   = $9.04 per direct labor hour

   Overhead assigned to proposed job = $9.04 × 1,000 direct labor hours
   = $9,040

   b. Total cost of proposed job:

Direct materials	$ 6,000
Direct labor	10,000
Overhead applied	9,040
Total cost	$25,040

c. Company's bid = Full manufacturing cost × 120%
= $25,040 × 120%
= $30,048

2. a. Maintenance: $200,000/20,000 machine hours = $10 per machine hour
Materials handling: $32,000/1,600 material moves = $20 per move
Setups: $100,000/2,500 setups = $40 per setup
Inspection: $120,000/4,000 inspections = $30 per inspection

Overhead assigned to proposed job:

Maintenance ($10 × 500)	$5,000
Materials handling ($20 × 12)	240
Setups ($40 × 2)	80
Inspections ($30 × 10)	300
Total overhead assigned to job	$5,620

b. Total cost of proposed project:

Direct materials	$ 6,000
Direct labor	10,000
Overhead applied	5,620
Total cost	$21,620

c. Company's bid = Full manufacturing cost × 120%
= $21,620 × 120%
= $25,944

3. Your memorandum should contain the following:

(a) A brief introductory sentence to inform the reader of the purpose of the memorandum.
Example: This memorandum regards the recommended bid price for proposed Job No. P902.

(b) A concise and specific recommendation.
Example: I recommend that Hanover Manufacturing submit a bid of $25,944 for Job No. P902.

(c) A discussion of the reasons why your recommendation should be followed.
Example: This bid price was developed using activity-based costing (ABC) because ABC produces more accurate product costs and more competitive bids.

(d) Supporting calculations included in the body of the memorandum or attached on a separate page.
Example: The bid price of $25,944 was determined as follows:

Direct materials		$ 6,000
Direct labor		10,000
Overhead assigned:		
Maintenance ($10 × 500)	$5,000	
Materials handling ($20 × 12)	240	
Setups ($40 × 2)	80	
Inspections ($30 × 10)	300	
Total overhead assigned to job		5,620
Total cost		$21,620
Markup		× 120%
Bid price		$25,944

(e) A closing sentence.
Example: If you have any questions, please contact me at Extension 76.

PROBLEM 4

1. a. Plantwide rate = Budgeted plant overhead/Budgeted direct labor hours
= ($240,000 + $180,000)/(30,000 + 12,000)
= $10 per direct labor hour

b. Applied overhead = Plantwide overhead rate × Actual activity
= $10 × (31,000 + 13,000)
= $440,000

c.

Overhead

Actual overhead	Applied overhead
$220,000	$440,000
215,000	
	$ 5,000 overapplied

2. a. Assembly departmental rate = $240,000/30,000 direct labor hours
= $8.00 per direct labor hour

Finished departmental rate = $180,000/10,000 machine hours
= $18.00 per machine hour

b. Applied overhead: Assembly = $8.00 × 31,000 direct labor hours
= $248,000

Applied overhead: Finishing = $18.00 × 11,000 machine hours
= $198,000

c.

Overhead: Assembly

Actual overhead	Applied overhead
$220,000	$248,000
	$ 28,000 overapplied

Overhead: Finishing

Actual overhead	Applied overhead
$215,000	$198,000
$ 17,000 underapplied	

CHAPTER 5
Job-Order Costing

CHAPTER REVIEW

JOB-ORDER ENVIRONMENT

- Unit cost information is needed for:
  1. the financial reporting requirements of costing inventory and determining income, and
  2. decision making, such as product pricing.
- Different cost information is needed for different purposes.
- Two cost assignment systems are:
  1. job-order costing, and
  2. process costing.

Job-Order Production and Costing

- A **job-order costing system** accumulates manufacturing costs by job.
- Such a system is used when separate jobs are identifiable, such as a furniture manufacturer.
- Unit costs in a job-order system are calculated by dividing the total manufacturing cost of the job by the number of units produced in the job.

Process Production and Costing

- A **process-costing system** is used where similar or homogeneous units are mass produced, such as the manufacture of paint or bricks.
- In a process-costing system, production costs are accumulated by process or by department for a given period of time.
- Unit costs are calculated by dividing the processing department's costs by the output for the period.
- A comparison of job-order and process costing follows:

Job-Order Costing	**Process Costing**
1. Wide variety of distinct products	**1.** Homogenous products
2. Costs accumulated by job	**2.** Costs accumulated by process or department
3. Unit cost is computed by dividing total job costs by the units produced.	**3.** Unit cost is computed by dividing process costs of the period by the units produced in the period.

Calculating Unit Cost with Job-Order Costing

- Using a normal costing system, the total cost of a job is calculated using:
  - actual costs for direct materials
  - actual costs for direct labor
  - a predetermined rate to apply overhead
- Overhead can be assigned using:
  - a single, unit-level activity driver, or
  - multiple activity drivers.
- Unit-level systems can be used effectively whenever one of three conditions is met: (1) the nonunit-level overhead is a small percentage of the total overhead, (2) the products produced in the job environment have the same overhead consumption ratios, or (3) the cost of using both unit-level and nonunit-level drivers exceeds the benefits.
- A **job-order cost sheet** is used to accumulate the manufacturing costs (direct materials, direct labor, and overhead) associated with a job.
- The job-order cost sheets are the subsidiary ledgers to the Work-in-Process account.

THE FLOW OF COSTS THROUGH THE ACCOUNTS

Accounting for Materials

- The materials account is used to account for:
  1. purchases of materials and supplies, and
  2. issuance of materials to production.
- The entry to record the purchase of materials would be:

  Debit: Raw Materials
  Credit: Accounts Payable

- The **materials requisition form** is the source document used to record direct materials on the job-cost sheet. Materials requisition forms are used to make requests for materials from inventory.
- The entry to record the issuance of direct materials for use in production would be:

  Debit: Work in Process
  Credit: Raw Materials

- Indirect materials are included in manufacturing overhead and assigned to jobs using the predetermined overhead rate.

Accounting for Direct Labor Cost

- **Time tickets** indicate the direct labor time worked on each job. Information on the time tickets are used to post direct labor costs to the job-order cost sheet for individual jobs.
- Indirect labor costs are included in overhead and assigned to jobs using the predetermined overhead rate.
- The entry to record direct labor costs would be:

  Debit: Work in Process
  Credit: Wages Payable

❒ The job-order cost sheets are updated to indicate the direct labor costs associated with each job.

Accounting for Overhead

❒ Overhead is applied to specific jobs using a predetermined overhead rate established at the beginning of the period.

ABC and Job-Order Costing

❒ ABC establishes activity-based overhead rates by estimating:

1. a budgeted cost for each activity pool, and
2. expected demand for the activity driver for each pool. Examples of activity drivers include direct labor hours, machine hours, purchase orders, etc.

❒ Activity-based rates are calculated as follows:

$$\textbf{Activity-based rate} = \frac{\textbf{Budgeted cost for activity pool}}{\textbf{Expected demand for activity driver}}$$

❒ Overhead is assigned to specific jobs by multiplying the activity-based rate by the actual activity for the specific job.

Applied overhead = Activity-based rate × Activity for job

❒ The summary entry to record total overhead applied would be:

Debit: Work in Process
  Credit: Overhead Control

❒ Overhead applied to specific jobs would be recorded on the job-cost sheet for the particular job.

Applying Overhead Using Functional Approaches

❒ Overhead can also be applied using:

- a plantwide rate (usually based on direct labor hours)
- departmental rates (usually based on unit-level drivers, such as direct labor hours or machine hours)

❒ The predetermined overhead rate is calculated as follows:

$$\textbf{Predetermined overhead rate} = \frac{\textbf{Budgeted overhead costs}}{\textbf{Budgeted activity}}$$

❒ Overhead is assigned or applied to each job by multiplying the activity for that particular job by the predetermined rate. For example, if a firm selected direct labor hours as the activity, overhead would be applied by multiplying the number of hours worked on the particular job by the predetermined rate.

Applied overhead = Predetermined overhead rate × Actual activity

❒ Differences between functional and activity-based costing are summarized at the top of page 78.

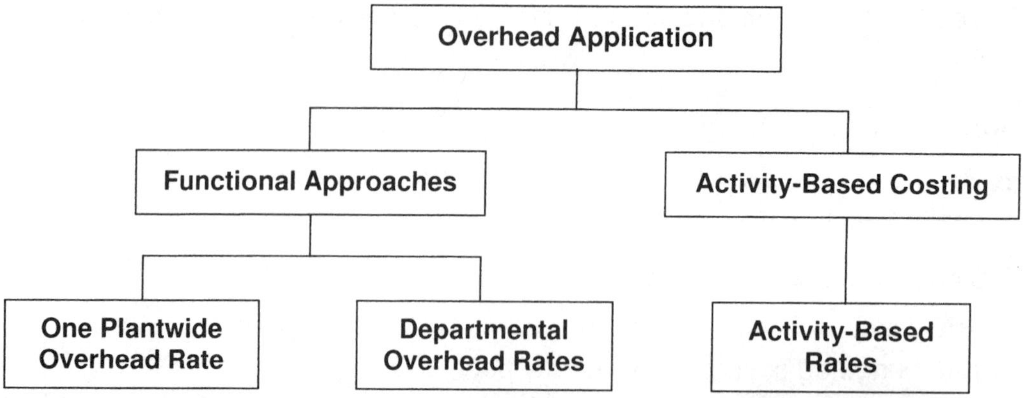

	One Plantwide Overhead Rate	Departmental Overhead Rates	Activity-Based Rates
Overhead rates:	one overhead rate using a unit-level driver	different overhead rates for different departments	multiple activity-based overhead rates
Examples of drivers:	direct labor hours	machine hours direct labor hours	machine hours direct labor hours purchase orders setups material moves, etc.
Predetermined overhead rate:	Estimated plant total overhead ÷ Estimated total activity	Estimated departmental overhead ÷ Total activity for department estimated	Estimated overhead cost of activity pool ÷ Activity driver for pool
Applied overhead:	Predetermined overhead rate × Activity for job	Predetermined overhead rate × Activity for job	Activity-based rate × Activity for job

Accounting for Actual Overhead Costs

- Actual overhead costs are recorded in the Overhead Control account.
- Actual overhead costs include:
  1. indirect materials
  2. indirect labor, overtime premium, and idle time
  3. invoices received from outside suppliers for utilities, rent, repairs, property taxes, etc. The entry to record these costs would be:

     Debit: Overhead Control
         Credit: Accounts Payable

  4. internal transfers of costs, such as depreciation and the expiration of prepaid insurance. The entry to record such items would be:

     Debit: Overhead Control
         Credit: Accumulated Depreciation—Building
         Credit: Accumulated Depreciation—Equipment
         Credit: Prepaid Insurance

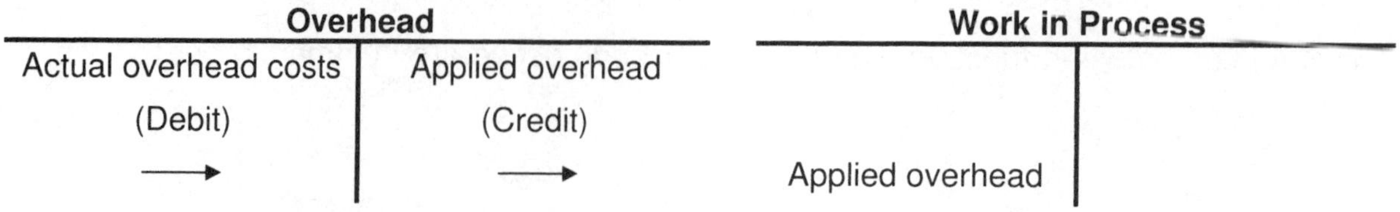

Overhead Variance

- The overhead variance is the difference between actual overhead and applied overhead.
- Underapplied overhead results when applied overhead is less than actual overhead for the period.
- Overapplied overhead results when applied overhead exceeds actual overhead for the period.
- If immaterial, underapplied or overapplied overhead may be treated as an adjustment to cost of goods sold.

Accounting for Finished Goods

- When a job is completed, the cost of the job is transferred from the Work-in-Process account to the Finished Goods account. The entry to record the transfer would be:

  Debit: Finished Goods
  Credit: Work in Process

- At the end of the period, the Work-in-Process account will have a balance only if there is uncompleted work in the factory.

Accounting for Cost of Goods Sold

- As goods are sold, the associated costs are transferred from the Finished Goods account to the Cost of Goods Sold account. The entry to record the transfer would be:

  Debit: Cost of Goods Sold
  Credit: Finished Goods

- The entry to record the sale would be:

  Debit: Accounts Receivable
  Credit: Sales Revenue

- If the overhead variance is immaterial, it is treated as an adjustment to cost of goods sold at the end of the year. The entry to close overapplied overhead to cost of goods sold would be:

  Debit: Cost of Goods Sold
  Credit: Overhead Control

- **Normal cost of goods sold** is the amount of cost of goods sold before adjustment for an overhead variance.
- **Adjusted cost of goods sold** is normal cost of goods sold after adjustment for an overhead variance.

Summary of Manufacturing Cost Flows

- The diagram at the top of page 80 summarizes the flow of manufacturing costs.
- Because Cost of Goods Sold is an expense, it appears on the company's income statement.
- Raw Materials, Work in Process, and Finished Goods would appear in the current assets section of the company's balance sheet.
- Work in Process would also appear in the schedule of cost of goods manufactured, while Finished Goods would also appear in the cost of goods sold section of the income statement.

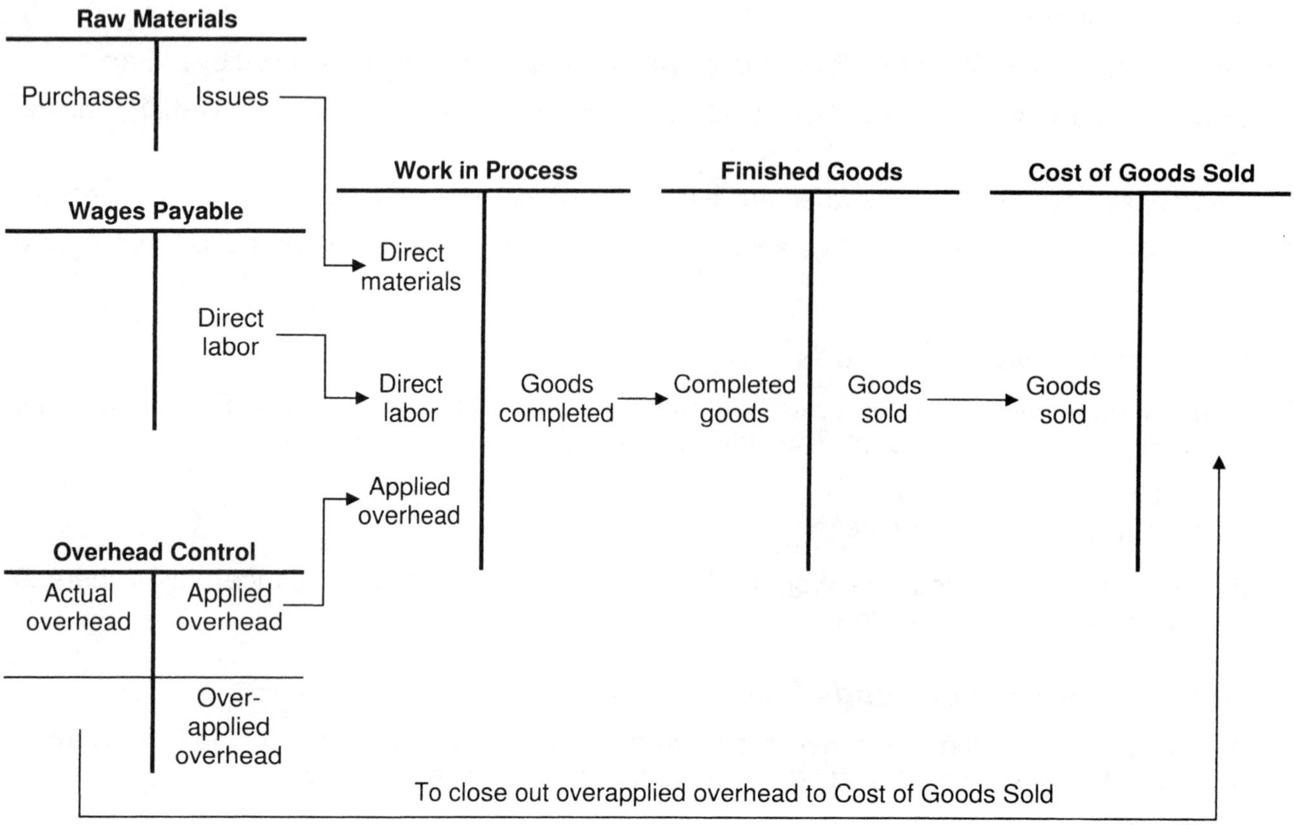

Accounting for Nonmanufacturing Costs

- Selling and general administrative costs (nonmanufacturing costs) are considered period costs and are not assigned to the product.
- The entry to record selling and general administrative costs would be:

  Debit: Selling Expense Control
  Debit: Administrative Expense Control
  Credit: Accounts Payable
  Credit: Wages Payable
  Credit: Accumulated Depreciation

- Selling and administrative expenses appear on the income statement.

KEY TERMS TEST

Test your recall of the key terms as follows. Try to recall as many key terms as possible without assistance. If you need assistance, refer to the list of key terms at the end of this section.

1. A document or record used to accumulate manufacturing costs for a job is a(n) ________-________ ________ ________.
2. A document used to record the cost of direct materials issued to each job is a(n) ________ ________ ________.
3. A cost accumulation method that accumulates costs by process or department is a(n) ________-________ ________.
4. A(n) ________-________ ________ ________ accumulates manufacturing costs by job.
5. A document used to identify the cost of direct labor for a job is a(n) ________ ________.
6. Normal cost of goods sold adjusted to include an overhead variance is called ________ ________ ________ ________ ________.
7. A(n) ________-________-________ ________ is a collection of open job-order cost sheets or job-order cost records.
8. The cost of goods sold amount calculated using per-unit normal cost is called ________ ________ ________ ________ ________.
9. A ________ is one distinct unit or set of units.

KEY TERMS:

adjusted cost of goods sold
job
job-order cost sheet
job-order costing system
materials requisition form
normal cost of goods sold
process-costing system
time ticket
work-in-process file

→ **Compare your answers with those at the end of the chapter. Review any key terms missed.**

CHAPTER QUIZ

Circle the single best answer.

1. Material requisitions are used for recording: (a) materials purchased; (b) materials issued and used in production; (c) materials on hand in the storeroom; (d) none of the above
2. A department that is equipment intensive would most likely use a predetermined departmental overhead rate based on which of the following cost drivers: (a) machine hours; (b) direct labor hours; (c) direct labor cost; (d) units of direct material used
3. The overhead costs of a given period might appear in all of the following accounts except: (a) Raw Materials; (b) Work in Process; (c) Finished Goods; (d) Cost of Goods Sold
4. A job-order cost system associates costs with particular jobs: (a) true; (b) false

5. A job-order cost system is especially appropriate for situations where basically homogeneous units flow through production on a fairly continuous basis: (a) true; (b) false

6. Time tickets indicate the direct labor time worked on each job: (a) true; (b) false

7. The Work-in-Process account will have a balance only if there is uncompleted work in the factory: (a) true; (b) false

8. Finished Goods is an expense account: (a) true; (b) false

9. Raw Materials, Work in Process, and Cost of Goods Sold would appear in the assets section of the balance sheet: (a) true; (b) false

10. Most firms use actual costing because it provides product cost information on a timely basis: (a) true; (b) false

11. A single, unit-level driver usually results in a more accurate cost assignment for overhead than activity-based costing: (a) true; (b) false

Use the following information to answer Questions 12 through 14:

Estimated overhead	$320,000
Actual overhead costs incurred	$344,400
Estimated direct labor hours	40,000
Actual direct labor hours worked	42,000

12. The predetermined overhead rate for applying overhead would be: (a) $7.62; (b) $8.00; (c) $8.20; (d) $8.61

13. If the predetermined overhead rate is used to apply overhead, applied overhead would be: (a) $321,000; (b) $328,000; (c) $336,000; (d) $344,400

14. The amount of the overhead variance would be: (a) $24,400 overapplied; (b) $24,400 underapplied; (c) $8,400 overapplied; (d) $8,400 underapplied

→ **Compare your answers with those at the end of the chapter. Review any questions missed.**

PRACTICE TEST

PROBLEM 1

Strief Industries identified the following budgeted overhead activities and drivers:

Activity Pools		Activity Drivers	
Machining	$80,000	Machine hours	10,000
Setups	$15,000	Number of setups	5,000
Purchasing	$10,000	Purchase orders	2,000

Data associated with Job 786 follows:

Direct materials	$1,000
Direct labor	$3,500
Machine hours	300
Number of setups	50
Purchase orders	20

PROBLEM 1 *(Continued)*

Instructions:

1. **a.** Calculate a unit-level overhead rate based on machine hours.

   b. What is the total cost of Job 786 using this rate?

2. **a.** Calculate activity-based overhead rates.

   b. What is the total cost of Job 786 using the three activity rates?

3. Which method of overhead application (activity-based rates or one plantwide rate) is more accurate?

PROBLEM 2

The Paine Company uses a predetermined overhead rate to apply overhead to production. The rate is based on direct labor hours.

Estimates for the year 2004 are given below:

Estimated overhead	$500,000
Estimated direct labor hours	50,000

During 2004, the Paine Company used 60,000 direct labor hours.

At the end of 2004, the Paine Company records revealed the following information:

Raw materials inventory	$ 40,000
Work-in-process inventory	100,000
Finished goods inventory	200,000
Cost of goods sold	700,000
Overhead	510,000

Instructions:

1. Calculate the predetermined overhead rate for 2004.

2. Determine the amount of underapplied or overapplied overhead for 2004.

3. If underapplied or overapplied overhead is treated as an adjustment to cost of goods sold, determine the cost of goods sold amount that would appear on the company's income statement.

PROBLEM 3

Getz, Inc., has two producing departments: Assembly and Finishing. The company has been using a plantwide predetermined overhead rate based on direct labor cost.

The following estimates were made for the current year:

	Assembly	Finishing	Total
Overhead	$240,000	$160,000	$400,000
Direct labor cost	$300,000	$500,000	$800,000
Machine hours.......................	15,000	10,000	25,000

Instructions:

1. Calculate a plantwide predetermined overhead rate for the current year based on direct labor cost.

2. Calculate separate departmental overhead rates based upon direct labor cost for Assembly and machine hours for Finishing.

PROBLEM 4

Cornell Industries uses a job-order costing system and applies overhead on the basis of direct labor hours. At the beginning of 2004, management estimated that 200,000 direct labor hours would be worked and $600,000 of overhead costs would be incurred.

During the year, the company actually worked 220,000 direct labor hours and incurred the following production costs:

Indirect labor	$140,000
Indirect materials	100,000
Insurance	50,000
Utilities	90,000
Repairs and maintenance	80,000
Depreciation	180,000
Direct materials used in production	540,000
Direct labor	700,000

Instructions:

1. Calculate the predetermined overhead application rate for 2004.

2. Determine the amount of overhead applied to work in process during 2004.

PROBLEM 4 *(Continued)*

3. Determine the amount of underapplied or overapplied overhead for the year.

4. If goods with a cost of $1,500,000 were completed and transferred to finished goods during 2004, determine the cost of goods in process at the end of the period.

5. Prepare the journal entry to close underapplied or overapplied overhead to cost of goods sold.

PROBLEM 5

Voellenger, Incorporated, uses a job-order costing system and a predetermined overhead rate based on machine hours.

At the beginning of the year, Voellenger estimated overhead for the year would be $50,000 and 8,000 machine hours would be used.

The following information pertains to December of the current year:

	Job No. 77	Job No. 79	Job No. 73	Totals
Work in process, December 1	$6,000	$2,500	$1,500	$10,000
December production activity:				
Materials requisitioned	$1,200	$800	$650	$2,650
Direct labor costs	$1,000	$400	$250	$1,650
Machine hours	300	200	100	600

Actual overhead costs incurred in December were $5,000, of which $1,000 was depreciation on the factory building and $500 was depreciation on the production equipment.

Instructions:

1. Compute the predetermined overhead rate.

2. Prepare the journal entries to record the activity for the month of December.

PROBLEM 5 *(Continued)*

3. Determine the cost associated with each job.

4. If Job No. 77 was completed during December, what is the balance of the Work-in-Process account at December 31?

5. If there was no balance in the Overhead Control account on December 1, what is the balance at December 31?

6. Prepare the journal entry to close underapplied or overapplied overhead to cost of goods sold.

PROBLEM 6

Thompson Industries uses a job-order costing system and a predetermined overhead rate based on direct labor cost.

Estimated overhead for 2004 was $540,000 and estimated direct labor costs were $900,000.

On January 1, 2004, the company had the following inventories:

Raw materials	$ –0–
Work in process (Job No. 96)	16,000
Finished goods	–0–

The following information pertains to the company's activities for the month of January 2004:

a. Purchased $150,000 of materials on account.

b. Job Nos. 97 and 98 were started during the month.

c. Materials requisitioned for production totaled $144,000, of which $6,000 was for indirect materials.

Job No. 96	$46,000
Job No. 97	70,000
Job No. 98	22,000

d. Factory payroll for the month totaled $100,000, of which $15,000 was for indirect labor. The direct labor was distributed as follows:

Job No. 96	$20,000
Job No. 97	35,000
Job No. 98	30,000

e. The company made adjusting entries at the end of January to record the following expenses:

Depreciation	$5,000
Expired insurance	1,000

f. Other manufacturing costs not yet paid totaled $30,650.

g. Overhead was applied using the predetermined overhead rate based upon direct labor cost.

h. Job Nos. 96 and 97 were completed during the month.

i. Job No. 96 was sold on account during the month at a selling price of 120% of manufacturing cost.

Instructions:

1. (Appendix) Prepare journal entries to record the manufacturing activities of the company for January and post to job-cost sheets, where appropriate.

PROBLEM 6 *(Continued)*

Use this page to continue your answer.

PROBLEM 6 *(Continued)*

2. Prepare T accounts for Raw Materials, Manufacturing Overhead Control, Work in Process, Finished Goods, and Cost of Goods Sold. Enter beginning balances, where appropriate, and post the transactions for January.

3. (Appendix) Prepare the journal entry to dispose of the underapplied or overapplied overhead if the underapplied or overapplied overhead is immaterial.

PROBLEM 7

AEU Industries uses a job-order costing system. There are two production departments: Machining and Assembly. A predetermined overhead rate is used in each department.

The Machining Department bases its rate on machine hours, and the Assembly Department bases its rate on direct labor hours.

The company made the following estimates at the beginning of the current year:

	Machining	Assembly
Machine hours	20,000	15,000
Direct labor hours	7,000	40,000
Overhead cost	$200,000	$800,000

The following information was available for Job No. 12-5, which was started and completed during December.

JOB NO. 12-5

	Machining	Assembly
Direct materials	$2,000	$–0–
Direct labor cost	$1,200	$5,500
Direct labor hours	30	200
Machine hours	150	50

Instructions:

1. Calculate the predetermined overhead rate used by each producing department.

2. Compute the total cost of Job No. 12-5.

ANSWERS

KEY TERMS TEST

1. job-order cost sheet
2. materials requisition form
3. process-costing system
4. job-order costing system
5. time ticket
6. adjusted cost of goods sold
7. work-in-process file
8. normal cost of goods sold
9. job

CHAPTER QUIZ

1. b
2. a
3. a
4. a True
5. b False Process costing would be appropriate for situations where basically homogeneous units flow through production on a fairly continuous basis.
6. a True
7. a True
8. b False Of the six control accounts, Cost of Goods Sold is the only expense account. Finished Goods is an inventory account that would appear in the current assets section of the balance sheet.
9. b False The three inventory accounts are Raw Materials, Work in Process, and Finished Goods. Cost of goods sold appears on the income statement.
10. b False Most firms do not use actual costing because actual costs cannot be determined until the end of the period.
11. b False Multiple activity drivers used in activity-based costing usually result in a more accurate cost assignment than a single, unit-level driver.
12. b $320,000/40,000 = $8.00
13. c $8 × 42,000 = $336,000
14. d $344,400 – $336,000 = $8,400 underapplied

PRACTICE TEST

PROBLEM 1

1. **a.** Unit-level overhead rate:

$$= \frac{\text{Total overhead costs}}{\text{Activity}}$$

$$= \frac{(\$80{,}000 + \$15{,}000 + \$10{,}000)}{10{,}000 \text{ machine hours}}$$

$$= \frac{\$105{,}000}{10{,}000 \text{ machine hours}}$$

= $10.50 per machine hour

b. Job 786 total cost:

Direct materials	$1,000
Direct labor	3,500
Overhead (300 machine hours × $10.50)	3,150
	$7,650

2. **a.** Activity-based overhead rates:

Machining rate: $80,000/10,000 machine hours = $8 per machine hour
Setup rate: $15,000/5,000 setups = $3 per setup
Purchasing rate: $10,000/2,000 purchase orders = $5 per purchase order

b. Job 786 total cost:

Direct materials	$1,000
Direct labor	3,500
Overhead (300 machine hours × $8.00)	2,400
Setups (50 setups × $3.00)	150
Purchasing (20 purchase orders × $5.00)	100
	$7,150

3. Activity-based rates

PROBLEM 2

1. Predetermined overhead rate:

$$= \frac{\text{Estimated total overhead}}{\text{Estimated total activity}}$$

$$= \frac{\$500{,}000}{50{,}000 \text{ direct labor hours}}$$

= $10 per direct labor hour

2. Overapplied overhead for 2004:

Overhead Control

Actual overhead	Applied overhead
$510,000	$600,000 (60,000 DLH × $10)
	$ 90,000 overapplied

3. Adjusted cost of goods sold:

Cost of goods sold	$700,000
Overapplied overhead	(90,000)
Adjusted cost of goods sold	$610,000

Since overhead was overapplied, cost of goods sold is reduced.

PROBLEM 3

1. Plantwide rate $= \frac{\text{Overhead}}{\text{Direct labor cost}}$

$$= \frac{\$400{,}000}{\$800{,}000}$$

= 50% of direct labor cost

2. Departmental rates:

Assembly application rate $= \frac{\text{Overhead}}{\text{Direct labor cost}}$

$$= \frac{\$240{,}000}{\$300{,}000}$$

= 80% of direct labor cost

Finishing application rate $= \frac{\text{Overhead}}{\text{Machine hours}}$

$$= \frac{\$160{,}000}{10{,}000 \text{ hours}}$$

= $16 per machine hour

PROBLEM 4

1. Predetermined overhead rate $= \frac{\text{Estimated overhead}}{\text{Estimated activity}}$

$$= \frac{\$600{,}000}{200{,}000 \text{ direct labor hours}}$$

= $3.00 per direct labor hour

2. Overhead applied to work in process during 2004:

= Actual activity × Predetermined rate
= 220,000 direct labor hours × $3 per direct labor hour
= $660,000

3. Overapplied overhead for 2004:

Overhead Control

(Actual costs)		(Applied)	
Indirect labor	$140,000		
Indirect materials	100,000		
Insurance	50,000		
Utilities	90,000		
Repairs and maintenance	80,000		
Depreciation	180,000		
		Overhead applied	$660,000
		Overapplied	$ 20,000

4.

Work in Process

Direct materials	$540,000		
Direct labor	700,000		
Overhead applied	660,000		
		Goods completed	$1,500,000
Ending balance	$400,000		

5. Journal entry to close overapplied overhead to Cost of Goods Sold:

Manufacturing Overhead Control	20,000	
Cost of Goods Sold		20,000

Since overhead was overapplied, Cost of Goods Sold is reduced by $20,000.

PROBLEM 5

1. Predetermined overhead rate $= \dfrac{\$50{,}000}{8{,}000 \text{ machine hours}}$

$= \$6.25$ per machine hour

2. Journal entries to record the activity for the month of December:

Entry to record issuance of direct materials for production:

Work in Process	2,650	
Raw Materials		2,650

Entry to record direct labor used in production:

Work in Process	1,650	
Wages Payable		1,650

Entry to record actual overhead costs incurred during December:

Overhead Control	5,000	
Accounts Payable		3,500
Accumulated Depreciation—Building		1,000
Accumulated Depreciation—Equipment		500

Entry to record overhead applied during December:

Work in Process	3,750*	
Overhead Control		3,750

*($6.25 × 600)

3.

	Job No. 77	Job No. 79	Job No. 73
Work in process, December 1	$ 6,000	$2,500	$1,500
December production activity:			
Materials	1,200	800	650
Direct labor	1,000	400	250
Overhead:			
$6.25 × 300 machine hours	1,875		
$6.25 × 200 machine hours		1,250	
$6.25 × 100 machine hours			625
Totals	$10,075	$4,950	$3,025

4. If Job No. 77 was completed during December, Work in Process at December 31 would have a balance of $7,975. (The Job No. 79 balance would be $4,950, and the Job No. 73 balance would be $3,025.)

5. The balance in the Overhead Control account at December 31 could be calculated as follows:

Overhead Control

(Actual costs)		(Applied)
	$5,000	$3,750
Underapplied	$1,250	

6. Journal entry to close underapplied overhead to cost of goods sold:

Cost of Goods Sold	1,250	
Manufacturing Overhead Control		1,250

Since overhead was underapplied, Cost of Goods Sold is increased by the entry.

PROBLEM 6

1. Journal entries to record manufacturing activities for January:

a. Purchased materials on account:

Raw Materials	150,000	
Accounts Payable		150,000

b. No entry required.

c. Materials requisitioned for production:

Work in Process	138,000	
Overhead Control	6,000	
Raw Materials		144,000

d. Factory payroll for January:

Work in Process	85,000	
Overhead Control	15,000	
Wages Payable		100,000

e. Expenses recorded with adjusting entries:

Overhead Control	6,000	
Accumulated Depreciation		5,000
Prepaid Insurance		1,000

f. Other manufacturing costs not yet paid:

Overhead Control	30,650	
Accounts Payable		30,650

g. Overhead applied using a predetermined overhead rate:

$$\text{Predetermined overhead rate} = \frac{\text{Estimated total overhead}}{\text{Estimated total direct labor cost}}$$

$$= \frac{\$540{,}000}{\$900{,}000}$$

$$= 60\% \text{ of direct labor cost}$$

Entry to apply manufacturing overhead in January:

Work in Process	51,000*	
Overhead Control		51,000

*(60% × $85,000)

h. Job Nos. 96 and 97 were completed and transferred to finished goods. (See the job-order cost sheets on page 100 for how the amounts were determined.)

Finished Goods	220,000*	
Work in Process		220,000

*(Job No. 96 at $94,000 and Job No. 97 at $126,000)

i. Job No. 96 was sold during the month. (See the job-order cost sheets below for how the amount was determined.)

Cost of Goods Sold	94,000	
Finished Goods		94,000
Accounts Receivable	112,800*	
Sales Revenue		112,800

*($94,000 × 120%)

Job No. 96		**Job No. 97**		**Job No. 98**	
Balance	$16,000	Balance	$ –0–	Balance	$ –0–
DM	46,000	DM	70,000	DM	22,000
DL	20,000	DL	35,000	DL	30,000
OH	12,000[1]	OH	21,000[2]	OH	18,000[3]
Total	$94,000	Total	$126,000	Total	$70,000

[1]($20,000 × 60%)
[2]($35,000 × 60%)
[3]($30,000 × 60%)

2. T accounts for the inventory accounts, Cost of Goods Sold, and Overhead Control:

Raw Materials

Debit	Credit
$150,000	$144,000
$ 6,000	

Work in Process

Debit	Credit
Bal. $ 16,000	
DM 138,000	
DL 85,000	
OH 51,000	
	$220,000
$ 70,000	

Finished Goods

Debit	Credit
$220,000	
	$94,000
$126,000	

Cost of Goods Sold

Debit	Credit
$94,000	
$94,000	

Overhead Control

(Actual costs)		(Applied)	
Indirect materials	$ 6,000		
Indirect labor	15,000		
Depreciation and insurance	6,000		
Other costs	30,650		
		Overhead applied	$51,000
Underapplied	$ 6,650		

3. Underapplied overhead is closed to Cost of Goods Sold:

Cost of Goods Sold	6,650	
Manufacturing Overhead Control		6,650

PROBLEM 7

1. $$\text{Machining overhead rate} = \frac{\text{Estimated overhead}}{\text{Estimated machine hours}} = \frac{\$200{,}000}{20{,}000 \text{ machine hours}} = \$10 \text{ per machine hour}$$

$$\text{Assembly predetermined overhead rate} = \frac{\text{Estimated overhead}}{\text{Estimated DLH}} = \frac{\$800{,}000}{40{,}000 \text{ DLH}} = \$20 \text{ per DLH}$$

2. **JOB NO. 12-5**

Direct materials—Machining	$ 2,000
Direct labor—Machining	1,200
Direct labor—Assembly	5,500
Overhead—Machining ($10 × 150 machine hours)	1,500
Overhead—Assembly ($20 × 200 direct labor hours)	4,000
Total	$14,200

CHAPTER 6
Process Costing

CHAPTER REVIEW

CHARACTERISTICS OF PROCESS MANUFACTURING

- Cost accounting systems should be designed to fit the nature of the manufacturing operation.
- *Process costing* works well whenever relatively homogeneous products pass through a series of processes and receive *similar* amounts of manufacturing costs.
- A process is a series of operations performed on the product, such as mixing, molding, or packaging.
- *Job-order costing* works well whenever products pass through a series of processes that deal out *different* amounts of manufacturing costs.
- The manufacture of nearly any product requires three types of cost:
  1. Direct materials
  2. Direct labor
  3. Manufacturing overhead
- The job-order costing system is designed to trace costs to a job.
- A process-costing system traces the costs to the process, instead of the job.
- **Operation costing** is a costing method that uses job-order costing to assign material costs and process costing to assign conversion costs (direct labor and manufacturing overhead).
- The same accounts are used in the process-costing system as in a job-order costing system with the exception of the number of Work-in-Process accounts. A different Work-in-Process account is required for each processing department.
- The major differences between process costing and job-order costing are summarized as follows:

Process Costing	Job-Order Costing
1. Homogeneous units pass through a series of similar processes.	**1.** Unique jobs are worked on during a time period.
2. Costs are accumulated by processing department.	**2.** Costs are accumulated by individual job.
3. Unit costs are computed by dividing the processing departments' costs by output. In addition, output is measured in equivalent units, not in units produced.	**3.** Unit costs are determined by dividing the total costs on the job-order cost sheet by the number of units in the job.
4. The production report provides the detail for the Work-in-Process account for each processing department.	**4.** The job-order cost sheet provides the detail for the Work-in-Process account.

Types of Process Manufacturing

- In a process-manufacturing firm, units produced pass through a series of manufacturing steps or processes.
- The product may flow through the processing departments in different ways.
- The product may flow through the factory's processing departments using:
  1. sequential processing, or
  2. parallel processing.
- **Sequential processing** is a method of process manufacturing in which units pass from one process to another in a sequential pattern and each unit is processed using the same series of steps.

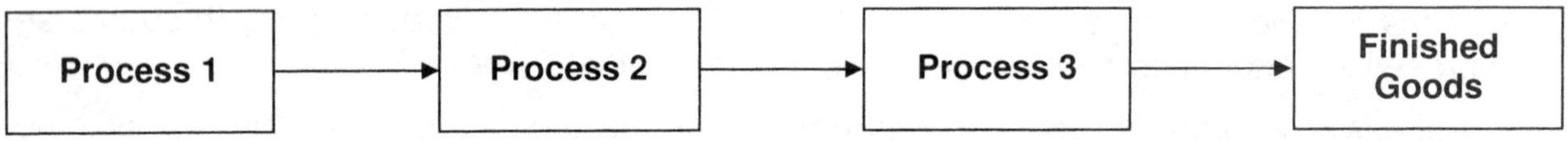

- Two examples of **parallel processing** are as follows:
  1. Two different products emerge from a common process, and then each flows through its own separate series of processes for completion.

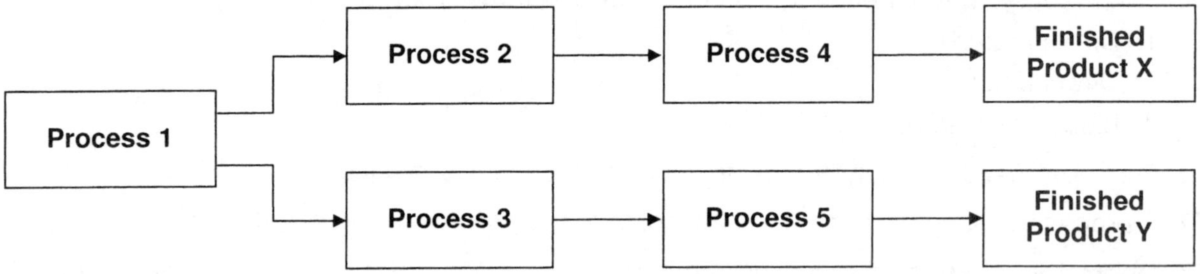

  2. The products flow through their separate series of processes and then eventually flow through a common department.

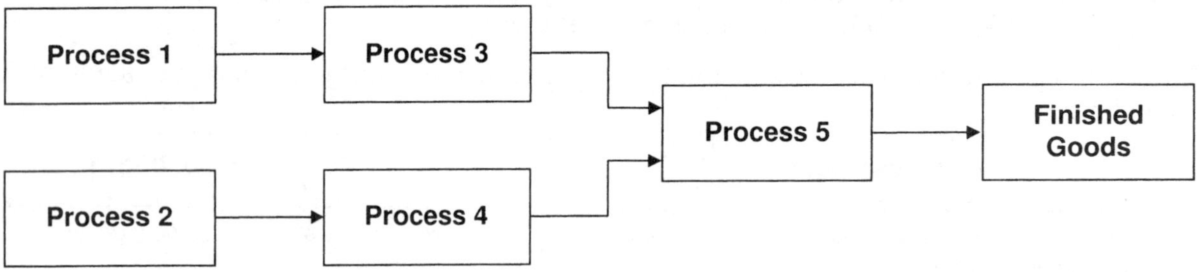

- No matter what the product flow, a unit cost is determined for each process, and the cost of the finished product is the total of the unit costs accumulated as the product passes through the processing departments.

How Costs Flow Through the Accounts in Process Costing

- As raw materials are purchased, the cost of the materials is recorded in a Raw Materials inventory account.
- As used, raw materials, direct labor, and manufacturing overhead are recorded in the Work-in-Process account.

- When goods are completed, their cost is transferred from the Work-in-Process account to the Finished Goods account.
- As goods are sold, their cost is transferred from the Finished Goods account to the Cost of Goods Sold account.
- In process costing, each processing department has its own Work-in-Process account.
- Costs transferred from a prior process to a subsequent process are called **transferred-in costs**.

Accumulating Costs in the Production Report

- The **production report** summarizes the manufacturing activity for a processing department during a period.
- The production report is divided into two main sections:
  1. Unit information
     a. Units to account for
     b. Units accounted for
  2. Cost information
     a. Costs to account for
     b Costs accounted for

Service and Manufacturing Firms

- Process costing can be used for any product or service that is basically homogeneous and repetitively produced, including service firms, manufacturing firms using JIT, and traditional manufacturing firms.

THE IMPACT OF WORK-IN-PROCESS INVENTORIES ON PROCESS COSTING

- **Equivalent units of output** is the expression of a processing department's activity in terms of fully completed units.
- For example, two units that are 50 percent complete are the equivalent of one unit fully completed.

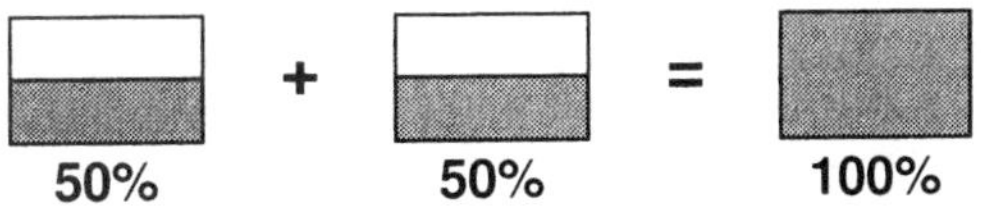

- Work done on partially completed units in beginning work-in-process inventory represents prior period work. Manufacturing costs assigned to these units represent prior period costs.
- Two approaches used for dealing with prior period output and prior period costs found in beginning work in process are:
  1. weighted average method, and
  2. first-in, first-out (FIFO) method.
- Both the weighted average method and the FIFO method use the following general pattern to determine the cost of production:
  1. Analysis of the flow of physical units
  2. Calculation of equivalent units
  3. Computation of unit costs

4. Valuation of inventories
   a. Cost of units transferred out, and
   b. Cost of units in ending work in process
5. Cost reconciliation

WEIGHTED AVERAGE COSTING

- The **weighted average costing method** combines the partially completed units in beginning work-in-process inventory with units produced in the current period to determine a weighted average equivalent units of production.
- Equivalent units of output using the weighted average method is calculated as:

Units completed and transferred out*
+ Equivalent units of production in ending work in process
= Equivalent production

*Note that the weighted average method includes the partially completed units in beginning inventory with the units that were started and completed in the current period.

- The weighted average method also merges prior-period costs with current-period costs by adding manufacturing costs in beginning work in process to manufacturing costs incurred during the current period.
- The major advantage of the weighted average method is simplicity.

Five Steps in Preparing a Production Report

Step One: Physical Flow Analysis

Units to account for:
Units in beginning work in process
+ Units started during the period
= Total units to account for

Units accounted for:
Units completed and transferred out
+ Units in ending work in process
= Total units accounted for

Step Two: Calculation of Equivalent Units (Weighted Average)

Units completed and transferred out
+ Units in ending work in process × Fraction complete
= Equivalent units of output

Step Three: Computation of Unit Cost

Costs to account for:
Beginning work in process
+ Costs added (incurred) during the period
= Total costs to account for

Cost per equivalent unit = Total costs to account for/Total equivalent units

Step Four: Valuation of Inventories

Costs accounted for:

  Goods transferred out (unit cost × equivalent units)
+ Goods in ending work in process (unit cost × equivalent units)
= Total costs accounted for

Step Five: Cost Reconciliation

Compare total costs to account for with total costs accounted for to determine that they are equal.

MULTIPLE INPUTS AND MULTIPLE DEPARTMENTS

Nonuniform Application of Manufacturing Inputs

- ❒ Equivalent units must be calculated for *each* category of manufacturing input.
- ❒ Equivalent units are calculated for:
  1. each type of material
  2. transferred-in costs (if any), and
  3. conversion costs.
- ❒ For example, if ending work in process contained 1,000 units and materials were 100% complete but conversion was only 40% complete, equivalent units would be calculated as follows:

  Equivalent units for materials = 1,000 × 100% = 1,000
  Equivalent units for conversion = 1,000 × 40% = 400
- ❒ A unit cost for materials and a unit cost for conversion would be calculated based upon the equivalent units for each.

APPENDIX: PRODUCTION REPORT—FIFO COSTING

- ❒ FIFO costing excludes the equivalent units and costs in beginning work in process (prior-period costs) from the current-period unit cost calculations.
- ❒ Only current-period work and current-period costs are used to compute FIFO unit costs.
- ❒ If the costs of the manufacturing inputs remain fairly stable, the weighted average and FIFO method will produce very similar results.
- ❒ If the costs of the manufacturing inputs fluctuate from period to period, the FIFO method may be more useful for cost control, pricing decisions, and performance evaluation because the FIFO method concentrates on the current period's activity.

KEY TERMS TEST

Test your recall of the key terms as follows. Try to recall as many key terms as possible without assistance. If you need assistance, refer to the list of key terms at the end of this section.

1. ________ ________________ involves determining whether the costs assigned to units transferred out and to units in ending work in process are equal to the costs in beginning work in process plus the manufacturing costs incurred in the current period.
2. The ________ __________ _________ is a process-costing method that separates units in beginning inventory from those produced during the current period.
3. A method of process manufacturing in which subunits pass through different sequential processes before being brought together in a final process is called ____________ ______________.
4. A method of process manufacturing in which units flow from one process to another in a set order is called _____________ _____________.
5. The __________ __________ __________ __________ combines prior-period work and costs with current-period work and costs.
6. The expression of a processing department's activity in terms of fully completed units is called _____________ ________ _____ _________.
7. ___________ __________ uses job-order costing to assign material costs and process costing to assign conversion costs.
8. The _____________ __________ summarizes the manufacturing activity for a department during a period and discloses physical flow, equivalent units, total costs to account for, unit cost computation, and costs assigned to goods transferred out and to units in ending work in process.
9. _______________-_____ _________ are the costs of a prior process.
10. A(n) __________ _________ ___________ is a schedule that accounts for all units flowing through a department during a period.

KEY TERMS:

cost reconciliation
equivalent units of output
FIFO costing method
operation costing
parallel processing
physical flow schedule
production report
sequential processing
transferred-in costs
weighted average costing method

→ **Compare your answers with those at the end of the chapter. Review any key terms missed.**

CHAPTER QUIZ

Write your answers in the spaces provided.

1. Cost accounting systems should be designed to fit the nature of the manufacturing operation. ____________ costing works well whenever relatively homogeneous products pass through a series of processes and receive similar amounts of manufacturing costs. ________-__________ costing works well whenever products pass through a series of processes that deal out different amounts of manufacturing costs.

2. The manufacture of nearly any product requires the following three types of costs:

   a. ________________________________

   b. ________________________________

   c. ________________________________

3. In a process-manufacturing firm, units pass through a series of processes. The product may flow through the processing departments using:

   a. ____________________ processing, or

   b. ____________________ processing.

4. Equivalent production is the expression of all activity of a processing department in terms of __________ ______________ units.

5. Equivalent units using the weighted average method is calculated as:

   ____

   \+ ____

   = Equivalent units of output

6. Cost per equivalent unit using the weighted average method is calculated as:

   Cost per equivalent unit = __________________________ / ____________________

7. List the five sections of the cost of production report.

   a. ____

   b. ____

   c. ____

   d. ____

   e. ____

Circle the single best answer.

8. In a process-costing system, costs are accumulated by jobs: (a) true; (b) false

9. In a process-costing system, a cost of production report contains the detail for the Work-in-Process account: (a) true; (b) false

10. In a job-order costing system, unit costs are determined by dividing the total costs on the job-order cost sheet by the number of units in the job: (a) true; (b) false

11. The FIFO method is more useful for cost control purposes because the FIFO method concentrates on the current period's activity: (a) true; (b) false

12. Job-order costing works well whenever relatively homogeneous products are produced on a continuous basis: (a) true; (b) false

13. Operation costing is a costing method that uses job-order costing to assign material costs and process costing to assign conversion costs: (a) true; (b) false

14. Costs transferred in from a prior process are handled in the same manner as materials: (a) true; (b) false

15. As raw materials are purchased, the cost of the materials is recorded in the Work-in-Process account: (a) true; (b) false

16. When using FIFO costing, work done on partially completed units in beginning work-in-process inventory is considered current-period work: (a) true; (b) false

17. The major advantage of the weighted average method is simplicity: (a) true; (b) false

Use the following information to answer Questions 18 through 23:

The Jones Company manufactures medicated shampoo. It passes through two processes: (1) mixing, where ingredients are added and blended together, and (2) packaging, where the shampoo is put into bottles and packed for shipment.

The following information pertains to the Mixing Department for September 2004:

	Units (Pounds)
Work in process, September 1 (80% complete, materials; 70% complete, labor and overhead)	10,000
Started during September	120,000
Work in process, September 30 (60% complete, materials; 40% complete, labor and overhead)	12,000

The costs of work in process at September 1 for the Mixing Department were as follows:

	Mixing Department
Work in process, September 1:	
Materials	$ 60,000
Direct labor	40,000
Overhead	25,000
Total	$125,000

Costs added by the Mixing Department during September were as follows:

	Mixing Department
Materials	$ 880,000
Direct labor	520,500
Overhead	208,600
Total costs added	$1,609,100

Using the weighted average costing method, calculate the following for the Mixing Department for September:

18. The equivalent units of production for materials is: (a) 118,000; (b) 125,200; (c) 130,000; (d) 142,000

19. The unit cost for materials is: (a) $5.69; (b) $7.07; (c) $7.23; (d) $7.51

20. The equivalent units of production for conversion is: (a) 112,000; (b) 118,000; (c) 122,800; (d) 130,000

21. The unit cost for conversion costs is: (a) $4.23; (b) $5.94; (c) $6.26; (d) $6.47

22. Cost of goods transferred out is: (a) $1,649,640; (b) $1,652,000; (c) $1,716,744; (d) $1,817,400

23. Cost of ending work in process is: (a) $77,640; (b) $82,632; (c) $85,128; (d) $90,120

→ **Compare your answers with those at the end of the chapter. Review any questions missed.**

PRACTICE TEST

PROBLEM 1

Jax, Inc., manufactures a product that passes through two processes: assembly and finishing. All manufacturing costs are added uniformly for both processes.

Information for the Assembly Department for the month of November follows:

Work in process, November 1:	
Direct materials	$10,000
Direct labor	$15,000
Overhead	$8,000
Number of units (20% complete)	6,000

During November, 20,000 units were completed and transferred to the Finishing Department. The following costs were incurred by the Assembly Department during November:

Direct materials	$35,000
Direct labor	50,000
Overhead	28,280

On November 30, 2,000 units that were 60% complete remained in assembly.

Instructions:

On the following page, complete the production report for the Assembly Department for November using the weighted average method.

PROBLEM 1 *(Continued)*

Jax, Inc.
Assembly Department
Production Report for November 2004
(Weighted Average Method)

UNIT INFORMATION

Units to account for:			
Units in beginning work in process			
Units started during the period			
Total units to account for			

		Equivalent Units	
	Physical Flow	**Materials**	**Conversion Cost**
Units completed			
Units in ending work in process			
Total equivalent units			

COST INFORMATION

Calculation of Unit Costs

	Materials	**Conversion Cost**	**Total**
Costs to account for:			
Beginning work in process			
Costs incurred during the period			
Total costs to account for			
Cost per equivalent unit			

Costs Transferred Out and Cost of Ending Inventory

	Transferred Out	**Ending Work in Process**	**Total**
Costs accounted for:			
Goods transferred out (Total unit cost × Units)			
Goods in ending work in process:			
Materials (Unit cost for materials × Equivalent units)			
Conversion (Unit cost for conversion × Equivalent units)			
Total costs accounted for			

PROBLEM 2

Jim's Paint Products manufactures house paint. The ingredients are combined in the Mixing Department, then put in gallon cans in the Packaging Department.

The following information pertains to the Mixing Department for May 2004:

	Units (Gallons)
Work in process, May 1 (100% complete, materials; 60% complete, labor and overhead)	5,000
Started during May	80,000
Work in process, May 31 (100% complete, materials; 35% complete, labor and overhead)	9,000

The costs of the Mixing Department's work in process at May 1 were as follows:

	Mixing Department
Work in process, May 1:	
Materials	$34,000
Direct labor	23,000
Overhead	15,000
Total	$72,000

The costs added by the Mixing Department during May were as follows:

	Mixing Department
Materials	$ 680,000
Direct labor	293,600
Overhead	182,875
Total costs added	$1,156,475

Instructions:

On the following page prepare a production report for the Mixing Department for May using the weighted average method. The report should include the following:

1. Physical flow of units
2. Equivalent units
3. Calculation of unit costs
4. Costs accounted for, showing costs transferred out and cost of ending work in process

PROBLEM 2 *(Continued)*

Use this page for your answer.

PROBLEM 3

The following information pertains to the Packaging Department of Jim's Paint Products for May 2004:

	Units (Gallons)
Work in process, May 1 (20% converted)	2,000
Transferred in from Mixing Department	76,000
Work in process, May 31 (70% converted)	8,000

The costs of the Packaging Department's work in process at May 1 were as follows:

	Packaging Department
Work in process, May 1:	
Costs transferred in from Mixing Department	$25,900
Direct labor	17,040
Manufacturing overhead	22,120
Total	$65,060

The costs added by the Packaging Department during May were as follows:

	Packaging Department
Direct labor	$240,000
Manufacturing overhead	560,000
Total	$800,000

Instructions:

Using the information from Problem 2 and the above information, on the following page prepare a production report for the Packaging Department for May using the weighted average method. The report should include the following:

1. Physical flow of unit
2. Calculation of equivalent units
3. Calculation of unit costs
4. Costs accounted for, showing costs transferred out and the cost of ending work in process

PROBLEM 3 *(Continued)*

Use this page for your answer.

PROBLEM 4 (Appendix)

Instructions:

Using the information from Problems 2 and 3, prepare a production report for the Mixing Department for May 2004 using the first-in, first-out method.

(Round unit costs to four decimal places and round other amounts to dollars.)

PROBLEM 5

Instructions:

1. Refer to the information presented in Problems 2 and 3 regarding Jim's Paint Products. Prepare journal entries to summarize the activities in the Mixing and Packaging Departments for May 2004 using the weighted average method.

2. Prepare T accounts for work in process for the Mixing and Packaging Departments of Jim's Paint Products.

ANSWERS

KEY TERMS TEST

1. Cost reconciliation
2. FIFO costing method
3. parallel processing
4. sequential processing
5. weighted average costing method
6. equivalent units of output
7. Operation costing
8. production report
9. Transferred-in costs
10. physical flow schedule

CHAPTER QUIZ

1. Process, Job-order
2. **a.** Direct materials
   b. Direct labor
   c. Manufacturing overhead
3. **a.** sequential
   b. parallel
4. fully completed
5. Units completed and transferred out + Units in ending work in process × Fraction complete
6. Total costs to account for/Equivalent units
7. **a.** Physical flow of units
   b. Equivalent units
   c. Calculation of unit cost
   d. Costs accounted for (calculation of costs transferred out and cost of ending work-in-process inventory)
   e. Cost reconciliation
8. b False A job-order costing system accumulates costs by jobs while a process-costing system accumulates costs by processing department.
9. a True
10. a True
11. a True
12. b False Process costing works well whenever relatively homogeneous products are produced on a continuous basis.
13. a True
14. a True
15. b False As raw materials are purchased, the cost is recorded as inventory. As raw materials are used in production, the cost is transferred to work in process.
16. b False The FIFO method does not include prior-period costs in the current-period unit cost.
17. a True
18. b (10,000 + 120,000 – 12,000) = 118,000 units completed; [118,000 units completed + (12,000 units in ending inventory × 60%)] = 125,200
19. d (60,000 + 880,000)/125,200 EUP = $7.51
20. c [118,000 units completed + (12,000 units in ending inventory × 40%)] = 122,800
21. d ($40,000 + $25,000 + $520,500 + $208,600)/122,800 = $6.47
22. a [118,000 × ($7.51 + $6.47)] = $1,649,640
23. c [(7,200 × $7.51) + (4,800 × $6.47)] = $85,128

PRACTICE TEST

PROBLEM 1

Jax, Inc.
Assembly Department
Production Report for November 2004
(Weighted Average Method)

UNIT INFORMATION

Units to account for:			
Units in beginning work in process	6,000		
Units started during the period	16,000		
Total units to account for	22,000		

		Equivalent Units	
	Physical Flow	**Materials**	**Conversion Cost**
Units completed	20,000	20,000	20,000
Units in ending work in process	2,000	1,200	1,200
Total equivalent units	22,000	21,200	21,200

COST INFORMATION

Calculation of Unit Costs

	Materials	**Conversion Cost**	**Total**
Costs to account for:			
Beginning work in process	$10,000	$ 23,000	$ 33,000
Costs incurred during the period	35,000	78,280	113,280
Total costs to account for	$45,000	$101,280	$146,280
Cost per equivalent unit	$2.123	$4.777	$6.90

Costs Transferred Out and Cost of Ending Inventory

	Transferred Out	**Ending Work in Process**	**Total**
Costs accounted for:			
Goods transferred out ($6.90 × 20,000)	$138,000.00		$138,000.00
Goods in ending work in process:			
Materials ($2.123 × 1,200)		$2,547.60	2,547.60
Conversion ($4.777 × 1,200)		5,732.40	5,732.40
Total costs accounted for	$138,000.00	$8,280.00	$146,280.00

PROBLEM 2

Jim's Paint Products
Mixing Department
Production Report for May 2004
(Weighted Average Method)

UNIT INFORMATION

Units to account for:			
Units in beginning work in process	5,000		
Units started during May	80,000		
Total units to account for	85,000		

		Equivalent Units	
	Physical Flow	**Materials**	**Conversion Cost**
Units completed	76,000	76,000	76,000
Units in ending work in process:			
Materials (100% × 9,000)	9,000	9,000	
Conversion (35% × 9,000)			3,150
Total equivalent units	85,000	85,000	79,150

COST INFORMATION

Calculation of Unit Costs

	Materials	**Conversion Cost**	**Total**
Costs to account for:			
Beginning work in process	$ 34,000	$ 38,000	$ 72,000
Costs incurred during the period	680,000	476,475	1,156,475
Total costs to account for	$714,000	$514,475	$1,228,475
Cost per equivalent unit	$8.40	$6.50	$14.90

Costs Transferred Out and Cost of Ending Inventory

	Transferred Out	**Ending Work in Process**	**Total**
Costs accounted for:			
Goods transferred out ($14.90 × 76,000)	$1,132,400		$1,132,400
Goods in ending work in process:			
Materials ($8.40 × 9,000)		$75,600	75,600
Conversion ($6.50 × 3,150)		20,475	20,475
Total costs accounted for	$1,132,400	$96,075	$1,228,475

PROBLEM 3

Jim's Paint Products
Packaging Department
Production Report for May 2004
(Weighted Average Method)

UNIT INFORMATION

Units to account for:			
Units in beginning work in process	2,000		
Units started during May (transferred in from Mixing)	76,000		
Total units to account for	78,000		

		Equivalent Units	
	Physical Flow	Transferred In	Conversion Cost
Units completed	70,000	70,000	70,000
Units in ending work in process:			
Materials (100% × 8,000)	8,000	8,000	
Conversion (70% × 8,000)			5,600
Total equivalent units	78,000	78,000	75,600

COST INFORMATION

Calculation of Unit Costs

	Transferred In	Conversion Cost	Total
Costs to account for:			
Beginning work in process	$ 25,900	$ 39,160	$ 65,060
Costs incurred during the period	1,132,400	800,000	1,932,400
Total costs to account for	$1,158,300	$839,160	$1,997,460
Cost per equivalent unit	$14.85	$11.10	$25.95

Costs Transferred Out and Cost of Ending Inventory

	Transferred Out	Ending Work in Process	Total
Costs accounted for:			
Goods transferred out ($25.95 × 70,000)	$1,816,500		$1,816,500
Goods in ending work in process:			
Materials ($14.85 × 8,000)		$118,800	118,800
Conversion ($11.10 × 5,600)		62,160	62,160
Total costs accounted for	$1,816,500	$180,960	$1,997,460

PROBLEM 4 (APPENDIX)

Jim's Paint Products
Mixing Department
Production Report for May 2004
(FIFO Method)

UNIT INFORMATION

Units to account for:			
Units in beginning work in process	5,000		
Units started during May	80,000		
Total units to account for	85,000		
		Equivalent Units	
	Physical Flow	**Materials**	**Conversion Cost**
Units started and completed	71,000	71,000	71,000
Units completed from beginning work in process	5,000		2,000
Units in ending work in process:			
Materials (100% × 9,000)	9,000	9,000	
Conversion (35% × 9,000)			3,150
Total equivalent units	85,000	80,000	76,150

COST INFORMATION

Calculation of Unit Costs

	Materials	**Conversion Cost**	**Total**
Costs to account for:			
Beginning work in process	$ 34,000	$ 38,000	$ 72,000
Costs incurred during the period	680,000	476,475	1,156,475
Total costs to account for	$714,000	$514,475	$1,228,475
Cost per equivalent unit (Cost added/Equivalent units)	$8.50	$6.2571	$14.7571

Costs Transferred Out and Cost of Ending Inventory

	Transferred Out	**Ending Work in Process**	**Total**
Costs accounted for:			
Units in beginning work in process:			
From prior period	$ 72,000		$ 72,000
From current period ($6.2571 × 2,000)	12,514		12,514
Units started and completed ($14.7571 × 71,000)	1,047,754		1,047,754
Goods in ending work in process:			
Materials ($8.50 × 9,000)		$76,500	76,500
Conversion ($6.2571 × 3,150)		19,710	19,710
Total costs accounted for	$1,132,268	$96,210	$1,228,478*

*Difference due to rounding

PROBLEM 5

1. Journal entries for the Mixing and Packaging Departments:

Entry to record materials used in production:

Work in Process—Mixing	680,000	
Raw Materials		680,000

Entry to record direct labor:

Work in Process—Mixing	293,600	
Wages Payable		293,600

Entry to record manufacturing overhead:

Work in Process—Mixing	182,875	
Manufacturing Overhead Control		182,875

Entry to record transfer of costs from the Mixing Department to the Packaging Department:

Work in Process—Packaging	1,132,400	
Work in Process—Mixing		1,132,400

Entry to record direct labor and manufacturing overhead costs in the Packaging Department in May:

Work in Process—Packaging	800,000	
Wages Payable		240,000
Manufacturing Overhead Control		560,000

Entry to record the transfer of costs from the Packaging Department to finished goods:

Finished Goods	1,816,500	
Work in Process—Packaging		1,816,500

2. T account for the Mixing Department:

Work in Process—Mixing Department

Beginning balance	$ 72,000		
Materials	680,000		
Direct labor	293,600	Transferred out to	
Overhead	182,875	Packaging	$1,132,400
Ending balance	$ 96,075*		

*Agrees with costs assigned to ending work in process in Problem 2 ($75,600 + $20,475 = $96,075).

T account for the Packaging Department:

Work in Process—Packaging Department

Beginning balance	$ 65,060		
Transferred in costs	1,132,400		
Direct labor	240,000	Transferred out to	
Overhead	560,000	Finished Goods	$1,816,500
Ending balance	$ 180,960*		

*Agrees with costs assigned to ending work in process in Problem 3 ($118,800 + $62,160 = $180,960).

CHAPTER 7
Support Department Cost Allocation

CHAPTER REVIEW

- Allocation is a means of assigning a portion of a pool of costs to various subunits, such as departments or products.
- Cost allocation can affect bid prices, profitability of products, and managers' behavior.

AN OVERVIEW OF COST ALLOCATION

- A **common cost** is the cost of a resource used in the output of two or more services or products. Common costs must be assigned to products or services produced.

Types of Departments

- When using allocations, costs are allocated or assigned to cost objects.
- If departments are the cost objects, departments are classified as either **producing departments** or **support departments**.

	Producing Departments	Support Departments
Definition:	responsible for creating the products or services sold to customers	provide support services for producing departments
Examples:	assembly department, finishing department	maintenance, personnel, security

- Although support departments do not work directly on the products of an organization, the costs of providing these support services are part of the total product cost.
- Three steps in allocating costs are:
  1. trace all overhead costs to a support or producing department
  2. allocate support-department costs to the producing departments, and
  3. allocate overhead costs to units of individual products using a predetermined overhead rate. The predetermined overhead rate is calculated as follows:

$$\textbf{Predetermined overhead rate} = \frac{\textbf{Budgeted overhead}}{\textbf{Budgeted activity}}$$

- Note that a producing department's overhead consists of two parts:
  - overhead directly associated with the producing department
  - overhead allocated to the producing department from the support departments

Types of Allocation Bases

- **Causal factors** are variables or activities within a producing department that cause the incurrence of service costs.

- In general, causal factors should be used as the basis for allocating service costs.
- For example, if power costs were to be allocated, kilowatt hours would be the causal factor that could be used as the allocation base.
- Using causal factors results in more accurate product costs, and if causal factors are known, managers are better able to control the consumption of services.

Objectives of Allocation

- The major objectives associated with the allocation of support-department costs to producing departments and ultimately to specific products are:
  - to obtain a mutually agreeable price
  - to compute product-line profitability
  - to predict economic effects for planning and control purposes
  - to value inventory
  - to motivate managers

ALLOCATING ONE DEPARTMENT'S COSTS TO ANOTHER DEPARTMENT

- A charging rate is used to allocate the costs of a support department to user departments.

A Single Charging Rate

- If a single charging rate is used, fixed costs and variable costs are combined and then divided by estimated activity.

$$\text{Single charging rate} = \frac{(\text{Fixed costs} + \text{Variable costs})}{\text{Total estimated usage}}$$

- The amount charged to producing departments is calculated as follows:

$$\text{Single charging rate} \times \text{Producing department usage}$$

- Instead of using a single charging rate, a company may break support department resources and causal factors into multiple charging rates, even to the point of approaching activity-based costing. However, the benefits of extra precision of more charging rates must be balanced against the cost of determining and applying those rates.

Budgeted versus Actual Usage

- Budgeted, not actual, costs should be allocated so that support departments' efficiencies or inefficiencies are not passed on to the producing departments.
- Two reasons for allocating support-department costs are:
  1. to determine the cost of units produced, and
  2. for performance evaluation.
- For product costing, the allocation is made at the beginning of the year based on budgeted usage so that a predetermined overhead rate can be computed to cost products during the year.

❒ For performance evaluation purposes, the allocation is made at the end of the period based on actual usage.

	Product Costing	**Performance Evaluation**
Usage:	Budgeted usage	Actual usage
Service department allocation:	**Budgeted rate × Budgeted usage**	**Budgeted rate × Actual usage**

CHOOSING A SUPPORT DEPARTMENT COST ALLOCATION METHOD

❒ Three methods used to allocate support-department costs to producing departments are:

1. direct method
2. sequential method, and
3. reciprocal method.

Direct Method of Allocation

❒ The **direct method** allocates support-department costs directly to the producing departments based on relative use.

❒ This method ignores reciprocal services (services provided by one support department to another support department). For example, this method would ignore service provided by the data processing department to other support departments, such as personnel or maintenance.

❒ If a firm has two support departments (maintenance and data processing) and two producing departments (assembly and finishing), the allocation of support-department costs using the direct method could be diagramed as follows:

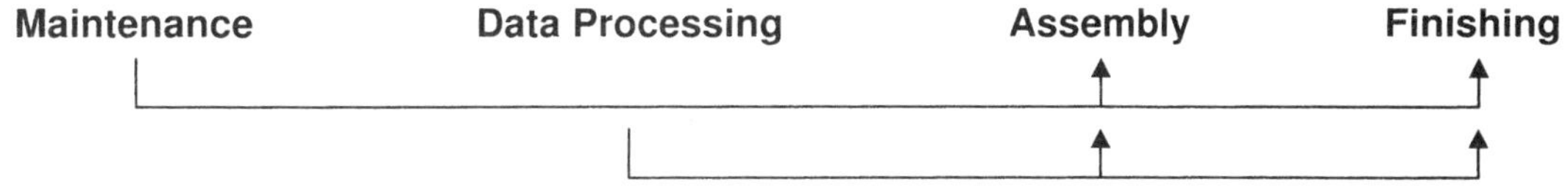

Sequential Method of Allocation

❒ The **sequential (or step) method** allocates support-department costs to the producing departments *and* to some support departments. Thus, the sequential method partially recognizes reciprocal services.

❒ The sequential method is applied in the following manner:

1. Select a support department and allocate its costs to the producing departments and support departments to which it provides services. (The support department with the greatest total costs is allocated first.)
2. Select another support department and allocate its cost to the producing departments and the remaining support departments.
3. Proceed in this manner until all of the support-department costs have been allocated to the producing departments.

❒ Notice that once the costs of a support department are allocated, no further allocations are made to that support department.

- The allocation of support-department costs under the sequential method can be diagramed as follows:

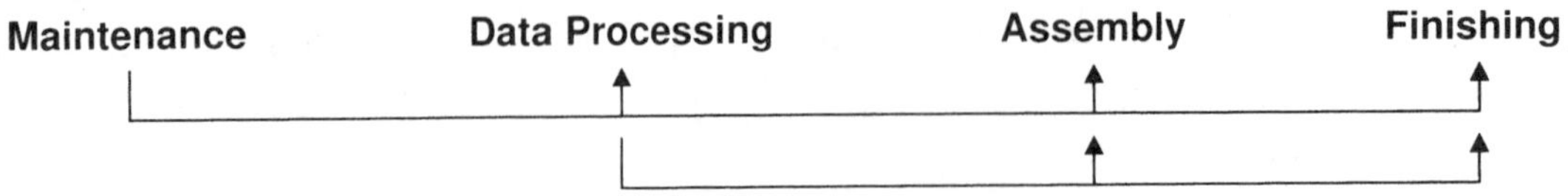

Reciprocal Method of Allocation

- The **reciprocal method** fully recognizes the reciprocal services provided by support departments to other support departments.
- The reciprocal method requires the use of simultaneous equations.
- The total cost of a support department is calculated:

Total cost of support department = Direct costs + Allocated costs of other support departments

- The allocation of support-department costs under the reciprocal method can be diagramed as follows:

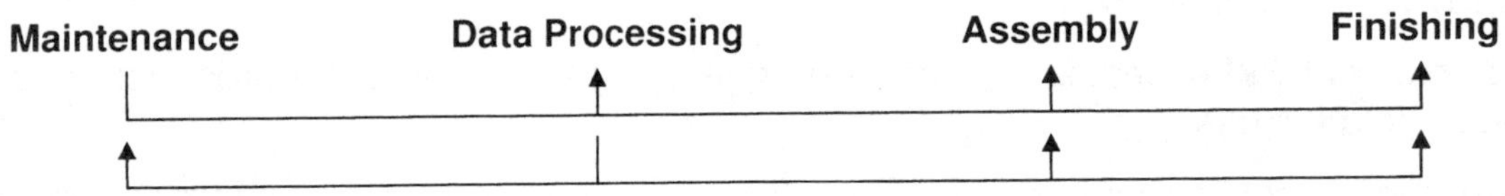

DEPARTMENTAL OVERHEAD RATES AND PRODUCT COSTING

- Support-department costs are allocated to the producing departments, and then the support-department costs are included in the producing departments' overhead application rates.
- The flow of costs could be diagramed as follows:

Support Department Costs		Producing Department Overhead Costs		Units of Product
		$400,000		
$200,000	→	<u>$200,000</u>		
		$600,000	→	

- The $600,000 of producing department overhead would be allocated to units of product using a cost driver such as direct labor hours or machine hours.

SUMMARY

- To summarize, the four steps involved in support-department allocation are as follows:
  1. Prepare departmental budgets for producing and support departments.
  2. Select an allocation base for use in allocating the support-department costs.
  3. Allocate the budgeted support-department costs to the producing departments using either the direct, sequential, or reciprocal method.
  4. Calculate a predetermined overhead application rate for each producing department to apply total overhead costs to units of product produced.

KEY TERMS TEST

Test your recall of the key terms as follows. Try to recall as many key terms as possible without assistance. If you need assistance, refer to the list of key terms at the end of this section.

1. A unit within an organization responsible for producing the products or services that are sold to customers is called a(n) ______________ ______________.
2. A unit within an organization that provides essential support services for producing departments is called a(n) ______________ ______________.
3. The ______________ ______________ simultaneously allocates service costs to all user departments. It gives full consideration to interactions among support departments.
4. The ______________ ______________ is a method of allocating service costs that ignores any interactions that may exist among support departments.
5. ______________ ______________ are activities or variables that cause the incurrence of service costs.
6. The ______________ ______________ is a method of allocating support-department costs that gives partial consideration to interactions among support departments.
7. The cost of a resource used in the output of two or more services or products are ______________ ______________.

KEY TERMS:

causal factors
common costs
direct method
producing department
reciprocal method
sequential (or step) method
support department

→ **Compare your answers with those at the end of the chapter. Review any key terms missed.**

CHAPTER QUIZ

Circle the single best answer.

1. The direct method of allocating support-department costs partially recognizes services that support departments provide to each other: (a) true; (b) false
2. The reciprocal method of allocating support-department costs fully recognizes services that support departments provide to each other: (a) true; (b) false
3. Producing departments are responsible for producing the products sold to customers: (a) true; (b) false
4. Support departments are responsible for providing services directly to customers: (a) true; (b) false
5. Accounting in an automobile factory is an example of a producing department: (a) true; (b) false
6. Maintenance is an example of a support department: (a) true; (b) false
7. The company cafeteria is an example of a producing department: (a) true; (b) false
8. Packaging is an example of a support department: (a) true; (b) false
9. One of the main objectives of allocation is to motivate managers: (a) true; (b) false
10. One of the main objectives of allocation is to value inventory: (a) true; (b) false
11. One of the main objectives of allocation is to compute product line profitability: (a) true; (b) false

12. Actual costs should always be used when allocating support-department costs: (a) true; (b) false
13. Support-department costs should be allocated directly to units of product: (a) true; (b) false
14. If the allocation is for performance evaluation, support-department costs should be allocated based on the actual rate and actual usage: (a) true; (b) false
15. If the allocation is for product costing, variable support-department costs should be allocated based on the budgeted rate and budgeted usage: (a) true; (b) false

Use the following information to answer Questions 16 through 22:

Mollet, Inc., often bids on jobs using a cost-plus basis; therefore, in order to be competitive, it is important to determine costs as accurately as possible. The company operates two support departments (Department A and Department B) and two producing departments (Department C and Department D).

Budgeted costs and normal activity levels are given below:

	Support Departments		Producing Departments	
	A	B	C	D
Overhead costs	$120,000	$160,000	$300,000	$240,000
Number of employees	8	12	40	60
Maintenance hours	3,000	400	8,000	2,000
Machine hours	—	—	12,000	15,000
Direct labor hours	—	—	1,800	15,000

The costs of Department A are allocated on the basis of number of employees, and the costs of Department B are allocated on the basis of maintenance hours.

Assume the direct method is used for Questions 16 through 20.

16. If the direct method is used, Department A costs allocated to Department C would be: (a) $48,000; (b) $96,000; (c) $72,000; (d) $120,000
17. If the direct method is used, Department B costs allocated to Department C would be: (a) $192,000; (b) $160,000; (c) $128,000; (d) $80,000
18. If Department C uses machine hours to allocate overhead to units of product, the overhead rate per machine hour for Department C would be: (a) $35.67; (b) $29.00; (c) $32.66; (d) $39.67
19. If Department D uses direct labor hours to allocate overhead to units of product, the overhead rate per direct labor hour for Department D would be: (a) $22.93; (b) $18.13; (c) $16.80; (d) $16.00
20. Estimates relating to a job that Mollet, Inc., plans to bid on are as follows:

Direct materials	$1,000
Direct labor	$600
Machine hours in Department C	20
Direct labor hours in Department D	30

The estimate for the cost of the job would be: (a) $2,393; (b) $2,288; (c) $1,481; (d) $3,081

21. If the sequential method is used and the costs of the support department with the greatest total cost are allocated first, Department B costs allocated to Department D would be: (a) $36,923; (b) $30,463; (c) $24,615; (d) $21,450
22. If the sequential method is used and the costs of the support department with the greatest total cost are allocated first, Department A costs allocated to Department C would be: (a) $60,649; (b) $62,769; (c) $62,980; (d) $69,280

→ **Compare your answers with those at the end of the chapter. Review any questions missed.**

PRACTICE TEST

PROBLEM 1

Husmann Company has three support departments and two producing departments. Information for each department for 2004 is as follows:

	Support Departments			Producing Departments	
	Plant Administration	Plant Maintenance	Plant Cafeteria	Machining	Assembly
Budgeted overhead cost........	$120,000	$100,000	$50,000	$200,000	$400,000
Direct labor hours	6,000	10,000	4,000	20,000	30,000
Square feet occupied............	2,000	3,000	5,000	35,000	65,000
Number of employees	5	6	3	15	25

Plant administration costs are allocated based on direct labor hours, plant maintenance costs are allocated based on square footage occupied, and plant cafeteria costs are allocated based on the number of employees.

The company uses a single charging rate. Predetermined overhead rates for the producing departments are based on direct labor hours.

Instructions:

Allocate the support-department costs using the direct method. Then calculate the predetermined overhead rates the producing departments would use to apply overhead to units of product.

	Support Departments			Producing Departments	
	Plant Administration	Plant Maintenance	Plant Cafeteria	Machining	Assembly
Budgeted overhead cost	$120,000	$100,000	$50,000	$200,000	$400,000

PROBLEM 2

Instructions:

Using the information from the previous problem, allocate the support-department costs using the sequential method, starting with the support department with the greatest total cost. Then, calculate the predetermined overhead rates the producing departments would use to apply overhead to units of product.

	Support Departments			Producing Departments	
	Plant Administration	**Plant Maintenance**	**Plant Cafeteria**	**Machining**	**Assembly**
Budgeted overhead cost	$120,000	$100,000	$50,000	$200,000	$400,000

PROBLEM 3

Taylor Bus Lines provides school bus service to two area school districts—Unit 1 and Unit 2.

Taylor has one support center that is responsible for service, maintenance, and cleanup of its buses. The costs of the support center are allocated to each operating unit on the basis of total miles driven.

During the first month of the year, the support center was expected to incur fixed costs of $25,000 and variable costs of $0.30 per mile. During the month, the support center incurred actual variable costs of $105,000 and actual fixed costs of $20,000.

The estimated and actual miles logged by each unit are given below:

	Unit 1	Unit 2
Estimated activity (miles)	170,000	80,000
Actual activity (miles)	175,000	90,000

Instructions:

1. Calculate a single charging rate per mile driven for support center services.

2. Calculate the support center costs that would be allocated at the end of the month to each district if a single charging rate is used.

PROBLEM 3 *(Continued)*

3. Based on the fixed and variable amounts budgeted, how much should it have cost the support center for the actual number of miles driven?

4. Is the amount in Requirement 3 different from the cost allocated in Requirement 2? Why?

ANSWERS

KEY TERMS TEST

1. producing department
2. support department
3. reciprocal method
4. direct method
5. Causal factors
6. sequential method (or step method)
7. common costs

CHAPTER QUIZ

1. b False The step method partially recognizes reciprocal services.
2. a True
3. a True
4. b False Support departments provide support services to the producing departments.
5. b False Accounting is an example of a support department.
6. a True
7. b False The company cafeteria would be an example of a support department.
8. b False Since packaging would work directly with the product, packaging would be considered a producing department.
9. a True
10. a True
11. a True
12. b False Budgeted costs, not actual costs, should be allocated.
13. b False First, support-department costs are allocated to the producing departments. Then producing department overhead (including the allocated support-department costs) is allocated to units of product.
14. b False If the allocation is for performance evaluation, variable support-department costs should be allocated based on the budgeted rate and actual usage.
15. a True
16. a \$120,000 × 40/100 = \$48,000
17. c \$160,000 × 8,000/10,000 = \$128,000
18. d (\$300,000 + \$48,000 + \$128,000)/12,000 = \$39.67
19. a (\$240,000 + \$72,000 + \$32,000)/15,000 = \$22.93
20. d \$1,000 + \$600 + (\$39.67 × 20) + (\$22.93 × 30) = \$3,081
21. c \$160,000 × (2,000/13,000) = \$24,615
22. b \$160,000 × (3,000/13,000) = \$36,923; (\$120,000 + \$36,923) × (40/100) = \$62,769

PRACTICE TEST

PROBLEM 1

	Support Departments			Producing Departments	
	Plant Administration	Plant Maintenance	Plant Cafeteria	Machining	Assembly
Budgeted overhead cost	\$ 120,000	\$ 100,000	\$ 50,000	\$200,000	\$400,000
Allocate plant administration (20,000/50,000; 30,000/50,000)	(120,000)			48,000	72,000
Allocate plant maintenance (35,000/100,000; 65,000/100,000)		(100,000)		35,000	65,000
Allocate plant cafeteria (15/40; 25/40)			(50,000)	18,750	31,250
Total producing department overhead to apply				\$301,750	\$568,250
Divided by direct labor hours				÷ 20,000	÷ 30,000
Predetermined overhead rate				\$15.0875	\$18.9417

PROBLEM 2

	Support Departments			Producing Departments	
	Plant Administration	Plant Maintenance	Plant Cafeteria	Machining	Assembly
Budgeted overhead cost	$ 120,000	$ 100,000	$ 50,000	$200,000	$400,000
Allocate plant administration (10/64; 4/64; 20/64; 30/64)	(120,000)	18,750	7,500	37,500	56,250
Total cost in plant maintenance		$ 118,750			
Allocate plant maintenance (5/105; 35/105; 65/105)		(118,750)	5,655	39,583	73,512
Total cost in plant cafeteria			$ 63,155		
Allocate plant cafeteria (15/40; 25/40)			(63,155)	23,683	39,472
Total producing department overhead to apply				$300,766	$569,234
Divided by direct labor hours				÷ 20,000	÷ 30,000
Predetermined overhead rate				$15.0383	$18.9745

PROBLEM 3

1. Single charging rate per mile driven would be calculated as follows:

Variable costs [$0.30 × (170,000 + 80,000)]	$ 75,000
Fixed costs	25,000
Total estimated costs	$100,000

Single charging rate = Total estimated costs/Number of estimated miles
= $100,000/(170,000 + 80,000)
= $0.40 per mile

2. Support center costs that would be allocated to each district if a single charging rate is used would be calculated as follows:

District	Miles Driven	Charge per Mile	Total Charges
Unit 1	175,000	$0.40	$ 70,000
Unit 2	90,000	0.40	36,000
Total	265,000		$106,000

3. Based on budgeted fixed and variable costs, the support department should have incurred the following costs for the actual number of miles driven:

Variable costs ($0.30 × 265,000 miles driven)	$ 79,500
Fixed costs	25,000
Total costs	$104,500

4. Yes, the support center costs allocated to the districts total $106,000. However, the total cost budgeted for 265,000 miles driven is only $104,500. This difference of $1,500 is due to treating the $25,000 of fixed costs as a variable cost for allocation purposes. The $25,000 fixed cost is divided by 250,000 budgeted miles to arrive at a fixed cost per mile of $0.10 for allocation purposes. If the actual number of miles driven differs from the budgeted miles of 250,000 used to calculated the fixed cost per mile, then there will be a resulting difference between total costs budgeted versus total costs allocated. This is a disadvantage of using a single charging rate that combines variable and fixed costs.

CHAPTER 8
Functional and Activity-Based Budgeting

CHAPTER REVIEW

DESCRIPTION OF BUDGETING

Budgeting and Planning and Control

- A **budget** is a plan of action expressed in financial terms.
- Budgeting is a planning and control tool used by managers.

Planning Tool	Control Tool
Identify objectives.	Compare actual results with budgeted (planned) amounts.
Identify actions needed to achieve objectives.	Corrective action can be taken, if needed.

- The steps involved in the planning and control process are as follows:
  - Develop a strategic plan. A **strategic plan** identifies strategies for future activities and operations, generally covering at least five years.
  - Translate the strategic plan into long-term and short-term objectives.
  - From the objectives, develop short-term plans.
  - Develop budgets based upon the short-term plans.
  - Compare actual results with planned (budgeted) amounts.
  - Take corrective action, if necessary.

Advantages of Budgeting

- Advantages of budgeting include the following:
  - Budgets force managers to plan.
  - Budgets provide information that can be used to improve decision making.
  - Budgets provide standards used for performance evaluation and control. **Control** involves comparing actual results with budgeted amounts and taking corrective action whenever actual performance deviates significantly from planned performance.
  - Budgets improve communication and coordination.

PREPARING THE MASTER BUDGET

- Most budgets are for a one-year period, further broken down into quarterly and/or monthly budgets.
- A **continuous budget** is a moving twelve-month budget. As a month expires in the budget, an additional month is added so that the company always has a twelve-month plan on hand.

The Master Budget

❒ The **master budget** is a comprehensive financial plan consisting of various individual budgets.

Master Budget

	Operating Budgets	**Financial Budgets**
Definition:	budgets concerned with income-generating activities	budgets concerned with cash flows and financial position at end of period
Examples:	sales budget production budget direct materials purchases budget direct labor budget overhead budget selling and administrative expenses budget ending finished goods inventory budget cost of goods sold budget budgeted income statement	cash budget budgeted balance sheet budget for capital expenditures

Preparing the Operating Budget

❒ The sales forecast is the basis for the sales budget and is usually the responsibility of the marketing department.

❒ Sales may be forecast using:

- the *bottom-up approach* based on feedback from salespeople
- time-series analysis
- correlation analysis
- econometric modeling

Sales Budget

❒ The **sales budget** is the projection of expected sales in units and dollars.

Production Budget

❒ The **production budget** indicates the number of units of finished product to be produced in order to meet:

- sales needs
- inventory requirements

❒ If production is related to sales of the next period, production needs for a manufacturer can be calculated as follows:

	Budgeted sales in units
+	**Desired ending inventory in units**
=	**Total units needed**
–	**Beginning inventory (units on hand)**
=	**Units to be produced**

Direct Materials Purchases Budget

- The **direct materials purchases budget** is a budget of the expected usage of materials in production and the purchase of the direct materials required.
- The steps involved in preparing a direct materials purchases budget are as follows:
  1. Determine the amount of direct materials necessary to manufacture the number of units to be produced.
  2. Determine the *quantity* of direct materials to be purchased as follows:

     Quantity of direct materials needed for production
     + Desired ending inventory of direct materials
     = Total quantity of direct materials needed
     – Beginning inventory of direct materials
     = Quantity of direct materials to be purchased

  3. Determine the cost of the direct materials to be purchased by multiplying the quantity of direct materials to be purchased by the expected cost per unit of direct material.

Direct Labor Budget

- The **direct labor budget** is a budget of planned expenditures for direct labor. The direct labor budget indicates the rate per hour and the number of hours necessary to meet production requirements.

Overhead Budget

- The **overhead budget** shows the expected cost of all manufacturing costs other than direct materials and direct labor.
- Budgeted variable overhead costs are based on a budgeted variable overhead rate multiplied by budgeted activity.
- Budgeted fixed overhead costs remain unchanged as the activity level changes within the relevant range.

Ending Finished Goods Inventory Budget

- The **ending finished goods inventory budget** contains:
  1. calculations of the unit cost of the product, and
  2. the cost of the planned ending inventory.

Cost of Goods Sold Budget

- The **cost of goods sold budget** calculates the expected costs of the goods to be sold.
- Budgeted cost of goods sold is calculated as follows:

  Direct materials used
  + Direct labor used
  + Overhead
  = Budgeted manufacturing costs
  + Beginning finished goods
  = Goods available for sale
  – Ending finished goods
  = Budgeted cost of goods sold

Selling and Administrative Expenses Budget

- The **selling and administrative expenses budget** is a budget of planned expenditures for nonmanufacturing activities, such as sales commissions and office salaries.
- Selling and administrative expenses have a variable component that varies with the level of production or sales and a fixed component that remains constant within the relevant range.

Budgeted Income Statement

- The budgeted income statement calculates net income as follows:

Sales
– Cost of goods sold
= Gross margin
– Selling and administrative expenses
= Operating income
– Interest expense
= Income before taxes
– Income taxes
= Net income

Preparing the Financial Budget

- The financial budgets are:
  1. the cash budget
  2. the budgeted balance sheet, and
  3. the budget for capital expenditures.

Cash Budget

- The **cash budget** is a summary of planned cash receipts and cash payments. A cash budget might include the following items:

Beginning cash balance
+ Cash receipts:
Cash collections on accounts receivable
Cash sales
= Cash available
– Cash payments:
Cash payments on accounts payable (for material purchases)
Direct labor wages
Variable overhead
Fixed overhead[a]
Variable selling and administrative expenses[b]
Fixed selling and administrative expenses[a]
Income taxes
Dividends
Purchases of property or equipment requiring cash[c]
Total cash payments
– Minimum cash balance
= Excess cash (or deficiency)
Investments:
– Investment of excess cash
+ Liquidation of investment of excess cash

Financing:
+ Borrowings to cover deficiency
– Repayment of loan
– Interest payments
= **Ending cash balance**

[a]Depreciation is considered a fixed cost; however, it is not a cash outflow. Therefore, depreciation would not be included in the cash budget.

[b]Bad debt expense is included in the selling and administrative expenses budget; however, it is not included in the cash budget. Instead, bad debt expense is shown as a reduction in the amount the firm expects to collect on accounts receivable.

[c]Only purchases of property and equipment *requiring cash* would be shown on the cash budget. If the property or equipment purchase was financed by long-term debt, cash repayments of the debt would be shown as a cash payment in the cash budget.

- A firm may desire or be required to maintain a minimum cash balance.
- Excess cash should be invested to earn a return.
- If the firm has a cash deficiency, borrowing will be necessary to maintain the minimum cash balance.

Budgeted Balance Sheet

- The final statement to be prepared in the budgeting process is the pro forma balance sheet. Most of the amounts appearing in the pro forma balance sheet can be traced to one of the other budgets or schedules.
- See text Exhibit 8–4 for a diagram of the interrelationships of the budgets.

USING BUDGETS FOR PERFORMANCE EVALUATION

Static Budgets versus Flexible Budgets

- A **static budget** is a budget for a particular level of activity, such as a sales level of 1,000 units. Static budgets are not very useful for performance reports because the actual activity level may differ from the static budget activity level.
- **Flexible budgets** compute expected costs at different levels of activity. A flexible budget is used to compute what costs should have been for the actual activity level. Flexible budgets permit management to prepare performance reports that compare actual and budgeted costs for the actual level of activity. When preparing a flexible budget, variable costs and fixed costs are identified and calculated for the different activity levels.
- **Flexible budget variance** is the difference between the actual amount and the flexible budget amount for the actual activity level.

The Behavioral Dimension of Budgeting

- Budgets are often used to judge the performance of managers.
- A manager's bonuses, salary increases, and promotions are affected by the manager's ability to achieve budgeted goals; therefore, budgets can have a significant effect on a manager's behavior.
- Whether the effect is positive or negative depends upon how the budgets are administered.

- An ideal budgetary system:
  - promotes **goal congruence** (the manager's personal goals are congruent or consistent with the organization's goals), and
  - creates a drive in managers to achieve the goals.
- **Dysfunctional behavior** is behavior that is in conflict with the organization's goals. If the budget is improperly administered, dysfunctional behavior may result.
- Key features of a budgeting system that encourage positive behavior are:
  - frequent feedback on performance
  - monetary and nonmonetary incentives
  - participative budgeting
  - realistic standards
  - controllability of costs
  - multiple measures of performance

Frequent Feedback on Performance

- Frequent feedback on performance lets managers know how they are doing as the year unfolds. This gives managers the opportunity to take corrective action and adapt to changing conditions.
- *Management by exception* uses performance reports that show variances (deviations from planned results). This allows managers to focus only on the areas that need attention.

Monetary and Nonmonetary Incentives

- **Incentives** are measures used to induce a manager to work toward achieving the organization's goals.
- Negative incentives use fear of punishment to motivate.
- Positive incentives use the expectation of a reward to motivate.
- **Monetary incentives** are economic rewards, such as salary increases, bonuses, and promotions.
- **Nonmonetary incentives** are psychological and social rewards to motivate managers, such as the satisfaction of a job well done, recognition, and increased responsibility.
- Monetary awards alone are not sufficient to highly motivate managers.

Participative Budgeting

- **Participative budgeting** allows managers to participate in creating the budget used to evaluate their performance.
- Participative budgeting can:
  - increase goal congruence
  - provide nonmonetary incentives (Individuals involved in setting their own standards work harder to achieve them.)
  - use the knowledge of individuals who are aware of local conditions
- Three potential problems of participative budgeting are:
  - standard-setting problems—If the goals are too low and too easily achieved, the manager's performance may drop because there is no challenge. If the goals are set too high, the man-

ager may become frustrated and give up when he or she does not meet the goal. In participative budgeting, the goals should be high but achievable.

- **budgetary slack**—Participatory budgeting creates the opportunity for managers to build slack into the budget (pad the budget). Top management should conduct a careful review of budgets proposed by subordinate managers to eliminate slack.
- **pseudoparticipation**—Top management assumes total control and subordinate manager participation is limited to endorsing the budget.

Realistic Standards

- Realistic standards should include allowances for seasonal variations and general economic conditions.

Controllability of Costs

- **Controllable costs** are costs a manager can influence.
- Managers should not be held accountable for costs they cannot control.
- Many firms still include noncontrollable costs in a manager's budget to make the manager aware of these costs. However, if noncontrollable costs are included in a manager's budget, they should be labeled as noncontrollable and separated from controllable costs.

Multiple Measures of Performance

- Budgets should not be the only measure used to evaluate manager performance.
- If budget performance is overemphasized, **myopic behavior** can occur where the manager takes actions that improve budgetary performance in the short run but cause long-run harm to the firm.
- Since managers of responsibility centers usually spend only three to five years before being promoted or moving to another position, their successors are the ones who must deal with the effects of myopic behavior.
- The best way to prevent myopic behavior is to measure manager performance based on several measures of performance, such as market share, productivity, quality, and personnel development.

ACTIVITY-BASED BUDGETING

- **Activity-based budgeting** identifies activities, demands for activity output, and the cost of resources needed to support the activity output demanded.
- Activities consume resources and thus are the causes of costs. Therefore, activity-based budgeting can be used to emphasize cost reduction through:
  - elimination of wasteful activities, and
  - improvement of efficiency of necessary activities.
- The principal difference between a traditional, functional-based budget approach and an activity-based approach is a detailed listing of activities and their expected costs within the overhead, selling, and administrative categories.

Activity Flexible Budgeting

- **Activity flexible budgeting** allows prediction of what activity costs will be as activity usage (output) changes.
- In a functional-based budget, budgeted costs are based on a single unit-based driver (usually direct labor hours). A cost formula is developed for each cost item as a function of direct labor hours. The formula is then used to predict what costs should be at any level of activity.
- An alternative is to develop flexible budget formulas using multiple drivers instead of a single driver. For example,
  - Labor and supplies costs might be driven by direct labor hours.
  - Maintenance costs might be driven by machine hours.
  - Setup costs might be driven by the number of setups.
- Cost formulas are developed for each activity.
- The variable-cost component for each activity corresponds to resources acquired as needed (flexible resources). The fixed-cost component corresponds to resources acquired in advance of usage (committed resources).
- This multiple-formula approach permits managers to predict more accurately what costs should be at different levels.
- The flexible budget amounts based on multiple cost drivers can be compared to actual costs for control purposes. Variances are calculated as the differences between the flexible budget amount and the actual amount as shown below:

Activity	Actual Cost	Budgeted Cost	Variance (F or U)
Maintenance costs:			
Fixed	$15,000	$14,000	$1,000 U
Variable	42,000	45,000	3,000 F
Total	$57,000	$59,000	$2,000 F

- Breaking variances into fixed and variable components provides more insight into the source of the variation in planned and actual expenditures.

KEY TERMS TEST

Test your recall of the key terms as follows. Try to recall as many key terms as possible without assistance. If you need assistance, refer to the list of key terms at the end of this section.

1. A(n) ____________ is a plan of action expressed in financial terms.
2. A(n) ________________ ___________ is the long-term plan for future activities and operations, usually involving at least five years.
3. The ____________ _________________ is responsible for setting budgetary policies and goals, reviewing and approving the budget, and resolving any differences that arise in the budgetary process.
4. A moving twelve-month budget where a future month is added as the current month expires is called a(n) ________________ ___________.
5. The ________________ __________ is the portion of the master budget that includes the cash budget, the budgeted balance sheet, and the capital budget.
6. The collection of all area and activity budgets, representing a firm's comprehensive plan of action is the ________________ __________.
7. Budgets associated with the income-producing activities of an organization are called ________________ __________.
8. The ________________ __________ shows the planned expenditures for all indirect manufacturing items.
9. The ________________ __________ shows how many units must be produced to meet sales needs and satisfy ending inventory requirements.
10. The ________________ __________ describes expected sales in units and dollars for the coming period.
11. The ____________ ______ ___________________ ___________ __________ outlines planned expenditures for nonmanufacturing activities.
12. A(n) ________________ __________ is a detailed plan that outlines all sources and uses of cash.
13. The __________ __________ __________ shows total direct labor hours needed and the associated cost for the number of units in the production budget.
14. The __________ ____________ ____________ __________ outlines the expected usage of materials in production and the purchases of the direct materials required.
15. The process of padding the budget by overestimating costs and underestimating revenues is called ______________ __________.
16. ___________ is the process of setting standards, receiving feedback on actual performance, and taking corrective action whenever actual performance deviates significantly from planned performance.
17. _________________ _________ are costs that managers have the power to influence.
18. Individual behavior that is in conflict with the goals of the organization is ________________ ______________.

19. Claiming that a participative budgetary system exists when, in reality, budgets are dictated from above is called ______________________________.

20. __________ ____________________ is the alignment of a manager's personal goals with those of the organization.

21. Managerial actions that improve budgetary performance in the short-run at the expense of the long-run welfare of the organization is called ____________ ______________.

22. _______________ are positive or negative measures taken by an organization to induce a manager to exert effort toward achieving the organization's goals.

23. ____________________ _______________ are economic rewards to motivate managers.

24. ____________________ _______________ are psychological and social rewards to motivate managers.

25. ____________________ _______________ allows managers who will be held accountable for budgetary performance to participate in the budget's development.

26. A(n) __________-__________ _______________ __________ estimates the demand for each activity's output and assesses the cost of resources required to produce this output.

27. A(n) ____________ ____________ is a budget for a particular level of activity.

28. A(n) ____________ ____________ computes budgeted costs for different levels of activity.

KEY TERMS:

activity-based budgeting system
budget
budget committee
budgetary slack
cash budget
continuous budget
control
controllable costs
direct labor budget
direct materials purchases budget
dysfunctional behavior
financial budget
flexible budget
goal congruence
incentives
master budget
monetary incentives
myopic behavior
nonmonetary incentives
operating budgets
overhead budget
participative budgeting
production budget
pseudoparticipation
sales budget
selling and administrative expenses budget
static budget
strategic plan

→ **Compare your answers with those at the end of the chapter. Review any key terms missed.**

CHAPTER QUIZ

Circle the single best answer.

1. Budgeting is a means of coordinating the activities of the organization and communicating the goals of the company: (a) true; (b) false
2. Budgeting is important only as a planning tool: (a) true; (b) false
3. The first step in the budgeting process is the preparation of the production budget: (a) true; (b) false
4. Bad debt expense is not included in the cash budget because it is shown as a reduction in the amount collected from accounts receivable: (a) true; (b) false
5. Depreciation is included in the cash budget because it is a cash outflow for equipment: (a) true; (b) false
6. On an income statement prepared using a contribution margin approach, costs would be classified by function (production costs versus selling and administrative costs): (a) true; (b) false
7. When participative budgeting is used, the flow of information for budgeting purposes is from the upper to the lower levels of the company: (a) true; (b) false
8. Equipment purchased using long-term debt would be shown in the cash budget as a cash outflow at the time the equipment is purchased: (a) true; (b) false
9. Budgets can affect managers' behavior because the managers' bonuses, salary increases, and promotions are often affected by the managers' ability to achieve budgeted goals: (a) true; (b) false

Write your answers in the spaces provided.

10. List the order in which the following budgets and schedules are prepared.

Cash budget	1. ____________
Direct labor budget	2. ____________
Manufacturing overhead budget	3. ____________
Production budget	4. ____________
Direct materials purchases budget	5. ____________
Sales budget	6. ____________
Sales forecast	7. ____________

11. The production needed for the period would be determined as follows:

  Budgeted sales in units
+ ____________
= Total units needed
– ____________
= Units to be produced

12. The purchases budget for direct materials for a manufacturer is based upon the quantity of direct materials to be purchased. The quantity of direct materials to be purchased would be determined as follows:

____

\+ ______________________________

= Total quantity of direct materials needed

− ______________________________

= Quantity of direct materials to be purchased

13. List six key features of a budgetary system that encourage positive behavior:

1. ______________________________

2. ______________________________

3. ______________________________

4. ______________________________

5. ______________________________

6. ______________________________

Circle the single best answer.

Use the following information to answer Questions 14 through 19:

Projected sales for Silver, Inc., for next year and beginning and ending inventory data are as follows:

Sales	40,000 units
Unit price	$20
Beginning inventory	20,000 units
Targeted ending inventory	10,000 units

Each unit requires 5 pounds of material which costs $3.00 per pound. The beginning inventory of raw materials is 5,000 pounds. The company wants to have 3,000 pounds of material in inventory at the end of the year. Each unit produced requires 2 hours of direct labor time, which is billed at $8 per hour.

14. Budgeted sales would be: (a) $580,000; (b) $600,000; (c) $800,000; (d) $840,000

15. According to the production budget, how many units should be produced? (a) 30,000; (b) 42,000; (c) 46,000; (d) 50,000

16. Pounds of material to be purchased would be: (a) 142,000; (b) 148,000; (c) 150,000; (d) 152,000

17. The budgeted total purchase cost of direct materials would be: (a) $456,000; (b) $450,000; (c) $444,000; (d) $426,000

18. The budgeted number of total direct labor hours needed would be: (a) 30,000; (b) 40,000; (c) 46,000; (d) 60,000

19. The budgeted total direct labor cost would be: (a) $320,000; (b) $442,000; (c) $480,000; (d) $496,000

→ **Compare your answers with those at the end of the chapter. Review any questions missed.**

PRACTICE TEST

NOTE: The following problems are interrelated.

PROBLEM 1

The Baumberger Company manufactures oak bookcases that sell for $400 each. Budgeted sales for the first four months of the year are as follows:

Month	Budgeted Sales (Units)
January	1,000
February	1,500
March	2,500
April	2,000

Instructions:

Prepare a sales budget in dollars for each month and in total for the first quarter of the year.

	January	February	March	Total

PROBLEM 2

Each bookcase requires 20 square feet of oak at a cost of $10 per square foot. The company wants to maintain an inventory of bookcases equal to 10% of the following month's sales. Inventory on January 1 consisted of 80 bookcases.

Instructions:

1. Prepare a production budget in units for each month and in total for the first quarter.

	January	February	March	Total

2. The company wants to maintain an inventory of oak equal to 20% of the next month's requirements. Materials inventory on January 1 consisted of 11,000 square feet of oak. The company estimates an inventory of oak on hand at the end of March of approximately 8,000 square feet.

   Prepare a purchases budget in dollars for direct materials for each month and in total for the first quarter.

	January	February	March	Total

PROBLEM 3

Each bookcase requires 5 hours of direct labor at a cost of $8.00 per hour. Variable manufacturing overhead is budgeted at $2 per direct labor hour.

Monthly fixed overhead consists of the following:

Supervisors' salaries	$ 6,000
Insurance	2,000
Depreciation on production equipment	500
Depreciation on production facility	10,000
Total	$18,500

Instructions:

1. Prepare a direct labor budget for each month and in total for the first quarter.

	January	February	March	Total

2. Prepare a manufacturing overhead budget for each month and in total for the first quarter.

	January	February	March	Total

PROBLEM 4

The company expects 60% of the sales each month will be collected in that month, with 35% collected in the following month. Five percent of all sales are uncollectible and written off in the following month.

The accounts receivable balance at the beginning of the year is $200,000, which is 40% of last year's December sales of $500,000.

Instructions:

Prepare a schedule of cash collections on accounts receivable for each month and in total for the first quarter.

	January	February	March	Total

PROBLEM 5

The company normally pays for 70% of its purchases in the month of purchase. The remaining 30% is paid in the following month.

Accounts payable at the beginning of the year is $54,000, which is 30% of December purchases of $180,000.

Instructions:

Prepare a schedule of cash payments on accounts payable for each month and in total for the first quarter.

	January	February	March	Total

PROBLEM 6

Use the information from the previous problems. In addition, assume variable selling costs equal 5% of sales and are paid in the month following the sale.

Fixed selling, general, and administrative costs are $50,000 and, except for $10,000 of depreciation, are paid in the month incurred. Estimated tax payments equal to 40% of estimated income for the quarter are made at the end of each quarter.

See Problem 7 regarding interest income and interest expense information.

Instructions:

Prepare a pro forma income statement for each month and in total for the first quarter.

	January	February	March	Total

PROBLEM 7

Use the information from the previous problems and assume the company attempts to maintain a cash balance of $100,000 at all times. Any excess is invested in marketable securities of $10,000 denominations earning an 8% return.

Any deficiencies are covered by borrowing from a local bank at 10% interest.

The cash balance at the beginning of the year is $105,000.

Instructions:

Prepare a cash budget for each month and in total for the first quarter.

	January	February	March	Total

PROBLEM 8

Barth Company produces two types of herbal remedies: Formula X and Formula Z.

The product is sold in cases of 12 bottles. The company expects to produce and sell 100,000 cases of each product during the coming year. Formula X requires 1 direct labor hour per case, and Formula Z requires 1.2 direct labor hours per case.

The following variable and fixed cost estimates have been developed for four overhead items used in producing the products:

Overhead Item	Fixed Cost	Variable Rate per DLH
Maintenance	$ 8,000	$0.20
Utilities		0.10
Indirect labor	25,000	1.00
Rent	12,000	

Instructions:

1. Calculate the expected activity level in direct labor hours if the expected activity level is 100,000 cases per product.

2. Prepare an overhead budget for the expected activity level of 100,000 cases for each product.

Barth Company
Overhead Budget
For the Year 2004

	Formula	Budgeted Costs at Activity Level of 100,000 Cases Each or ____ DLHs	
Variable costs:			
Maintenance	$0.20	$______	
Utilities	______	______	
Indirect labor	______	______	
Total variable costs			$______
Fixed costs:			
Maintenance		$______	
Utilities		______	
Rent		______	
Total fixed costs			______
Total overhead costs			$______

PROBLEM 8 *(Continued)*

3. Given the recent increase in demand for herbal remedies, the president of the company asks you to prepare an overhead budget for the production budget that is 20% higher than expected activity level of 100,000 cases per product.

Barth Company
Overhead Budget
For the Year 2004

	Formula	Budgeted Costs at Activity Level of _______ Cases Each or ____ DLHs	
Variable costs:			
Maintenance............................	$______	$______________	
Utilities....................................	______	______________	
Indirect labor	______	______________	
Total variable costs			$______________
Fixed costs:			
Maintenance...........................		$______________	
Utilities....................................		______________	
Rent..		______________	
Total fixed costs			______________
Total overhead costs..................			$______________

PROBLEM 9

In order to improve the accuracy of budget estimates, Hampton Corporation has instituted the use of an activity-based budgeting system. The number of setups drives the cost of activities of inspections and setups. Cost estimates for inspections and setups are as follows:

	Fixed	Variable
Inspections	$40,000	$1,050
Setups	2,000	900

Instructions:

1. Calculate the budgeted cost of inspections and setups if the activity level is 50 setups.

	Fixed	Variable	Budgeted Cost (50 Setups)
Inspections cost	$40,000	$1,050	$________
Setups cost	2,000	900	$________

2. Calculate the budgeted cost of inspection and setups if the activity level is 60 setups.

	Fixed	Variable	Budgeted Cost (60 Setups)
Inspections cost	$40,000	$1,050	$________
Setups cost	2,000	900	$________

3. Calculate variable and fixed budget variances for inspection and setup costs if the activity level is 60 setups and actual costs are as follows:

	Actual Fixed Costs	Actual Variable Costs
Inspections cost	$41,000	$60,000
Setups cost	1,800	55,500

ANSWERS

KEY TERMS TEST

1. budget
2. strategic plan
3. budget committee
4. continuous budget
5. financial budget
6. master budget
7. operating budgets
8. overhead budget
9. production budget
10. sales budget
11. selling and administrative expenses budget
12. cash budget
13. direct labor budget
14. direct materials purchases budget
15. budgetary slack
16. Control
17. Controllable costs
18. dysfunctional behavior
19. pseudoparticipation
20. Goal congruence
21. myopic behavior
22. Incentives
23. Monetary incentives
24. Nonmonetary incentives
25. Participative budgeting
26. activity-based budgeting system
27. static budget
28. flexible budget

CHAPTER QUIZ

1. a True
2. b False Budgeting is also an important means of controlling operations by comparing actual results with budgeted amounts.
3. b False The first step in the budgeting process is preparation of the sales forecast.
4. a True
5. b False Depreciation is not a cash outflow; therefore, it is not included in the cash budget.
6. b False On an income statement prepared using a contribution margin approach, costs would be classified by behavior (fixed versus variable costs).
7. b False When participatory budgeting is used, the flow of information is from the lower to the upper levels of the company.
8. b False Equipment purchased using long-term debt would result in a cash outflow as the debt is repaid.
9. a True
10. 1. Sales forecast
    2. Sales budget
    3. Production budget
    4. Direct materials purchases budget
    5. Direct labor budget
    6. Manufacturing overhead budget
    7. Cash budget
11. Desired level of ending inventory
    Beginning inventory
12. Quantity of direct material needed for production
    Ending inventory of direct material
    Beginning inventory of direct material
13. 1. frequent feedback on performance
    2. monetary and nonmonetary incentives
    3. participative budgeting
    4. realistic standards
    5. controllability of costs
    6. multiple measures of performance
14. c (40,000 × $20) = $800,000
15. a 40,000 + 10,000 – 20,000 = 30,000 units
16. b (30,000 × 5 pounds) + 3,000 pounds – 5,000 pounds = 148,000 pounds
17. c 148,000 pounds × $3/pound = $444,000
18. d 30,000 units × 2 hours = 60,000 hours
19. c 60,000 hours × $8 = $480,000

PRACTICE TEST

PROBLEM 1

Sales Budget (in dollars)

	January	February	March	Total
Budgeted sales in units	1,000	1,500	2,500	5,000
Multiplied by: Selling price	× $400	× $400	× $400	× $400
Budgeted sales	$400,000	$600,000	$1,000,000	$2,000,000

PROBLEM 2

1.

Production Budget (in units)

	January	February	March	Total
Budgeted sales in units	1,000	1,500	2,500	5,000
Add: Desired ending inventory (10% of next month's sales)	150	250	200*	200
Total units needed	1,150	1,750	2,700	5,200
Less: Beginning inventory	80	150	250	80
Units to be produced	1,070	1,600	2,450	5,120

*2,000 units budgeted sales for April multiplied by 10%

2.

Purchases Budget (in dollars)

	January	February	March	Total
Units to be produced	1,070	1,600	2,450	5,120
Multiplied by: Sq. ft. of oak per unit	× 20	× 20	× 20	× 20
Sq. ft. of material needed for production	21,400	32,000	49,000	102,400
Add: Desired ending inventory (20% of next month's needs)	6,400	9,800	8,000	8,000
Total sq. ft. needed	27,800	41,800	57,000	110,400
Less: Beginning inventory	11,000	6,400	9,800	11,000
Sq. ft. to be purchased	16,800	35,400	47,200	99,400
Multiplied by: Cost per sq. ft.	× $10	× $10	× $10	× $10
Cost of raw material purchases	$168,000	$354,000	$472,000	$994,000

PROBLEM 3

1.

Direct Labor Budget

	January	February	March	Total
Units to be produced	1,070	1,600	2,450	5,120
Multiplied by: Direct labor hours per unit	× 5	× 5	× 5	× 5
Direct labor hours needed	5,350	8,000	12,250	25,600
Multiplied by: Labor cost per hour	× $8	× $8	× $8	× $8
Total direct labor cost	$42,800	$64,000	$98,000	$204,800

2.

Manufacturing Overhead Budget (in dollars)

	January	February	March	Total
Budgeted direct labor hours	5,350	8,000	12,250	25,600
Multiplied by: Variable overhead rate	× $2	× $2	× $2	× $2
Budgeted variable overhead	$10,700	$16,000	$24,500	$ 51,200
Budgeted fixed overhead:				
Supervisors' salaries	$ 6,000	$ 6,000	$ 6,000	$ 18,000
Insurance	2,000	2,000	2,000	6,000
Depreciation—equipment	500	500	500	1,500
Depreciation—facility	10,000	10,000	10,000	30,000
Total fixed overhead	$18,500	$18,500	$18,500	$ 55,500
Total budgeted overhead	$29,200	$34,500	$43,000	$106,700

PROBLEM 4

Cash Collections on Accounts Receivable

	January	February	March	Total
Accounts receivable, beginning of month	$ 200,000[a]	$ 160,000	$ 240,000	$ 200,000
Add: Sales	400,000	600,000	1,000,000	2,000,000
Total amount due from customers	$ 600,000	$ 760,000	$1,240,000	$ 2,200,000
Deduct cash collections:				
60% of sales for current month	$(240,000)	$(360,000)	$ (600,000)	$(1,200,000)
35% of sales for previous month	(175,000)[b]	(140,000)	(210,000)	(525,000)
Deduct writeoffs:				
5% of previous month's sales	(25,000)	(20,000)	(30,000)	(75,000)
Accounts receivable, end of month	$ 160,000	$ 240,000	$ 400,000	$ 400,000

[a]40% of December sales of $500,000
[b]35% of December sales of $500,000

PROBLEM 5

Cash Payments on Accounts Payable

	January	February	March	Total
Accounts payable, beginning of month	$ 54,000[a]	$ 50,400	$106,200	$ 54,000
Add: Purchases	168,000	354,000	472,000	994,000
Total amount owed	$222,000	$404,400	$578,200	$1,048,000
Deduct cash payments:				
70% of purchases for current month	$117,600	$247,800	$330,400	$ 695,800
30% of purchases for previous month	54,000	50,400	106,200	210,600
Total cash payments	$171,600	$298,200	$436,600	$ 906,400
Accounts payable, end of month	$ 50,400	$106,200	$141,600	$ 141,600

[a]30% of December purchases of $180,000

PROBLEM 6

Pro Forma Statements of Income

	January *1,000 Units*	February *1,500 Units*	March *2,500 Units*	Total *5,000 Units*
Sales revenue	$400,000	$600,000	$1,000,000	$2,000,000
Variable expenses:				
Production expenses[a]	$250,000	$375,000	$ 625,000	$1,250,000
S & A expenses (5% of sales)	20,000	30,000	50,000	100,000
Bad debt expenses (5% of sales)	20,000	30,000	50,000	100,000
Total variable expenses	$290,000	$435,000	$ 725,000	$1,450,000
Contribution margin	$110,000	$165,000	$ 275,000	$ 550,000
Fixed expenses:				
Fixed mfr. overhead	$ 18,500	$ 18,500	$ 18,500	$ 55,500
Fixed S & A expenses	50,000	50,000	50,000	150,000
Total fixed expenses	$ 68,500	$ 68,500	$ 68,500	$ 205,500
Operating income	$ 41,500	$ 96,500	$ 206,500	$ 344,500
Interest income	–0–	1,000[b]	1,417[c]	2,417
Net income before tax	$ 41,500	$ 97,500	$ 207,917	$ 346,917
Income tax expense	16,600	39,000	83,167	138,767
Net income	$ 24,900	$ 58,500	$ 124,750	$ 208,150

[a]Consists of the following costs per unit:

Direct materials (20 sq. ft. × $10 per sq. ft.)	$200
Direct labor (5 hours per unit × $8 per hour)	40
Variable overhead (5 hours per unit × $2 per hour)	10
Total variable production costs per unit	$250

[b]$120,000 invested at the end of January × 10% return × 1/12 = $1,000
[c]$120,000 + $50,000 invested at the end of February × 10% return × 1/12 = $1,417

PROBLEM 7

Cash Budget

	January	February	March	Total
Cash balance, beginning of month	$105,000	$101,900	$105,700	$ 105,000
Add: Cash collected on accounts receivable	415,000	500,000	810,000	1,725,000
Cash available	$520,000	$601,900	$915,700	$1,830,000
Deduct cash payments:				
Accounts payable	$171,600	$298,200	$436,600	$ 906,400
Direct labor	42,800	64,000	98,000	204,800
Variable mfr. overhead	10,700	16,000	24,500	51,200
Fixed mfr. overhead[a]	8,000	8,000	8,000	24,000
Variable S & A[b]	25,000	20,000	30,000	75,000
Fixed S & A[b]	40,000	40,000	40,000	120,000
Income taxes[c]	–0–	–0–	138,767	138,767
Total cash payments	$298,100	$446,200	$775,867	$1,520,167
Excess cash	$221,900	$155,700	$139,833	$ 309,833
Investing activities:				
Investment in marketable securities	120,000	50,000	30,000	200,000
Ending cash balance	$101,900	$105,700	$109,833	$ 109,833

[a]Excludes $10,500 of depreciation each month (non-cash expense)
[b]5% of previous month's sales
[c]The amount of taxes to be paid in March is determined from the income statement for the quarter prepared in Problem 6.

PROBLEM 8

1. If the expected activity level is 100,000 cases per product, expected activity in direct labor hours is calculated as follows:

Product X: 100,000 cases × 1.0 DLH =	100,000 DLH
Product Z: 100,000 cases × 1.2 DLH =	120,000 DLH
Total direct labor hours	220,000 DLH

2. The overhead budget for the expected activity level of 100,000 cases for each product:

Barth Company
Overhead Budget
For the Year 2004

	Formula	Budgeted Costs at Activity Level of 100,000 Cases Each or 220,000 DLHs	
Variable costs:			
Maintenance	$0.20	$ 44,000	
Utilities	0.10	22,000	
Indirect labor	1.00	220,000	
Total variable costs			$286,000
Fixed costs:			
Maintenance		$ 8,000	
Utilities		25,000	
Rent		12,000	
Total fixed costs			45,000
Total overhead costs			$331,000

3. If production increases by 20%, then the number of cases produced would equal 120,000 cases for each product (100,000 × 120%).

   If the expected activity level is 120,000 cases per product, expected activity in direct labor hours is calculated as follows:

Product X:	120,000 cases × 1.0 DLH =	120,000 DLH
Product Z:	120,000 cases × 1.2 DLH =	144,000 DLH
Total direct labor hours		264,000 DLH

Barth Company
Overhead Budget
For the Year 2004

	Formula	Budgeted Costs at Activity Level of 120,000 Cases Each or 264,000 DLHs	
Variable costs:			
Maintenance	$0.20	$ 52,800	
Utilities	0.10	26,400	
Indirect labor	1.00	264,000	
Total variable costs			$343,200
Fixed costs:			
Maintenance		$ 8,000	
Utilities		25,000	
Rent		12,000	
Total fixed costs			45,000
Total overhead costs			$388,200

PROBLEM 9

1. Budgeted cost of inspections and setups if the activity level is 50 setups:

	Fixed	Variable	Budgeted Cost (50 Setups)
Inspections	$40,000	$1,050	$92,500[a]
Setups	2,000	900	47,000[b]

[a]$40,000 + ($1,050 × 50 setups) = $92,500
[b]$2,000 + ($900 × 50 setups) = $47,000

2. Budgeted cost of inspection and setups if the activity level is 60 setups:

	Fixed	Variable	Budgeted Cost (60 Setups)
Inspections	$40,000	$1,050	$103,000[a]
Setups	2,000	900	56,000[b]

[a]$40,000 + ($1,050 × 60 setups) = $103,000
[b]$2,000 + ($900 × 60 setups) = $56,000

3. Variable and fixed budget variances for inspection and setup costs would be calculated as follows:

Activity	Actual Cost	Budgeted Cost	Variance
Inspections:			
Fixed	$ 41,000	$ 40,000	$1,000 U
Variable	60,000	63,000	3,000 F
Total	$101,000	$103,000	$2,000 F
Setups:			
Fixed	$ 1,800	$ 2,000	$ 200 F
Variable	55,500	54,000	1,500 U
Total	$57,300	$56,000	$1,300 U

CHAPTER 9
Standard Costing: A Managerial Control Tool

CHAPTER REVIEW

UNIT STANDARDS

- A *standard cost* is the expected or budgeted cost of materials, labor, and manufacturing overhead required to produce one unit of product.
- The unit standard cost is calculated as follows:

Price standard × Quantity standard

- A **price standard** is the price that should be paid per unit of input (such as pound of material).
- A **quantity standard** is the quantity of input allowed per unit of output (for example, pounds of material allowed per one unit of product).
- A **standard cost sheet** calculates the total standard cost for one unit of product. It lists the standard costs for one unit of product for the following:
  - Materials (Price standard × Quantity standard)
  - Labor (Price standard × Quantity standard)
  - Variable manufacturing overhead (Price standard × Quantity standard)
  - Fixed manufacturing overhead (Price standard × Quantity standard)

How Standards Are Developed

- Standards can be based on:
  - historical experience
  - engineering studies, and
  - input from operating personnel.

Types of Standards

- **Ideal standards** are standards that reflect perfect operating efficiency. Ideal standards are virtually unattainable and can result in low employee morale and a decline in performance.
- **Currently attainable standards** are demanding but attainable under efficient operating conditions. Such standards allow for normal machine downtime and employee rest periods.
- Challenging but attainable standards tend to result in higher performance levels than ideal standards. If standards are too tight and never achievable, workers become frustrated and performance levels decline.

Why Standard Cost Systems Are Adopted

- Two reasons for adopting a standard cost system are:
  - *To improve planning and control.* A standard cost system compares actual amounts with standard amounts to determine variances from the standard. The use of a standard cost

system for operational control in an advanced manufacturing environment can produce dysfunctional behavior. However, standards in the advanced manufacturing environment are still useful for planning, such as developing bids.

- *To facilitate product costing.* Standard costing uses standard costs for direct materials, direct labor, and overhead. Standard cost systems provide readily available unit cost information that can be used for pricing decisions.

❒ Costs under the three product cost assignment approaches are summarized below:

PRODUCT COSTING SYSTEM	MANUFACTURING COSTS		
	Direct Materials	**Direct Labor**	**Overhead**
Actual costing system	Actual	Actual	Actual
Normal costing system	Actual	Actual	Budgeted
Standard costing system	Standard	Standard	Standard

STANDARD PRODUCT COSTS

❒ The standard cost sheet for one unit of product might appear as follows:

STANDARD COST SHEET
Production Costs for One Unit of Product

Direct materials
(Standard quantity of materials × Standard price for materials)

Direct labor
(Standard direct labor hours × Standard direct labor rate)

Variable manufacturing overhead
(Standard direct labor hours × Standard variable overhead rate)

Fixed manufacturing overhead
(Standard direct labor hours × Standard fixed overhead rate)

Total standard cost per unit of product

❒ The standard cost for direct materials is calculated as follows:

Standard cost for direct materials =
Standard quantity of materials × Standard price for the materials

❒ **Standard quantity of materials allowed** (*SQ*) is calculated:

***SQ* = Unit quantity standard × Actual output**

❒ The standard direct labor cost for a unit of product would be calculated as follows:

Standard direct labor cost =
Standard quantity of direct labor × Standard rate per direct labor hour

❒ **Standard hours allowed** (*SH*) is calculated:

***SH* = Unit labor standard × Actual output**

VARIANCE ANALYSIS: GENERAL DESCRIPTION

Price and Efficiency Variances

- The **total budget variance** is the difference between actual cost of inputs and the standard (or planned) cost of inputs.
- There are two variances for variable production costs:
  - price or rate variances
  - usage or efficiency variances
- **Price (rate) variances** focus on the difference between actual costs of inputs and what the inputs should have cost (standard prices).
- **Usage (efficiency) variances** focus on the difference between the actual quantity used and the standard quantity allowed for units produced.
- The general model for calculating variable cost variances appears below:

Actual quantity of input at actual price ($AP \times AQ$)	Actual quantity of input at standard price ($SP \times AQ$)	Standard quantity of input at standard price ($SP \times SQ$)
$(AP - SP)AQ$	$(AQ - SQ)SP$	
Price variance	Usage or efficiency variance	

Total variance = $(AP \times AQ) - (SP \times SQ)$

- If the actual price or quantity is less than the standard, the variance is considered **favorable**.
- If the actual price or quantity exceeds the standard, the variance is considered **unfavorable**.

VARIANCE ANALYSIS: MATERIALS AND LABOR

Direct Materials Variances

Materials Price Variance

- The **materials price variance (*MPV*)** for materials is calculated as follows:

Actual quantity purchased at actual price ($AP \times AQ$)	Actual quantity purchased at standard price ($SP \times AQ$)
$(AP - SP)AQ$	

Direct materials price variance

- The materials price variance can be computed at one of two points:
  1. When the raw materials are issued for use in production
  2. When the raw materials are purchased
- Variances should be calculated at the earliest point possible so management can take any necessary corrective action. Thus, the price variance for materials should be calculated at the time of purchase.
- Responsibility for the materials price variance is usually assigned to the purchasing agent.

- Using the materials price variance to evaluate performance can produce undesirable behavior. For example, if the purchasing agent feels pressured to produce favorable price variances:
  - materials of lower quality might be purchased (perhaps resulting in unfavorable usage variances), or
  - in order to take advantage of quantity discounts, large amounts of inventory might be purchased (eliminating some of the benefits of JIT).
- Variance analysis involves the following process:
  - Decide whether the variance is significant.
  - If insignificant, no further investigation is needed.
  - If significant, investigate the cause of the variance and take corrective action if necessary.

Direct Materials Usage Variance

- The **materials usage variance (*MUV*)** is calculated as follows:

Actual quantity used at standard price ($SP \times AQ$)	Standard quantity allowed at standard price ($SP \times SQ$)

$$(AQ - SQ)SP$$

Direct materials usage variance

- The production manager is usually responsible for materials usage because the production manager can minimize scrap, waste, and rework in order to meet the standard.
- Using the usage variance to evaluate performance can lead to undesirable behavior. For example, a production manager that is pressured to produce a favorable materials usage variance might allow defective units to be transferred to finished goods. Although this avoids the problem of wasted materials, it creates customer-relation problems.
- The materials usage variance is calculated at the time materials are issued or used in the manufacturing process.

Direct Labor Variances

Labor Rate Variance

- The **labor rate variance (*LRV*)** is calculated as follows:

Actual labor hours at actual rate ($AR \times AH$)	Actual labor hours at standard rate ($SR \times AH$)

$$(AR - SR)AH$$

Direct labor rate variance

- Labor rates are largely determined by external factors, such as labor markets and union contracts.
- When labor rate variances occur, it is usually due to:
  - using the average wage rate as the standard rate, or
  - using more skilled and higher paid laborers for less skilled tasks.
- Responsibility for the labor rate variance is often assigned to the individual, such as the production manager, who decides how labor will be used.

Labor Efficiency Variance

- The **labor efficiency variance (*LEV*)** is calculated as follows:

Actual labor hours at standard rate		**Standard labor hours allowed at standard rate**
($AH \times SR$)		**($SH \times SR$)**
	$(AH - SH)SR$	
	Direct labor efficiency variance	

- Usually production managers are responsible for the direct labor efficiency variance; however, once the cause of the variance is discovered, responsibility may be assigned elsewhere.
- The total variance for direct labor would be the sum of the rate variance and the efficiency variance. The total variance can also be calculated as follows:

Total direct labor variance =
(Actual quantity × Actual price) – (Standard quantity × Standard price)

VARIANCE ANALYSIS: OVERHEAD COSTS

- One method of analyzing overhead variances is as follows:
  1. Divide manufacturing overhead costs into two categories:
     - variable costs
     - fixed costs
  2. Determine separate overhead rates for variable and fixed overhead because the two costs react differently to changes in activity.

     The variable overhead rate is determined by analyzing how variable overhead costs react to changes in activity. For example, if a firm determines that $10 of variable manufacturing overhead is incurred for each direct labor hour worked, then the standard variable overhead rate (*SVOR*) would be $10 per direct labor hour.

     The standard fixed overhead rate (*SFOR*) is calculated as follows:

$$\textbf{Standard fixed overhead rate} = \frac{\textbf{Budgeted fixed overhead costs}}{\textbf{Standard hours allowed for denominator volume}}$$

     Denominator volume is the expected production volume selected at the beginning of the year when the standard fixed overhead rate is established. The standard fixed overhead rate is determined on an annual basis.
  3. Apply manufacturing overhead using the standard variable overhead rate (*SVOR*) and the standard fixed overhead rate (*SFOR*).

     Manufacturing overhead in a standard costing system is applied based on *the standard hours allowed for production achieved* rather than on the actual hours worked.

     The Manufacturing Overhead Control account would include the following items:

Manufacturing Overhead Control

Actual overhead costs	Applied overhead costs (based on standard hours allowed for production)

4. Calculate the two variable overhead variances:
   - variable overhead spending variance
   - variable overhead efficiency variance
5. Calculate the two fixed overhead variances:
   - fixed overhead spending variance
   - fixed overhead volume variance

Variable Overhead Variances

Variable Overhead Spending Variance

❒ The variable overhead spending variance indicates if a firm is paying the budgeted price for the variable manufacturing overhead used.

❒ The **variable overhead spending variance** is calculated as follows:

Actual variable overhead rate × Actual hours	Standard variable overhead rate × Actual hours
(*AVOR* × *AH*)	(*SVOR* × *AH*)

(*AVOR* – *SVOR*)*AH*

Variable overhead spending variance

❒ Price changes of variable overhead items are essentially beyond the control of supervisors; therefore, the variable overhead spending variance is usually assigned to the production departments.

❒ In order to determine how well costs of individual variable overhead items were controlled, a line-by-line analysis of each variable overhead item is essential.

Variable Overhead Efficiency Variance

❒ The variable overhead efficiency variance results from the efficient or inefficient use of the base used to apply variable manufacturing overhead.

❒ For example, if variable manufacturing overhead is applied using direct labor hours as the base and there is an unfavorable labor efficiency variance, there will also be an unfavorable variable overhead efficiency variance.

❒ The **variable overhead efficiency variance** is calculated as follows:

Standard variable overhead rate × Actual hours	Standard variable overhead rate × Standard hours
(*AH* × *SVOR*)	(*SH* × *SVOR*)

(*AH* – *SH*)*SVOR*

Variable overhead efficiency variance

❒ If variable overhead costs change in proportion to changes in the base, such as direct labor hours, then responsibility for the variable overhead efficiency variance should be assigned to the production manager because the production manager has responsibility for the use of direct labor.

Total Variable Overhead Variance

- The total variable overhead variance is calculated as follows:

Actual variable overhead	**Variable overhead rate × Actual hours (*SVOR* × *AH*)**	**Applied variable overhead** **Variable overhead rate × Standard hours (*SVOR* × *SH*)**
Variable overhead spending variance		**Variable overhead efficiency variance**
	Total variable overhead variance	

Fixed Overhead Variances

- Variance analysis for fixed manufacturing overhead differs from variance analysis for variable manufacturing costs because fixed costs react differently to changes in activity.
- Two variances calculated for fixed manufacturing overhead are:
  1. the fixed overhead spending or budget variance, and
  2. the fixed overhead volume variance.

Fixed Overhead Spending Variance

- The **fixed overhead spending variance** compares actual fixed overhead to the fixed overhead budgeted for the production level achieved.
- The fixed overhead spending variance is calculated as follows:

Actual fixed overhead	**Budgeted fixed overhead**
Fixed overhead spending variance	

- Because many fixed overhead items are not subject to change in the short run, fixed overhead costs are often beyond the immediate control of management.
- In addition, because fixed overhead consists of a number of items, such as salaries, depreciation, property taxes, and insurance, a line-by-line comparison of actual costs and budgeted costs provides more information about the causes of budget variances.

Fixed Overhead Volume Variance

- The **fixed overhead volume variance** is the difference between *budgeted* fixed overhead and *applied* fixed overhead. It is a measure of the utilization of plant facilities.
- The *standard fixed overhead rate (SFOR)* used to apply fixed overhead is calculated as follows:

$$\text{Standard fixed overhead rate} = \frac{\text{Budgeted fixed overhead costs}}{\text{Standard hours allowed for expected capacity}}$$

- The expected production volume is selected at the beginning of the year when the standard fixed overhead rate is established.

- The output used to calculate the fixed overhead rate can be viewed as the activity capacity acquired. Actual output can be viewed as the activity capacity used.
- The fixed overhead volume variance is calculated as follows:

Budgeted fixed overhead	Applied fixed overhead (Standard hours allowed × *SFOR*)
Fixed overhead volume variance	

- The volume variance tells management if they operated at the expected production volume used to calculate the standard fixed overhead rate.
- The volume variance can also be calculated as follows:

Fixed overhead volume variance =
***SFOR* × [Expected activity used in *SFOR* – Standard allowed for actual production]**

- A volume variance occurs when *actual* production differs from the *expected* production volume used to calculate the standard fixed overhead rate.
- There will be no volume variance if actual output equals expected output.
- If actual production exceeds expected production, the volume variance is labeled favorable. If actual production is less than expected, the volume variance is labeled unfavorable.
- When a volume variance occurs, it might indicate that:
  - management did not use the correct expected production level when calculating the standard fixed overhead rate, or
  - if the expected output is correct and the volume variance is unfavorable, production facilities were not fully utilized.

Total Fixed Overhead Variance

- The total fixed overhead variance is the sum of the fixed overhead spending and volume variances and is calculated as follows:

Actual fixed overhead	Budgeted fixed overhead	Applied fixed overhead (*SH* × *SFOR*)
Fixed overhead spending variance	Fixed overhead volume variance	
Total fixed overhead variance		

The Decision to Investigate

- Variances indicate that actual performance is not going according to plan.
- Variances do not indicate the cause of the variance or responsibility.
- Usually the cause of a variance can be determined only by an investigation. For example, an unfavorable materials quantity variance may not be the fault of the production supervisor. Instead, it may be the result of the purchasing agent buying inferior-quality material.
- As a general principle, variances should be investigated if the anticipated benefits of the investigation exceed the expected costs of investigating.

- Most firms adopt the general guideline of investigating variances only if they fall outside an acceptable range.

Lower control limit — **Upper control limit**

Acceptable range

- The **control limits** of the acceptable range are calculated as follows:

Upper control limit = Standard + Allowable deviation

Lower control limit = Standard – Allowable deviation

- The control limits are often expressed as:
  - a specified amount, and/or
  - a specified percentage of the variance.
- For example, management may investigate any variance that exceeds $1,000 or 5% of the standard amount to which the variance relates.

SUMMARY

- The following summarizes variances:

Variances

Direct materials variance	**Actual cost** ***AP × AQ***	***SP × AQ***	**Standard cost** ***SP × SQ***
	Direct materials price variance	**Direct materials efficiency variance**	
Direct labor variance	***AR × AH***	***SR × AH***	***SH × SR***
	Direct labor rate variance	**Direct labor efficiency variance**	
Variable overhead variances	**Actual variable overhead**	***AH × SVOR***	***SH × SVOR***
	Variable overhead spending variance	**Variable overhead efficiency variance**	
Fixed overhead variances	**Actual fixed overhead**	**Budgeted fixed overhead**	**Applied fixed overhead** ***SH × SFOR***
	Fixed overhead spending variance	**Fixed overhead volume variance**	

KEY TERMS TEST

Test your recall of the key terms as follows. Try to recall as many key terms as possible without assistance. If you need assistance, refer to the list of key terms at the end of this section.

1. ________ ________ ________ are demanding but achievable under efficient operating conditions. Such standards allow for normal machine downtime and employee rest periods.

2. ________ ________ reflect perfect operating conditions. Such standards are virtually unattainable and can result in low employee morale and a decline in performance.

3. A(n) ________ ________ ________ lists the standard costs and standard quantities of direct materials, direct labor, and overhead for a product.

4. ________ ________ establish the maximum allowable deviation from a standard.

5. ________ ________ ________ are the direct labor hours that should have been used to produce the actual output.

6. ________ ________ ________ ________ ________ is the quantity of materials that should have been used to produce the actual output.

7. A(n) ________ ________ results when the actual amounts are greater than the budgeted or standard allowances.

8. A(n) ________ ________ results whenever the actual amounts are less than the budgeted or standard allowances.

9. The ________ ________ ________ ________ is the difference between the actual direct labor hours used and the standard hours allowed, multiplied by the standard variable overhead rate.

10. The ________ ________ ________ ________ is the difference between the actual variable overhead and the budgeted variable overhead based on actual hours used to produce the actual output.

11. The ________ ________ ________ is the difference between the actual price paid per unit of materials and the standard price allowed per unit, multiplied by the actual quantity of materials purchased.

12. The ________ ________ ________ is the difference between the direct materials actually used and the direct materials allowed for the actual output, multiplied by the standard price.

13. The ________ ________ ________ ________ is the difference between budgeted fixed overhead and applied fixed overhead and is a measure of capacity utilization.

14. The ________ ________ ________ is the difference between the actual hourly rate paid and the standard hourly rate, multiplied by the actual hours worked.

15. The ________ ________ ________ is the difference between the actual direct labor hours used and the standard direct labor hours allowed, multiplied by the standard hourly wage rate.

16. The ________ ________ ________ ________ is the difference between actual fixed overhead and budgeted fixed overhead.

KEY TERMS:

control limits
currently attainable standards
favorable variance
fixed overhead spending variance
fixed overhead volume variance
ideal standards
labor efficiency variance
labor rate variance
materials price variance
materials usage variance
standard cost sheet
standard hours allowed
standard quantity of materials allowed
unfavorable variance
variable overhead efficiency variance
variable overhead spending variance

→ **Compare your answers with those at the end of the chapter. Review any key terms missed.**

CHAPTER QUIZ

Circle the single best answer.

1. All of the following are true of currently attainable standards except: (a) currently attainable standards are based on an efficiently operating workforce; (b) currently attainable standards are based on ideal conditions; (c) currently attainable standards allow for downtime and rest periods; (d) currently attainable standards are based on present production processes and technology.
2. There is a direct relationship between (circle two answers): (a) inputs of direct materials and output of finished product; (b) inputs of direct labor and output of finished product; (c) input of variable manufacturing overhead and output of finished product; (d) input of fixed manufacturing overhead and output of finished product
3. Standards can be based on: (a) historical experience; (b) engineering studies; (c) input from operating personnel; (d) all of the above
4. In order to facilitate control, actual overhead costs for the output level attained should be compared with budgeted costs at the expected activity level: (a) true; (b) false
5. Engineering relationships between inputs and outputs can be established for manufacturing overhead: (a) true; (b) false
6. Separate overhead rates should be calculated for variable and fixed manufacturing overhead because the two costs react differently to changes in activity: (a) true; (b) false
7. The standard fixed overhead rate is calculated as estimated fixed manufacturing overhead costs divided by estimated activity: (a) true; (b) false
8. The standard fixed overhead rate should be determined on a monthly basis: (a) true; (b) false
9. If the selected activity is direct labor hours, manufacturing overhead in a standard costing system would be applied based on the actual direct labor hours worked: (a) true; (b) false
10. The variable manufacturing overhead efficiency variance results from the efficient or inefficient use of the base upon which variable manufacturing overhead is budgeted: (a) true; (b) false
11. The fixed manufacturing overhead budget variance is a measure of the utilization of plant facilities: (a) true; (b) false

12. The fixed manufacturing overhead volume variance indicates to management whether they operated at the expected activity level used to calculate the standard fixed overhead rate. There will be no volume variance if the company operated at the expected activity level: (a) true; (b) false

13. As a general rule, variances should be investigated if the anticipated benefits of the investigation exceed the expected costs of investigating: (a) true; (b) false

Use the following information to answer Questions 14 through 21:

The standard cost sheet for one of the Carver Company's products is presented below:

Direct materials (4 feet @ $6.00)	$24.00
Direct labor (1 hour @ $12.00)	12.00
Variable overhead (1 hour @ $5.00)	5.00
Fixed overhead (1 hour @ $3.00[a])	3.00
Standard unit cost	$44.00

[a]Rate based on expected activity of 12,000 hours

The following results for last year were recorded:

Production	10,000 units
Direct materials (39,000 feet purchased and used)	$241,800
Direct labor (10,500 hours)	$131,250
Variable overhead	$48,000
Fixed overhead	$40,000

14. The materials price variance is: (a) $7,800 unfavorable; (b) $7,800 favorable; (c) $8,400 unfavorable; (d) $8,400 favorable

15. The materials usage variance is: (a) $4,000 favorable; (b) $4,000 unfavorable; (c) $6,000 favorable; (d) $6,000 unfavorable

16. The labor rate variance is: (a) $5,250 favorable; (b) $5,250 unfavorable; (c) $5,000 favorable; (d) $5,000 unfavorable

17. The labor efficiency variance is: (a) $5,250 favorable; (b) $5,250 unfavorable; (c) $6,000 favorable; (d) $6,000 unfavorable

18. The variable overhead spending variance is: (a) $4,500 favorable; (b) $4,500 unfavorable; (c) $4,800 favorable; (d) $4,800 unfavorable

19. The variable overhead efficiency variance is: (a) $2,500 favorable; (b) $2,500 unfavorable; (c) $2,250 favorable; (d) $2,250 unfavorable

20. The fixed overhead spending variance is: (a) $4,000 unfavorable; (b) $4,000 favorable; (c) $8,000 unfavorable; (d) $8,000 favorable

21. The fixed overhead volume variance is: (a) $4,000 unfavorable; (b) $4,000 favorable; (c) $6,000 unfavorable; (d) $6,000 favorable

→ **Compare your answers with those at the end of the chapter. Review any questions missed.**

PRACTICE TEST

PROBLEM 1

The Carver Manufacturing Company has developed the following standards for one of their products, a walnut fern stand:

STANDARD VARIABLE COST SHEET
One Walnut Fern Stand

Materials: 5 square feet × $8 per square foot	$40.00
Direct labor: 2 hours × $10/DLH	20.00
Variable manufacturing overhead: 2 hours × $5/DLH	10.00
Total standard variable cost per unit	$70.00

The company records materials price variances at the time of purchase. The following activity occurred during the month of April:

Materials purchased	5,000 square feet costing $46,000
Materials used	4,250 square feet
Units produced	900 units
Direct labor	2,200 hours costing $19,800
Actual variable manufacturing overhead	$10,500

Instructions:

1. Calculate the direct materials price and usage variances.

PROBLEM 1 *(Continued)*

2. Calculate the direct labor rate variance, the direct labor efficiency variance, and the total direct labor variance.

3. Compute the variable manufacturing overhead spending and efficiency variances.

PROBLEM 2

The Mills Company manufactures roofing shingles. The production process involves heating and compressing asphalt into sheets and then rolling coarse sand into the hot asphalt. The sheets are then cooled, cut into shingles, and packaged.

The following standard costs were developed:

STANDARD COST SHEET PER SHINGLE

Direct materials:		
Asphalt	2 lbs. × $0.08/lb.	$0.16
Sand	2 lbs. × $0.02/lb.	0.04
Direct labor	.01 hrs. × $7/hr.	0.07
Variable manufacturing overhead	.01 hrs. × $3/hr.	0.03
Fixed manufacturing overhead		?
Total standard cost per shingle		?

The following information is available regarding the company's operations for the period:

Shingles produced	500,000
Materials purchased:	
Asphalt	800,000 pounds @ $0.07 per pound
Sand	900,000 pounds @ $0.03 per pound
Materials used:	
Asphalt	775,000 pounds
Sand	850,000 pounds
Direct labor	5,100 hours costing $36,000
Manufacturing overhead incurred:	
Variable	$16,500
Fixed	$48,000

Budgeted fixed manufacturing overhead for the period is $60,000, and the standard fixed overhead rate is based on expected capacity of 6,000 direct labor hours.

Instructions:

1. Calculate the standard fixed manufacturing overhead rate.

PROBLEM 2 *(Continued)*

2. Complete the standard cost card for roofing shingles.

3. Calculate the following variances:

a. Materials price and usage variances for asphalt and sand

PROBLEM 2 *(Continued)*

Use this space to continue your answer.

b. Direct labor rate and efficiency variances

PROBLEM 2 *(Continued)*

c. Variable manufacturing overhead spending and efficiency variances

d. Fixed manufacturing overhead spending and volume variances

PROBLEM 3

The Commodore Company uses standard costing for direct materials and direct labor. Management would like to use standard costing for variable and fixed overhead also.

The following monthly cost functions were developed for manufacturing overhead items:

Overhead Item	Cost Function
Indirect materials	$0.10 per DLH
Indirect labor	$0.40 per DLH
Repairs and maintenance	$0.20 per DLH
Utilities	$0.25 per DLH
Insurance	$2,000
Rent	$4,000
Depreciation	$20,000

The cost functions are considered reliable within a relevant range of 30,000 to 55,000 direct labor hours.

Commodore expects to operate at 40,000 direct labor hours per month.

Information for the month of September is as follows:

Actual overhead costs incurred:	
Indirect materials	$ 4,500
Indirect labor	17,000
Repairs and maintenance	8,000
Utilities	10,000
Insurance	2,100
Rent	4,000
Depreciation	20,000
Total	$65,600
Actual direct labor hours worked	42,000
Standard direct labor hours allowed for production achieved	44,000

Instructions:

1. Calculate the standard manufacturing overhead rate based upon expected capacity, showing the breakdown between the fixed overhead rate and the variable overhead rate.

PROBLEM 3 *(Continued)*

Use this space to continue your answer.

2. Calculate the variable manufacturing overhead spending variance.

3. Calculate the variable manufacturing overhead efficiency variance.

PROBLEM 3 *(Continued)*

4. Calculate the fixed manufacturing overhead spending variance.

5. Calculate the fixed manufacturing overhead volume variance.

ANSWERS

KEY TERMS TEST

1. Currently attainable standards
2. Ideal standards
3. standard cost sheet
4. Control limits
5. Standard hours allowed
6. Standard quantity of materials allowed
7. unfavorable variance
8. favorable variance
9. variable overhead efficiency variance
10. variable overhead spending variance
11. materials price variance
12. materials usage variance
13. fixed overhead volume variance
14. labor rate variance
15. labor efficiency variance
16. fixed overhead spending variance

CHAPTER QUIZ

1. b
2. a and b
3. d
4. b False To facilitate control, actual overhead costs should be compared with budgeted costs for the same level of output.
5. b False
6. a True
7. a True
8. b False The fixed manufacturing overhead rate should be determined on a yearly basis.
9. b False Manufacturing overhead would be applied based on the standard hours allowed for production achieved.
10. a True
11. b False The fixed manufacturing overhead volume variance is a measure of the utilization of plant facilities.
12. a True
13. a True
14. a 39,000($6.20 – $6.00) = $7,800 unfavorable
15. c $6.00[39,000 – (4 feet × 10,000)] = $6,000 favorable
16. b 10,500 hours($12.50 – $12.00) = $5,250 unfavorable
17. d $12(10,500 – 10,000) = $6,000 unfavorable
18. a $48,000 – (10,500 × $5) = $4,500 favorable
19. b $5(10,500 – 10,000) = $2,500 unfavorable
20. a $40,000 – ($3 × 12,000) = $4,000 unfavorable
21. c $36,000 budgeted – ($3 × 10,000) applied = $6,000 unfavorable

PRACTICE TEST

PROBLEM 1

1. **Direct materials price variance:**

Actual quantity purchased at Actual price	Actual quantity purchased at Standard price
5,000 sq. ft. × $9.20/sq. ft.	5,000 sq. ft. × $8/sq. ft.
$46,000	$40,000

$6,000 Unfavorable

Direct materials price variance
5,000($9.20 – $8.00) = $6,000 Unfavorable

Direct materials usage variance:

Actual quantity used at Standard price	Standard quantity allowed at Standard price
4,250 sq. ft. × $8/sq. ft.	900 units × 5 sq. ft. × $8/sq. ft.
$34,000	$36,000

$2,000 Favorable

Direct materials usage variance
$8(4,250 – 4,500) = $2,000 Favorable

2. Direct labor rate variance:

Actual labor hours at Actual rate		Actual labor hours at Standard rate
2,200 hours × $9/hour		2,200 hours × $10/hour
$19,800		$22,000
	$2,200 Favorable	

Direct labor rate variance
2,200($9 – $10) = $2,200 Favorable

Direct labor efficiency variance:

Actual labor hours at Standard rate		Standard labor hours allowed at Standard rate
2,200 hours × $10/hour		(900 units × 2 hours) × $10/hour
$22,000		$18,000
	$4,000 Unfavorable	

Direct labor efficiency variance
$10(2,200 – 1,800) = $4,000 Unfavorable

Total direct labor variance:

Actual hours at actual price	$19,800	
Standard hours allowed for production [(900 × 2) × $10]	18,000	
Total direct labor variance	$ 1,800	U

The total direct labor variance can be broken down as follows:

Direct labor rate variance	$2,200	F
Direct labor efficiency variance	4,000	U
Total direct labor variance	$1,800	U

3. Variable manufacturing overhead spending variance:

Actual variable overhead		Standard variable overhead rate × Actual hours (*AQ* × *SVOR*)
		2,200 hours × $5/hour
$10,500		$11,000
	$500 Favorable	

Variable overhead spending variance

Variable manufacturing overhead efficiency variance:

Standard variable overhead rate × Actual hours (*AQ* × *SVOR*)		Standard variable overhead rate × Standard hours (*SQ* × *SVOR*)
2,200 hours × $5/hour		(900 units × 2 hours) × $5/hour
$11,000		$9,000
	$2,000 Unfavorable	

Variable overhead efficiency variance

PROBLEM 2

1. Standard fixed manufacturing overhead rate = $\frac{\text{Estimated fixed overhead}}{\text{Estimated direct labor hours}}$

$= \frac{\$60{,}000}{6{,}000 \text{ direct labor hours}}$

= $10 per direct labor hour

2. **STANDARD COST SHEET PER SHINGLE**

Direct materials:	
Asphalt	$0.16
Sand	0.04
Direct labor	0.07
Variable manufacturing overhead	0.03
Fixed manufacturing overhead (.01 hrs. × $10/hr.)	0.10
Total standard cost per shingle	$0.40

3. a. **Materials price variance—Asphalt:**

Actual quantity purchased × Actual price		Actual quantity purchased × Standard price
800,000 lbs. × $0.07/lb.		800,000 lbs. × $0.08/lb.
$56,000	$8,000 Favorable	$64,000
	Materials price variance—Asphalt	

Materials price variance—Sand:

Actual quantity purchased × Actual price		Actual quantity purchased × Standard price
900,000 lbs. × $0.03/lb.		900,000 lbs. × $0.02/lb.
$27,000	$9,000 Unfavorable	$18,000
	Materials price variance—Sand	

Materials usage variance—Asphalt:

Actual quantity used × Standard price		Standard quantity × Standard price
775,000 lbs. × $0.08/lb.		500,000 × 2 lbs. × $0.08/lb.
$62,000	$18,000 Favorable	$80,000
	Materials usage variance—Asphalt	

Materials usage variance—Sand:

Actual quantity used × Standard price		Standard quantity × Standard price
850,000 lbs. × $0.02/lb.		500,000 × 2 lbs. × $0.02/lb.
$17,000	$3,000 Favorable	$20,000
	Materials usage variance—Sand	

b. Direct labor rate variance:

Actual labor hours × Actual rate		Actual labor hours × Standard rate
5,100 DLH × $7.06*/hr.		5,100 DLH × $7/hr.
$36,000		$35,700
	$300 Unfavorable	
	Direct labor rate variance	

*rounded

Direct labor efficiency variance:

Actual labor hours × Standard rate		Standard labor hours × Standard rate
5,100 DLH × $7/hr.		500,000 units × .01 DLH × $7/hr.
$35,700		$35,000
	$700 Unfavorable	
	Direct labor efficiency variance	

c. Variable manufacturing overhead spending variance:

Actual variable overhead		Standard variable overhead rate × Actual hours (*SVOR* × *AH*)
		5,100 DLH × $3/hr.
$16,500		$15,300
	$1,200 Unfavorable	
	Variable overhead spending variance	

Variable manufacturing overhead efficiency variance:

Standard variable overhead rate × Actual hours (*SVOR* × *AH*)		Standard variable overhead rate × Standard hours (*SVOR* × *SH*)
5,100 DLH × $3/hr.		500,000 units × .01 DLH × $3/hr.
$15,300		$15,000
	$300 Unfavorable	
	Variable overhead efficiency variance	

d. Fixed manufacturing overhead spending variance:

Actual fixed overhead		Budgeted fixed overhead
$48,000		$60,000
	$12,000 Favorable	
	Fixed overhead spending variance	

Fixed manufacturing overhead volume variance:

Budgeted fixed overhead		Applied fixed overhead (Standard activity × *SFOR*)
		500,000 units × .01 DLH × $10/hr.
$60,000		$50,000
	$10,000 Unfavorable	
	Fixed overhead volume variance	

The volume variance could also be calculated as follows:

FMO volume variance = *SFOR* × [Expected capacity – Standard hours allowed for production level achieved]
= ($10)(6,000 DLH – 5,000 DLH allowed)
= ($10)(1,000 DLH)
= $10,000

The Mills Company produced 500,000 shingles, a level for which 5,000 direct labor hours are allowed.

The Mills Company budgeted 6,000 direct labor hours. The volume variance resulted from the company operating at a level other than the budgeted level of 6,000 direct labor hours.

PROBLEM 3

1. Standard manufacturing overhead rate:

Manufacturing overhead items:		
Indirect materials		$0.10 per DLH
Indirect labor		0.40 per DLH
Repairs and maintenance		0.20 per DLH
Utilities		0.25 per DLH
Insurance	$ 2,000	
Rent	4,000	
Depreciation	20,000	
Variable manufacturing overhead		$0.95 per DLH
Fixed manufacturing overhead	$26,000	

SVOR = $0.95 per direct labor hour

$$SFOR = \frac{\text{Estimated fixed manufacturing overhead}}{\text{Estimated direct labor hours}}$$

$$= \frac{\$26{,}000}{40{,}000 \text{ direct labor hours}}$$

= $0.65 per direct labor hour

Total manufacturing overhead rate = *SFOR* + *SVOR*
= $0.65 + $0.95
= $1.60 per direct labor hour

2. Variable manufacturing overhead spending variance:

Actual variable overhead	Standard variable overhead rate × Actual hours (*SVOR* × *AH*)
($4,500 + $17,000 + $8,000 + $10,000)	42,000 DLH × $0.95/hr.
$39,500	$39,900

$400 Favorable

Variable overhead spending variance

3. Variable manufacturing overhead efficiency variance:

Standard variable overhead rate × Actual hours (*SVOR* × *AH*)	Standard variable overhead rate × Standard hours (*SVOR* × *SH*)
42,000 DLH × $0.95/hr.	44,000 DLH × $0.95/hr.
$39,900	$41,800

$1,900 Favorable

Variable overhead efficiency variance

4. Fixed manufacturing overhead spending variance:

Actual fixed overhead		Budgeted fixed overhead
$26,100		$26,000
	$100 Unfavorable	
	Fixed overhead spending variance	

5. Fixed manufacturing overhead volume variance:

Budgeted fixed overhead		Applied fixed overhead (Standard activity × *SFOR*)
		44,000 DLH × $0.65/hr.
$26,000		$28,600
	$2,600 Favorable	
	Fixed overhead volume variance	

The volume variance could also be calculated as follows:

FMO volume variance = *SFOR* × [Expected capacity – Standard hours allowed for production level achieved]
= ($0.65)(40,000 DLH – 44,000 DLH allowed)
= ($0.65)(4,000 DLH)
= $2,600 Favorable

CHAPTER 10

Activity- and Strategic-Based Responsibility Accounting

CHAPTER REVIEW

RESPONSIBILITY ACCOUNTING SYSTEMS

- Responsibility accounting uses the accounting system to measure actions and outcomes.
- The responsibility control model has four elements:
  - assign responsibility
  - establish performance measure or benchmarks
  - evaluate performance
  - assign rewards
- Three types of responsibility accounting systems are:
  1. *functional-based* responsibility accounting
  2. *activity-based* responsibility accounting, and
  3. *strategic-based* responsibility accounting.
- The system selected is *contingent* on the environment in which the firm operates. Firms that operate in a stable environment with standardized products and low competitive pressures may use the functional-based responsibility accounting system. As the competitive environment becomes more dynamic, activity-based and strategic-based systems may be more suitable.
- Organizations operating in a dynamic, rapidly changing environment find that adaptation, change, and continuous improvement are necessary. Continuous improvement is the process of constantly searching for ways to eliminate waste. Waste reduction tools attempt to eliminate waste in the form of inventories, unnecessary activities, defective products, rework, setup time, and underutilization of employee talents and skills. Waste reduction tools include:
  - JIT purchasing and manufacturing
  - reengineering
  - total quality management
  - employee empowerment
  - computer-aided manufacturing
- A **functional-based responsibility accounting system**:
  - focuses on organizational units such as departments and plants
  - uses financial outcome measures and static standards and benchmarks to evaluation performance
  - emphasizes status quo and organizational stability

❒ **Activity-based responsibility accounting**:

- focuses on processes
- uses both operational and financial measures and dynamic standards
- emphasizes continuous improvement

❒ A **strategic-based responsibility accounting system** (or **Balanced Scorecard**) translates the mission and strategy of an organization into operational objectives and measures for the following four perspectives:

1. Financial perspective
2. Customer perspective
3. Process perspective
4. Infrastructure (learning and growth) perspective

Strategic-based responsibility accounting uses directed continuous improvement, whereby continuous improvement is related to the overall mission and strategy of the organization.

❒ The four responsibility elements for functional-based, activity-based, and strategic-based responsibility accounting is summarized below:

Responsibility Element	Functional-Based Responsibility Accounting	Activity-Based Responsibility Accounting	Strategic-Based Responsibility Accounting
Assign responsibility	■ Responsibility assigned to individual in charge of an organizational unit such as a department, division, or plant ■ Responsibility defined in financial terms (costs)	■ Responsibility assigned to teams or processes such as product development ■ Focuses on **process improvement** (incremental and constant increases in efficiency of an existing system), **process innovation** or **business reengineering** (performing processes in radically new ways to achieve dramatic improvements in response time, quality, and efficiency), and **process creation** (installation of a new process with the objective of meeting customer and financial objectives)	■ Responsibility system maintains perspectives that serve as a potential source for a competitive advantage ■ Focuses on financial, customer, process, and infrastructure (learning and growth) perspectives

Establish performance measures or benchmarks	■ Budgets
	■ Standard costing using currently attainable standards
		■ Performance measures are dynamic and process-oriented.
		■ Focuses on continual improvement and increasing customer value
			■ Performance measures are perspective oriented.
			■ Performance measures are integrated and linked to the organization's goals and initiatives.
			■ Measures balance between:[a]
			  ■ lag and lead measures
			  ■ objective and subjective measures
			  ■ financial and nonfinancial measures
			  ■ external and internal measures

Responsibility Element	Functional-Based Responsibility Accounting	Activity-Based Responsibility Accounting	Strategic-Based Responsibility Accounting
Evaluate performance	■ Compare actual costs with budgeted (or standard) costs ■ Individuals held accountable only for items they can control	■ Financial measures ■ Nonfinancial measures such as quality, efficiency, on-time delivery, cycle time, productivity	■ Performance measures relate to: ■ process efficiency ■ customer satisfaction ■ infrastructure factors that enable an organization to learn, change, and use new and improved process (employee satisfaction and skills) ■ economic or financial consequences of processes (cost trends)
Assign rewards	■ Rewards individuals based on financial performance ■ Rewards include promotions, salary increases, bonuses, and profit sharing.	■ Rewards based on multidimensional performance ■ Group-based or team rewards ■ Rewards include gainsharing—sharing in gains related to specific improvement projects.	■ Rewards based on multidimensional performance ■ Incentive compensation may be distributed among the four perspectives: financial, customer, process, and infrastructure (learning and growth) perspectives.

[a]**Lag measures** are outcome measures of results from past efforts, such as customer profitability.

Lead measures or **performance drivers** are factors that drive future performance, such as hours of employee training.

Objective measures are readily quantified and verified, such as market share.

Subjective measures are less quantifiable and more judgmental, such as employee capabilities.

Financial measures are expressed in monetary terms.

Nonfinancial measures are expressed in nonmonetary terms, such as effects of dissatisfied customers.

External measures relate to customers and shareholders, such as customer satisfaction.

Internal measures relate to processes and capabilities that create value for customers and shareholders, such as process efficiency and employee satisfaction.

❒ **Activity-based management (ABM)**, the management of activities—not costs, is the key to successful control for firms operating in dynamic environments.

❒ The activity-based management model has two dimensions:

- a *cost dimension*, which provides cost information about resources, activities, products, and customers. The cost of resources is traced to activities and then the cost of activities is assigned to products and customers.
- a *process dimension*, which provides information about what activities are performed, why activities are performed, and how well they are done.

PROCESS VALUE ANALYSIS

❒ **Process value analysis**:

- focuses on accountability for activities rather than costs
- emphasizes the maximization of system-wide performance instead of individual performance

- Process value analysis is concerned with:
  - driver analysis
  - activity analysis
  - activity performance measurement

Driver Analysis: The Search for Root Causes

- **Driver analysis** is the effort expended to identify those factors that are the root causes of activity costs. Once the root cause of activity costs is known, then action can be taken to improve the activity.

Activity Analysis: Identifying and Assessing Value Content

- **Activity analysis** is the process of identifying, describing, and evaluating the activities an organization performs.
- Activity analysis should produce four outcomes:
  1. What activities are done
  2. How many people perform the activities
  3. The time and resources required to perform the activities
  4. Determination of the value-added portion of the activities
- **Value-added activities** are activities that are necessary to achieve corporate objectives and remain in business.
- **Value-added costs** are costs caused by value-added activities.
- **Nonvalue-added activities** are unnecessary activities and are all activities other than those that are absolutely essential to remain in business.
- **Nonvalue-added costs** are costs caused by either:
  - nonvalue-added activities, or
  - the inefficient performance of value-added activities.
- Activity analysis attempts to:
  - identify and eliminate all unnecessary activities, and
  - increase the efficiency of necessary activities.
- An unnecessary activity is wasteful and should be eliminated. Managing costs may increase the efficiency of an activity—but if the activity is unnecessary, what does it matter if it is performed efficiently?
- Five major categories of nonvalue-added activities are:
  - *Scheduling*—an activity that uses time and resources to determine when different products have access to processes (or when and how many setups must be done) and how much will be produced.
  - *Moving*—an activity that uses time and resources to move materials, work in process, and finished goods from one department to another.
  - *Waiting*—an activity in which materials or work in process use time and resources by waiting on the next process.
  - *Inspecting*—an activity where time and resources are spent on ensuring that the product meets specifications.
  - *Storing*—an activity that uses time and resources while a good or raw material is held in inventory.

- None of the above activities adds any value for the customer. Activity management tries to manufacture the product without using any of these nonvalue-added activities.
- Competitive conditions dictate that companies deliver products the customers want, on time, and at the lowest possible cost.
- Activity analysis can reduce costs in four ways:
  1. **Activity elimination**—eliminating nonvalue-added activities.
  2. **Activity selection**—choosing among different sets of activities caused by competing strategies.
  3. **Activity reduction**—decreasing the time and resources required by an activity. This approach to cost reduction should be primarily aimed at:
     - improving the efficiency of necessary activities, or
     - improving the nonvalue-added activities until they can be eliminated.

     Reducing setup time is an example of improving the efficiency of a necessary activity.
  4. **Activity sharing**—increasing the efficiency of activities by using economies of scale. An example is designing a product to use components already used in other products. By using existing components, activities associated with these components, such as design and machine tooling, are not duplicated.

Activity Performance Measurement

- Activity performance measures can be financial or nonfinancial.
- Three dimensions of activity performance measures are:
  - *Efficiency*—focuses on the relationship of activity inputs and activity outputs. For example, activity efficiency is improved by producing the same activity output with less input.
  - *Quality*—concerned with doing the activity right the first time it is performed.
  - *Time*—longer times usually result in more resource consumption and less ability to respond to customer demands.

MEASURES OF ACTIVITY PERFORMANCE

- Financial measures identify dollar values for:
  - potential savings, and
  - actual savings.
- Financial measures of activity efficiency include:
  - value- and nonvalue-added activity cost reports
  - trends in activity cost reports
  - kaizen standard setting
  - benchmarking
  - life-cycle costing

Value- and Nonvalue-Added Cost Reporting

- An activity-based cost report should include:
  - value-added costs
  - nonvalue-added costs

- This enables management to focus on reducing and eventually eliminating nonvalue-added costs.
- A **value-added standard** is the optimal output level for an activity.
- Value-added standards focuses on continual improvement and movement toward the ideal.
- The steps involved in reporting value-added and nonvalue-added costs are as follows:
  - Identify output measures for each activity.
  - Determine value-added standard quantities for each activity.
  - Calculate value-added costs as the value-added standard quantities multiplied by the price standard.

$$\textbf{Value-added costs} = \textbf{Standard quantity} \times \textbf{Standard price} = SQ \times SP$$

  - Nonvalue-added costs are the difference between the actual quantity of the activity's output and the value-added level, multiplied by the unit standard cost.

$$\textbf{Nonvalue-added costs} = (\textbf{Actual quantity} - \textbf{Standard quantity}) \times \textbf{Standard price} = (AQ - SQ) \times SP$$

  - For flexible resources (resources acquired as needed), *AQ* is the actual quantity of activity used.
  - For committed resources (resources acquired in advance of usage), *AQ* is the actual quantity of activity capacity acquired (the activity's practical capacity).
  - For nonvalue-added activities that are unnecessary, the value-added standard quantity is zero.

Trend Reporting

- Trend reporting involves comparing costs for each activity over time. If activities are reduced, eliminated, selected, and shared, cost reductions should follow and there should be a decline in nonvalue-added costs from one period to the next.

The Role of Kaizen Standards

- **Kaizen costing** focuses on reducing the costs of existing products and processes using two major subcycles:
  1. The kaizen or continuous improvement cycle
  2. The maintenance cycle
- The kaizen or continuous improvement cycle consists of a Plan-Do-Check-Act sequence:
  1. *Plan.* Plan the amount of improvement (such as reduction in nonvalue-added costs). A **kaizen standard**, a type of currently attainable standard, reflects planned improvement for the upcoming period.
  2. *Do.* Implement the planned improvements.
  3. *Check.* Check the actual improvement attained with the kaizen standard.
  4. *Act.* Set a new minimum standard for future performance, initiate a maintenance cycle, and search for additional improvement opportunities.
- The maintenance cycle also uses a Plan-Do-Check-Act sequence; however, the standard is based on prior improvements to lock in realized improvements. For example, if actual improvement achieved resulted in setup costs of $125, then setup costs of $125 should be maintained until further improvements are made.

Benchmarking

- **Benchmarking** is an approach to standard setting that uses best practices as the standard for evaluating activity performance. For example, the plant with the best performance for a given activity sets the standard for all the plants.

Drivers and Behavioral Effects

- The activity output measure selected can affect the behavior of employees. For example, if the activity output measure for setup costs is setup time, an incentive is created for workers to reduce setup time.

Activity Capacity Management

- **Activity capacity** is the number of times an activity can be performed. Activity drivers measure activity capacity.
- There are two capacity variances:
  1. **Activity volume variance** is the difference between the actual activity level acquired (practical capacity or *AQ*) and the capacity that should be used (value-added standard quantity or *SQ*). The volume variance is the nonvalue-added cost of the activity. For a nonvalue-added activity, the standard quantity (*SQ*) equals zero.
  2. **Unused capacity variance** is the difference between activity availability (*AQ*) and activity usage (*AU*).
- The capacity variances are calculated as follows:

$SP \times SQ$		$SP \times AQ$		$SP \times AU$
	Volume variance		**Unused capacity variance**	

where *AQ* = activity capacity acquired (practical capacity)
SQ = activity capacity used
AU = actual usage of the activity
SP = fixed activity rate

- Activity improvement can create unused capacity, but managers must be willing to reduce resource spending to increase profits.

Life-Cycle Cost Budgeting

- **Product life cycle** is the time a product exists from conception to abandonment.
- **Life-cycle costs** are all costs associated with the product for its entire life cycle.
- Life-cycle costs include:
  - development (planning, design, and testing)
  - production (conversion activities)
  - logistics support (advertising, distribution, and warranty)
- **Whole-life cost** is the life-cycle cost of a product plus postpurchase costs that consumers incur, including operation, support, maintenance, and disposal.
- **Life-cycle cost management** focuses on managing value-chain activities so that a long-term competitive advantage is created.

- The *value chain* is the set of activities required to design, develop, produce, market, and service a product (or service).

Cost Reduction

- Because 90 percent or more of a product's costs are *committed* (but not incurred) during the development stage, it is logical to focus on managing activities during this stage.
- Studies have shown that every dollar spent on premanufacturing activities saves $8–$10 on manufacturing and postmanufacturing activities.
- More opportunities for cost reduction exist during product planning than in production.
- The traditional emphasis has been on controlling costs during the production stage. In addition, development and logistics costs have been virtually ignored when computing product profitability for managerial purposes.

Whole-Life Product Cost

- A whole-life product cost consists of four elements:
  - nonrecurring costs (planning, designing, and testing)
  - manufacturing costs
  - logistic costs
  - the customer's postpurchase costs

Role of Target Costing

- Target costing is a useful tool for establishing cost reduction goals.
- A **target cost** is the difference between the sales price needed to capture a predetermined market share and the desired profit per unit.

$$\textbf{Target cost per unit} = \textbf{Sales price needed to capture a predetermined market share} - \textbf{Desired profit unit}$$

- If the target cost is less than what is currently achievable, cost reductions are budgeted to achieve the target cost. Progress is measured by comparing actual costs with target costs.

THE BALANCED SCORECARD

- The **Balanced Scorecard** is a strategic responsibility accounting system that translates an organization's mission and strategy into operational objectives and performance measures for four different perspectives:
  1. **Financial perspective**, which describes the economic consequences of actions taken in the other three perspectives
  2. **Customer perspective**, which defines the customer and market segments in which the business operates
  3. **Internal business process perspective**, which describes the internal processes needed to provide value for customers and owners
  4. **Learning and growth (infrastructure) perspective**, which defines the capabilities that an organization needs to create long-term growth and improvement: employee capabilities, information systems capabilities, and employee attitudes of motivation, empowerment, and alignment
- A business's **strategy** specifies the desired relationships among the above four perspectives.
- *Strategy translation* specifies objectives, measures, targets, and initiatives for each perspective.

- **Single-loop feedback** provides information about the effectiveness of the strategy implementation.
- **Double-loop feedback** provides information about both the *effectiveness* of the strategy implementation and the *validity* of the assumptions underlying the strategy.

The Financial Perspective

- The financial perspective has three strategic themes:
  1. *Revenue growth.* Objectives may include increasing the number of new products, developing new markets, changing the pricing strategy.
  2. *Cost reduction.* Objectives might include reducing the cost per unit. Accuracy of cost assignment is important when evaluating cost reduction performance objectives.
  3. *Asset utilization.* Financial measures include return on investment and economic value added.

Customer Perspective

- The customer perspective defines and selects the customer and market segments in which the company chooses to compete.
- **Core objectives and measures** are common across all organizations.

Core Objectives	Measures
Increase market share	Market share (percentage of market)
Increase customer retention	Percentage growth from existing customers Percentage of repeating customers
Increase customer acquisition	Number of new customers
Increase customer satisfaction	Ratings from customer surveys
Increase customer profitability	Customer profitability

- **Customer value** is the difference between what the customer receives (realization) and what the customer gives up (sacrifices).
- Realization objectives and measures are summarized below:

Realization Objectives	Measures
Decrease price	Reduce price
Decrease postpurchase costs	Reduce postpurchase costs
Improve production functionality	Satisfaction ratings of product features
Improve product quality	Percentage of returns
Increase delivery reliability	On-time delivery percentage Aging schedule
Improve product image and reputation	Ratings from customer surveys

Process Perspective

- The process perspective identifies the processes needed to achieve the customer and financial perspectives.
- The **process value chain** consists of three processes:

1. The **innovation process** creates new products and services to satisfy the emerging and potential needs of customers.
2. The **operations process** produces and delivers existing products and services to customers. Cycle time and velocity are two operational measures of responsiveness to customer orders. **Cycle time** is the time it takes to produce a unit of output (cycle time = time/units produced). **Velocity** is the number of units of output that can be produced in a given period of time (velocity = units produced/time).
3. The **postsales service process** provides critical and responsive services to customers after the product or service has been delivered.

❐ Objectives and measures for the three processes of the process perspective are summarized below:

Objectives	Measures
Innovation process:	
Increase the number of new products	Number of new products versus planned products
Increase proprietary products	Percentage of revenue from proprietary products
Decrease new product development time	Time to market (from start to finish)
Operations process:	
Increase process quality	Quality costs Output yields Percentage of defective units
Increase process efficiency	Unit cost trends Output/input(s)
Decrease process time	Cycle time and velocity MCE (Manufacturing Cycle Efficiency)
Postsales service process:	
Increase service quality	First-pass yields
Increase service efficiency	Cost trends Output/Input
Decrease service time	Cycle time

Learning and Growth Perspective

❐ The learning and growth perspective provides the capabilities that enable the accomplishment of the other three perspectives' objectives.

❐ The objectives and measures of the learning and growth perspective are summarized below:

Objectives	Measures
Increase employee capabilities	Employee satisfaction ratings Employee turnover percentages Employee productivity (revenue/employee) Hours of training
Increase motivation, empowerment, and alignment	Suggestions per employee Suggestions implemented per employee
Increase information systems capabilities	Percentage of processes with real-time feedback capabilities Percentage of customer-facing employees with on-line access to customer and product information

KEY TERMS TEST

Test your recall of the key terms as follows. Try to recall as many key terms as possible without assistance. If you need assistance, refer to the list of key terms at the end of this section.

1. ____________-__________ ______________ are all activities other than those that are absolutely essential to remain in business.
2. ____________-__________ ______________ are activities necessary to achieve corporate objectives and remain in business.
3. A(n) ____________-__________ ______________ is the optimal output level for an activity.
4. Costs caused by value-added activities are ____________-__________ __________.
5. Costs caused by nonvalue-added activities or the inefficient performance of value-added activities are ____________-__________ __________.
6. __________ ________________ is the process of identifying, describing, and evaluating the activities an organization performs.
7. __________ ________________ is the process of eliminating nonvalue-added activities.
8. __________ ________________ decreases the time and resources required by an activity.
9. __________ ________________ is the process of choosing among sets of activities caused by competing strategies.
10. __________ ________________ increases the efficiency of necessary activities by using economies of scale.
11. ____________-__________ ______________ or ________ is a system-wide, integrated approach that focuses management's attention on activities with the objective of improving customer value.
12. __________ __________ __________ is the time a product exists from conception to abandonment.
13. ________-__________ ________ ______________ is managing value-chain activities so that a long-term competitive advantage is created.
14. Costs associated with the product for its entire life cycle are called ________-__________ ________.
15. ________-__________ ________ is the life-cycle cost of a product plus costs that consumers incur, including operation, support, maintenance, and disposal.
16. __________ ________________ is incremental and constant increases in the efficiency of an existing process.
17. __________ ________________ is the performance of a process in a radically new way with the objective of achieving dramatic improvements in response time, quality, and efficiency.
18. __________________ is an approach that uses best practices as the standard for evaluating activity performance.
19. A(n) ______________-________ ______________ ______________ ________ is a control system that centers responsibility on organizational units and individuals with budgets and standard costing used to evaluate and monitor performance.
20. ______________-________ ______________ ______________ is a control system that centers responsibility on processes and teams where activity performance is measured in terms of time, quality, and efficiency.
21. __________ ________ is the difference between the sales price needed to achieve a projected market share and the desired per unit profit.

22. __________ is the number of units that can be produced in a given period of time (e.g., output per hour).

23. ________ ________ is the length of time required to produce one unit of a product.

24. A(n) ____________-_______ ____________ ____________ ________ or __________ __________ is a responsibility accounting system that translates an organization's mission and strategy into operational objectives and measures for four different perspectives: the financial perspective, the customer perspective, the process perspective, and the learning and growth (infrastructure) perspective.

25. __________ __________ are resources consumed by the activity in producing its output.

26. __________ __________ is the result or product of an activity.

27. __________ __________ __________ is the number of times the activity is performed.

28. __________ __________ is a Balanced Scorecard viewpoint that defines the customer and market segments in which the business will compete.

29. __________ __________ is a Balanced Scorecard viewpoint that describes the financial consequences of actions taken in the other three perspectives.

30. __________ __________ __________ __________ is a Balanced Scorecard viewpoint that describes the internal processes needed to provide value for customers and owners.

31. __________ ______ __________ __________ is a Balanced Scorecard viewpoint that defines the capabilities that an organization needs to create long-term growth and improvement.

32. ____________ ______ are costs incurred by the customer after purchasing a product.

33. ________ __________ is an effort to reduce the costs of existing products and processes.

KEY TERMS:

activity analysis
activity-based management (ABM)
activity-based responsibility accounting
activity elimination
activity inputs
activity output
activity output measure
activity reduction
activity selection
activity sharing
Balanced Scorecard
benchmarking
customer perspective
cycle time
financial perspective
functional-based responsibility accounting system
internal business process perspective
kaizen costing
learning and growth (infrastructure) perspective
life-cycle cost management
life-cycle costs
nonvalue-added activities
nonvalue-added costs
postpurchase costs
process improvement
process innovation
product life cycle
strategic-based responsibility accounting system
target cost
value-added activities
value-added costs
value-added standard
velocity
whole-life cost

→ **Compare your answers with those at the end of the chapter. Review any key terms missed.**

CHAPTER QUIZ

Write your answers in the spaces provided.

1. The emphasis of functional-based responsibility accounting is on managing ______________.

2. The key to successful control in activity-based responsibility is to manage ______________.

3. Value-added costs = ______________________________ × ______________________________

4. Nonvalue-added costs =
   (________________________ – ________________________) × ____________________

5. For nonvalue-added activities that are unnecessary, the standard quantity is ____________.

6. Target cost = ____
   – ____

7. Life-cycle costs include:

   1. ______________________________
   2. ______________________________
   3. ______________________________

8. The traditional emphasis has been on controlling costs during the ________________ stage; however, because 90 percent or more of a products costs are committed during the ________________ stage, it is logical to focus on managing activities during this stage.

9. On-time delivery performance = Orders delivered on time ÷ ____.

10. Cycle time = ______________________________/______________________________

11. Delivery performance can be improved by decreasing __________ ________ or increasing ________.

12. It is important for bottleneck equipment to be:

    1. ____, and
    2. ____.

Circle the single best answer.

Use the following information to answer Questions 13 through 19:

King Manufacturing has developed optimal standards for labor usage, receiving, and packing. The optimal levels of the inputs for each of the activities, their actual levels achieved, and the standard prices are as follows:

	Cost Driver	*SQ*	*AQ*	*SP*
Labor usage	Labor hours	15,000	20,000	$ 10
Receiving	Purchase orders	600	750	120
Packing	Sales orders	700	1,000	90

The actual prices paid for the inputs equal the standard price.

13. Value-added costs for labor are: (a) $145,500; (b) $150,000; (c) $160,000; (d) $200,000

14. Nonvalue-added costs for labor are: (a) $50,000; (b) $60,200; (c) $68,400; (d) $105,000

15. Value-added costs for receiving are: (a) $68,000; (b) $72,000; (c) $84,600; (d) $90,000

16. Nonvalue-added costs for receiving are: (a) $15,600; (b) $16,200; (c) $16,800; (d) $18,000

17. Value-added costs for packing are: (a) $63,000; (b) $70,000; (c) $72,000; (d) $90,000

18. Nonvalue-added costs for packing are: (a) $18,900; (b) $25,200; (c) $27,000; (d) $28,400

19. If the company wants to reduce nonvalue-added costs for labor by 20 percent next year, the currently attainable standard for labor hours would be: (a) 17,000; (b) 18,600; (c) 19,000; (d) 20,000

→ **Compare your answers with those at the end of the chapter. Review any questions missed.**

PRACTICE TEST

PROBLEM 1

Instructions:

For each activity listed below, determine the amount of value-added and nonvalue-added costs.

1. A company has 10 days of finished goods inventory on hand to avoid stockouts. The carrying costs of the inventory average $20,000 per day.

   Value-added costs: $__________

   Nonvalue-added costs: $__________

2. Setup time for a product is 5 hours. A firm that produces the same product and uses JIT has reduced setup time to 15 minutes. Setup labor is $10 per hour.

   Value-added costs: $__________

   Nonvalue-added costs: $__________

3. Warranty work costs the firm $1,000,000 per year. A competitor's warranty costs are $200,000 per year.

   Value-added costs: $__________

   Nonvalue-added costs: $__________

4. Downtime for bottleneck machinery averages 200 hours per year resulting in $600,000 in lost sales.

   Value-added costs: $__________

   Nonvalue-added costs: $__________

5. A time and motion study revealed it should take 12 minutes to produce a product that currently takes 30 minutes to produce. Labor is $15 per hour.

   Value-added costs: $__________

   Nonvalue-added costs: $__________

6. The company keeps 5 days of raw materials on hand to avoid shutdowns due to raw materials shortages. Carrying costs average $10,000 per day.

   Value-added costs: $__________

   Nonvalue-added costs: $__________

7. By redesigning the manufacturing layout, the time required to move materials can be reduced from 2 hours to 30 minutes. The labor cost is $12 per hour.

   Value-added costs: $__________

   Nonvalue-added costs: $__________

8. Each unit of product requires 10 pounds of raw material. Due to scrap and rework, each unit has been averaging 10.8 pounds of raw material. The raw material costs $5 per pound.

   Value-added costs: $__________

   Nonvalue-added costs: $__________

PROBLEM 2

Bass Company has developed ideal standards for four activities: labor, materials, inspection, and receiving. Information about each activity is provided below:

Activity	Cost Driver	Standard Quantity	Actual Quantity	Standard Price
Labor	Hours	5,000	6,000	$ 6
Materials	Pounds	20,000	24,000	8
Inspection	Inspection hours	–0–	30,000	7
Receiving	Orders	200	225	500

The actual prices paid per unit of each cost driver were equal to the standard prices.

Instructions:

1. Prepare a cost report that lists the value-added costs, nonvalue-added costs, and actual costs for each activity using the following format.

Activity	Value-Added Costs	Nonvalue-Added Costs	Actual Costs
Labor	$ ________	$ ________	$ ________
Materials	________	________	________
Inspection	________	________	________
Receiving	________	________	________
Totals	________	________	________

2. Assume that continuous improvement efforts reduce the demand for inspection by 20% during the year (i.e., actual activity usage drops by 20%). Calculate the activity volume variance and the unused capacity variance below:

SP × *SQ*	*SP* × *AQ*	*SP* × *AU*
$________	$________	$________

Volume variance (SP × SQ to SP × AQ)   Unused capacity variance (SP × AQ to SP × AU)

PROBLEM 3

At the beginning of 2004, Mollett Company installed a JIT purchasing and manufacturing system. The following information has been gathered about one of the company's products:

	2004	2005
Theoretical annual capacity in units	20,000	20,000
Actual production in units	15,000	16,000
Production hours available	4,000	4,000
On-time deliveries	1,000	1,500
Total deliveries	2,000	2,200
Scrap (pounds)	6,000	5,500
Materials used (pounds)	60,000	62,000
Actual cost per unit	$25	$24
Days of inventory	4	2
Number of defective units	1,000	1,200

Instructions:

1. Compute the following measures for 2004 and 2005 as compared to the company's goal:

Activity	2004	2005	Goal
a. Actual velocity	________	________	________
b. Actual cycle time	________	________	________
c. On-time delivery percentage	________	________	________
d. Scrap as a percentage of total materials used	________	________	________
e. Days of inventory	________	________	________
f. Defective units as a percentage of total units produced	________	________	________

2. Indicate any areas that need further improvement.

PROBLEM 4

Ashley, Inc., sells one of its products for $120 each. Sales volume averages 1,000 units per year. Recently, its main competitor reduced the price of its product to $100. Ashley expects its own sales to plummet unless it matches the competitor's price. In addition, the current profit per unit must be maintained. Information about the product (for production of 1,000 units) is as follows:

	Standard Quantity	Actual Quantity	Actual Cost
Materials (pounds)	7,800	8,000	$40,000
Labor (hours)	1,800	2,000	20,000
Setups (hours)	–0–	1,000	10,000
Material handling (moves)	–0–	500	5,000
Warranties (number repaired)	–0–	300	15,000

Instructions:

1. Calculate the target cost for maintaining current market share and profitability.

2. Calculate the nonvalue-added cost per unit. If nonvalue-added costs can be reduced to zero, can the target cost be achieved?

PROBLEM 5

Oak, Inc., manufactures a product that experiences the following activities:

Processing (three departments)	15 hours
Moving (four moves)	4 hours
Waiting time	18 hours
Storage (before delivery)	3 hours

Instructions:

Calculate the MCE for the product.

PROBLEM 6

Michaels, Inc., developed the following budgeted life-cycle income statement for two proposed products. Each product's life cycle is expected to be two years.

	Product A	Product B	Total
Sales	$1,000,000	$1,400,000	$2,400,000
Cost of goods sold	800,000	1,000,000	1,800,000
Gross margin	$ 200,000	$ 400,000	$ 600,000
Period expenses:			
Research and development			(220,000)
Marketing			(180,000)
Life-cycle income			$ 200,000

An 11% return on sales is required for new products; therefore, because the proposed products did not have an 11% return on sales, the products were going to be dropped.

Relative to Product B, Product A requires more research and development costs but requires fewer resources to market the product. Seventy percent of the research and development costs are traceable to Product A, and 20% of the marketing costs are traceable to Product A.

PROBLEM 6 *(Continued)*

Instructions:

1. Prepare a revised life-cycle income statement for each product.

	Product A	Product B

2. If an 11% return on sales is required, should Product A be produced?

3. If an 11% return on sales is required, should Product B be produced?

ANSWERS

KEY TERMS TEST

1. Nonvalue-added activities
2. Value-added activities
3. value-added standard
4. value-added costs
5. nonvalue-added costs
6. Activity analysis
7. Activity elimination
8. Activity reduction
9. Activity selection
10. Activity sharing
11. Activity-based management, ABM
12. Product life cycle
13. Life-cycle management
14. life-cycle costs
15. Whole-life cost
16. Process improvement
17. Process innovation
18. Benchmarking
19. functional-based responsibility accounting system
20. Activity-based responsibility accounting
21. Target cost
22. Velocity
23. Cycle time
24. strategic-based responsibility accounting system, Balanced Scorecard
25. Activity input
26. Activity output
27. Activity output measure
28. Customer perspective
29. Financial perspective
30. Internal business process perspective
31. Learning and growth perspective (or Infrastructure perspective)
32. Postpurchase costs
33. Kaizen costing

CHAPTER QUIZ

1. costs
2. activities
3. Standard quantity × Standard price
4. (Actual quantity – Standard quantity) × Standard price
5. zero
6. Sales price needed to capture a predetermined market share – Desired profit per unit
7. 1. development
   2. production
   3. logistics support
8. production, development
9. Total number of orders delivered
10. Total production time/Number of units produced
11. cycle time, velocity
12. 1. available for use
    2. fully utilized when available
13. b 15,000 × $10 = $150,000
14. a (20,000 – 15,000) × $10 = $50,000
15. b 600 × $120 = $72,000
16. d (750 – 600) × $120 = $18,000
17. a 700 × $90 = $63,000
18. c (1,000 – 700) × $90 = $27,000
19. c 5,000 hours × 20% = 1,000 hours;
    20,000 – 1,000 = 19,000 hours

PRACTICE TEST

PROBLEM 1

1. Value-added costs: $–0–
   Nonvalue-added costs: $200,000
2. Value-added costs: $10 × (15/60) = $2.50
   Nonvalue-added costs: $10 × 4.75 = $47.50
3. Value-added costs: $–0–
   Nonvalue-added costs: $1,000,000
   Note that with zero defects there should be no warranty costs.
4. Value-added costs: $–0–
   Nonvalue-added costs: $600,000
5. Value-added costs: $15 × (12/60) = $3.00 per product
   Nonvalue-added costs: $15 × [(30 – 12)/60] = $4.50 per product
6. Value-added costs: $–0–
   Nonvalue-added costs: $50,000

7. Value-added costs: $12 × (30/60) = $6
   Nonvalue-added costs: $12 × 1.5 = $18

8. Value-added costs: $5 × 10 = $50
   Nonvalue-added costs: $5 × .8 = $4

PROBLEM 2

1.

Activity	Value-Added Costs	Nonvalue-Added Costs	Actual Costs
Labor	$ 30,000	$ 6,000	$ 36,000
Materials	160,000	32,000	192,000
Inspection	–0–	210,000	210,000
Receiving	100,000	12,500	112,500
Totals	$290,000	$260,500	$550,500

The previous amounts would be calculated as follows:

Activity	Value-Added Costs (*SQ* × *SP*)	Nonvalue-Added Costs (*AQ* – *SQ*)(*SP*)	Actual Costs (*AQ* × *AP*)
Labor	5,000 × $6	(6,000 – 5,000)($6)	6,000 × $6
Materials	20,000 × $8	(24,000 – 20,000)($8)	24,000 × $8
Inspection	0 × $7	(30,000 – 0)($7)	30,000 × $7
Receiving	200 × $500	(225 – 200)($500)	225 × $500

2.

SP × *SQ*		*SP* × *AQ*		*SP* × *AU*
$7 × 0		$7 × 30,000		$7 × 24,000
$0		$210,000		$168,000
	$210,000 U		$42,000 F	
	Volume variance		Unused capacity variance	

PROBLEM 3

1. a.

	2004	2005	Goal
Actual velocity			
15,000/4,000	3.75 units/hr.		
16,000/4,000		4 units/hr.	
20,000/4,000			5 units/hr.

b.

	2004	2005	Goal
Actual cycle time			
4,000/15,000	.27 hrs./unit		
4,000/16,000		.25 hrs./unit	
4,000/20,000			.20 hrs./unit

c.

	2004	2005	Goal
On-time delivery percentage			
1,000/2,000	50%		
1,500/2,200		68%	
			100%

d.

	2004	2005	Goal
Scrap as a percentage of total materials used			
6,000 lbs./60,000 lbs.	10%		
5,500 lbs./62,000 lbs.		8.87%	
			0%

e.

	2004	2005	Goal
Days of inventory	4	2	0

f.	2004	2005	Goal
Defective units as a percentage of total units produced			
1,000/15,000	6.67%		
1,200/16,000		7.5%	
			0%

2. All areas need further improvement in order to meet the goals.

PROBLEM 4

1.

Current selling price	$120
Current cost ($90,000/1,000)	90
Current profit per unit	$ 30
Selling price to maintain market share	$100
Desired profit per unit	30
Target cost	$ 70

2.

	Nonvalue-Added Costs
Materials:	
$40,000/8,000 = $5/pound	
(8,000 – 7,800) × $5	$ 1,000
Labor:	
$20,000/2,000 = $10/hour	
(2,000 – 1,800) × $10	2,000
Setups	10,000
Materials handling	5,000
Warranties	15,000
Nonvalue-added costs	$33,000
Nonvalue-added costs per unit ($33,000/1,000 units)	$33/unit

If nonvalue-added costs can be reduced to zero, the cost per unit would be $57 ($90 – $33), which is below the target cost of $70.

PROBLEM 5

MCE = 15/(15 + 4 + 18 + 3)
= 15/40
= .375

PROBLEM 6

1.

	Product A	Product B
Sales	$1,000,000	$1,400,000
Cost of goods sold	800,000	1,000,000
Gross margin	$ 200,000	$ 400,000
Traceable expenses:		
Research and development		
(70% × $220,000)	(154,000)	
(30% × $220,000)		(66,000)
Marketing expenses		
(20% × $180,000)	(36,000)	
(80% × $180,000)		(144,000)
Life-cycle income	$ 10,000	$ 190,000

2. Return on sales (Product A) = $10,000/$1,000,000
= 1%

If an 11% return on sales is required, Product A should not be produced.

3. Return on sales (Product B) = $190,000/$1,400,000
= 13.6%

If an 11% return on sales is required, Product B should be produced.

CHAPTER 11

Quality Costs and Productivity: Measurement, Reporting, and Control

CHAPTER REVIEW

MEASURING THE COSTS OF QUALITY

- Quality improvement can increase profitability in two ways:
  1. By increasing customer demand
  2. By decreasing costs
- Studies indicate that costs of quality for American companies are typically 20 to 30 percent of sales. Quality experts maintain that the optimal quality level should be about 2 to 4 percent of sales.

Quality Defined

- A **quality product** is a product that meets or exceeds customer expectations. Quality is customer satisfaction.
- A quality product or service meets or exceeds customer expectations on the following eight dimensions:
  - **Performance**—how consistent and well a product performs
  - **Aesthetics**—the appearance of the product as well as the appearance of the facilities, equipment, personnel, and communication materials associated with services
  - **Serviceability**—ease of maintaining and/or repairing a product
  - **Features (quality of design)**—characteristics of a product that serve the same function but have different design specifications, such as the type and quality of materials used in the product (for example, 14-karat gold jewelry and gold-plated jewelry)
  - **Reliability**—the probability that the product or service will perform its intended function for a specified length of time
  - **Durability**—the length of time a product functions
  - **Quality of conformance**—how a product meets its design specifications. Is the product manufactured as the design specifies?
  - **Fitness for use**—suitability of the product for carrying out its advertised functions
- Providing a higher quality product than a competitor means outperforming the competitor on at least one dimension while matching performance on the remaining dimensions.
- A **defective product** does not conform to specifications.
- **Zero defects** requires that all products and services conform to specifications. The *traditional view* of conformance assumes an acceptable range on either side of a target value for each specification or quality characteristic. The *robust quality view* redefines defective units as those that do not meet the target value.

Costs of Quality Defined

- **Costs of quality** are costs incurred because poor quality may exist or poor quality does exist.
- Quality costs are associated with two subcategories of quality-related activities:
  - **Control activities**—activities performed by an organization to prevent or detect poor quality (because poor quality may exist). Control activities consist of prevention and appraisal activities. **Control costs** are the costs of performing control activities.
  - **Failure activities**—activities performed by an organization or its customers in response to poor quality (poor quality does exist). **Failure costs** are the costs incurred by an organization because failure activities are performed.
- Four categories of quality costs include the following:
  1. **Prevention costs** are incurred to prevent poor quality. Examples of prevention costs include:
     - quality engineering
     - quality training programs
     - quality planning
     - quality reporting
     - supplier evaluation and selection
     - quality audits
     - quality circles
     - field trials
     - design reviews
  2. **Appraisal costs** are incurred to determine whether products and services are conforming to requirements or customer needs. The main objective is to prevent nonconforming goods from being shipped to customers. Examples of appraisal costs include:
     - inspecting and testing of materials
     - packaging inspection
     - supervising appraisal activities
     - *process acceptance* (sampling goods in process to see if the process is in control and producing nondefective goods)
     - *product acceptance* (sampling finished goods to determine if the finished goods meet an acceptable quality level)
     - measurement (inspection and test) equipment
     - outside endorsements
  3. **Internal failure costs** are incurred because products or services do not meet requirements and the defect is discovered before the external sale. Examples of internal failure costs include:
     - scrap
     - rework
     - downtime (due to defects)
     - reinspection
     - retesting
     - design changes

     If there are no defects, there are no internal failure costs.
  4. **External failure costs** are incurred because products fail to meet requirements after delivery to customers. Examples include:
     - the cost of recalling defective products
     - lost sales because of poor product performance

- returns and allowances because of poor quality
- warranty costs
- repair costs
- product liability
- customer dissatisfaction
- lost market share
- complaint adjustment

Measuring Quality Costs

- Quality costs can be classified as:
  - **observable quality costs**—quality costs available from an organization's accounting records.
  - **hidden quality costs**—opportunity costs resulting from poor quality. Hidden quality costs are usually not recorded in the accounting records. Three methods of estimating hidden quality costs are:
    - the multiplier method
    - the market research method, and
    - the Taguchi quality loss function.
- The multiplier method assumes that total failure costs are a multiple of measured failure costs.
- Market research methods, such as customer surveys, are used to assess the effect of poor quality on sales and market share.
- The **Taguchi loss function** assumes any variation from the target value of a quality characteristic causes hidden quality costs. The Taguchi loss function is:

$$L(y) = k(y - T)^2$$

where k = a proportionally constant dependent upon the organization's external failure cost structure
y = actual value of quality characteristic
T = target value of quality characteristic
L = quality loss

REPORTING QUALITY COST INFORMATION

- The first step in a quality cost reporting system is to prepare a detailed listing of actual quality costs by category.
- This serves two purposes:
  1. It permits managers to assess the financial impact of quality costs.
  2. It reveals the relative emphasis currently placed on each category.

Quality Cost Reports

- In the quality cost report, quality costs are grouped into one of four categories:
  - prevention costs
  - appraisal costs
  - internal failure costs
  - external failure costs
- In addition, each category of quality costs is expressed as a percentage of sales.

- An example of a quality cost report appears in Exhibit 11–3 in the text.
- There are two views concerning optimal quality costs:
  - the traditional view that uses an acceptable quality level
  - the contemporary view that uses total quality control

Quality Cost Function: Acceptable Quality View

- The acceptable quality view uses an **acceptable quality level (AQL)** that permits a predetermined level of defective units to be produced and sold. AQL is the level where the number of defects allowed minimizes total quality costs.
- The reasoning of this traditional approach is that there is a trade-off between failure costs and prevention and appraisal costs (control costs). As prevention and appraisal costs increase, internal and external failure costs are expected to decrease. As long as the decrease in failure costs is greater than the corresponding increase in prevention and failure costs, a company should continue increasing its efforts to prevent or detect defective units.

Quality Cost Function: Zero-Defects View

- The zero-defects model views the optimal level of quality costs as the level where zero defects are produced.
- The robust quality model redefines a defective unit. The robust model focuses on hitting the *target value* for product specifications rather than an acceptable range.

Activity-Based Management and Optimal Quality Costs

- Activity-based management classifies activities as:
  - value-added activities, and
  - nonvalue-added activities.
- Internal and external failure activities and their associated costs are nonvalue-added and should be eliminated.
- Prevention activities performed efficiently are value-added. (Costs caused by inefficiency in prevention activities are nonvalue-added costs.)
- Appraisal activities may be value-added or nonvalue-added, depending upon the activity. For example, quality audits may serve a value-added objective.

USING QUALITY COST INFORMATION

- The principal objective of reporting quality costs is to improve and facilitate managerial planning, control, and decision making.
- Potential uses of quality cost information include:
  - quality program implementation decisions
  - evaluation of the effectiveness of quality programs
  - strategic pricing decisions (For example, improved reporting of quality costs might be used by managers to target specific quality costs for reductions. A reduction in quality costs might enable a firm to reduce its selling price, improve its competitive position, and increase market share.)
  - inclusion of quality costs in cost-volume-profit analysis (For example, overlooking quality cost savings results in a higher break-even and possible rejection of a profitable project.)

PRODUCTIVITY: MEASUREMENT AND CONTROL

- **Productivity** is concerned with producing output efficiently.
- **Total productive efficiency** is the point at which the following two conditions are met:
  - **technical efficiency**—the point at which, for any mix of inputs that will produce a given output, no more of any one input is used than is absolutely necessary.
  - **input trade-off efficiency**—the least-cost, technically efficient mix of inputs.
- Productivity can be improved as follows:
  1. Improve technical efficiency by:
     - using less input to produce the same output, or
     - using the same input to produce more output.
  2. Improve input trade-off efficiency by using a less costly mix of inputs.

Partial Productivity Measurement

- **Productivity measurement** involves measuring productivity changes so that efforts to improve productivity can be evaluated.
- Productivity can be measured using:
  - a **partial productivity measure** that assesses productivity for each input separately, or
  - a **total productivity measure** that assesses productivity for all inputs combined.
- An **operational productivity measure** uses *physical quantities* to measure input and output.
- A **financial productivity measure** uses dollars to measure input and output.
- A partial productivity measure assesses productivity efficiency for one input by comparing output to input:

  Productivity ratio = Output/Input

- To assess changes in productivity, the actual productivity measure for the current period is compared with the **base period** (a prior period that serves as a benchmark for measuring changes).
- Advantages of partial productivity measures include the following:
  - They permit managers to focus on the use of a particular input.
  - They provide feedback that operating personnel can relate to and understand—measures that deal with the specific inputs they control.
- A disadvantage of partial productivity measures is that because partial productivity measures focus on a particular input, they do not consider trade-offs between the productivity of different inputs. For example, less direct labor might be used (direct labor productivity increased), but more scrap and waste might result (material productivity decreased).

Total Productivity Measurement

- A **total productivity measurement** is an assessment of productivity efficiency for all inputs combined in order to value a change in productivity.
- One way to value productivity changes is to calculate the effects of productivity changes on profits.

Profile Productivity Measurement

- **Profile measurement** is a series or vector of separate and distinct partial operational measures. Productivity ratio profiles are shown for a series of years.

Profit-Linked Productivity Measurement

- **Profit-linked productivity measurement** is an assessment of the amount of profit change from the base period to the current period attributable to productivity changes.
- The *profit-linkage rule* determines the profit effect by computing the difference between the cost of the inputs that would have been used without any productivity changes and the cost of the actual inputs used.

Profit-linked effect = Cost of inputs that would have been used without any productivity changes − Cost of actual inputs used

Profit-linked effect = (*PQ* × *P*) − (*AQ* × *P*)

where *PQ* = the inputs that would have been used for the current period without any productivity changes). PQ is calculated as follows:

PQ = Current output/Base-period productivity ratio

P = current input price
AQ = actual quantity

Price-Recovery Component

- The **price-recovery component** indicates the change in profit that would have occurred without the productivity improvement.
- The price-recovery component is calculated as follows:

Price recovery = Profit change − Profit-linked productivity change

Quality and Productivity

- Improving quality is one way to improve productivity. For example, by improving quality and reducing the number of defective units, rework time and materials are reduced. Thus, fewer inputs are used to produce the same output and productivity increases.

Gainsharing

- **Gainsharing** provides cash incentives for a company's entire workforce with the incentives keyed to quality and productivity gains. For example, instead of using profit-driven bonuses, a company might use performance-based measures such as product quality or customer loyalty.

KEY TERMS TEST

Test your recall of the key terms as follows. Try to recall as many key terms as possible without assistance. If you need assistance, refer to the list of key terms at the end of this section.

1. __________ ____________ is a quality performance standard that requires all products and services to be produced and delivered according to specifications.
2. _____________ ___________ _________ are incurred because products fail to conform to requirements after being sold to outside parties.
3. _____________ ___________ _________ are incurred because products and services fail to conform to requirements where lack of conformity is discovered prior to external sale.
4. ________________ _________ are incurred to determine whether products and services are conforming to requirements.
5. ________________ _________ are incurred to prevent defects in products or services being produced.
6. __________ _____ __________ are costs incurred because poor quality may exist or because poor quality does exist.
7. _______________ _________________ _____________ are expressed in physical terms.
8. A(n) _______________ _________________ _____________ is a productivity measure that expresses inputs and outputs in dollars.
9. _________________ concerns producing output efficiency, using the least quantity of inputs possible.
10. __________ _______________ _______________ is the point at which technical efficiency and price efficiency are achieved.
11. __________ _______________ _______________ is an assessment of productive efficiency for all inputs combined.
12. A(n) __________ _______________ _______________ is a ratio that measures productive efficiency for one input.
13. ______________ ______________ is the point at which for any mix of inputs that will produce a given output, no more of any one input is used than is absolutely necessary.
14. __________ _______-_____ _______________ is the least-cost, technically efficient mix of inputs.
15. _________-__________ _______________ _______________ is an assessment of the amount of profit change—from the base period to the current period attributable to productivity changes.
16. _______________ _______________ is an assessment of productivity changes.
17. A(n) _______________ ___________ _________ or ______ is a predetermined level of defective products that a company permits to be sold.
18. The difference between the total profit change and the profit-linked productivity change is the _________-_____________ ______________.

19. ____________ ______ ________________ is a measure of how well a product meets its design specifications.

20. ____________ ______________ are activities performed by an organization to prevent or detect poor quality because poor quality may exist.

21. ____________ _____________ are activities performed by an organization or its customers in response to poor quality (poor quality does exist).

22. ________________ __________ ________ are opportunity costs resulting from poor quality.

23. ________________ __________ ________ are quality costs available from an organization's accounting records.

24. __________________ provides cash incentives for a company's entire workforce with incentives keyed to quality and productivity gains.

KEY TERMS:

acceptable quality level (AQL)
appraisal costs
control activities
costs of quality
external failure costs
failure activities
financial productivity measure
gainsharing
hidden quality costs
input trade-off efficiency
internal failure costs
observable quality costs
operational productivity measures
partial productivity measurement
prevention costs
price-recovery component
productivity
productivity measurement
profit-linked productivity measurement
quality of conformance
technical efficiency
total productive efficiency
total productivity measurement
zero defects

→ **Compare your answers with those at the end of the chapter. Review any key terms missed.**

CHAPTER QUIZ

Write your answers in the spaces provided.

1. List the four categories of quality costs:
   1. ______________________________
   2. ______________________________
   3. ______________________________
   4. ______________________________
2. In a quality cost report, quality costs are grouped into categories and then each category of quality costs is expressed as a percentage of ____________.
3. There are two views concerning optimal quality costs:
   1. the traditional view that uses a(n) ______________ quality level
   2. the contemporary view that uses ______________ quality control
4. Productivity is concerned with producing output ________________.
5. Productivity is measured as ___________ divided by ___________.

Use the following information to answer Questions 6 through 15:

Classify the following costs as one of the following:

- prevention cost
- appraisal cost
- internal failure cost
- external failure cost

____________________ 6. Warranty work

____________________ 7. Quality training programs

____________________ 8. In-process inspection

____________________ 9. Reinspection of reworked products

____________________ 10. Product recalls

____________________ 11. Inspection labor costs

____________________ 12. Downtime attributed to quality problems

____________________ 13. Product inspection

____________________ 14. Consumer complaint department

____________________ 15. Labor and overhead incurred for rework of defective products

Circle the single best answer.

16. A quality product is a product that meets or exceeds customer expectations: (a) true; (b) false

17. As prevention and appraisal costs increase, internal and external failure costs are expected to increase: (a) true; (b) false

18. The robust quality model focuses on hitting the target value for product specifications rather than an acceptable range: (a) true; (b) false

Use the following information to answer Questions 19 through 27:

The following information pertains to the Sunshine Company.

	2004	**2005**
Output	8,000	10,000
Output prices	$12	$12
Materials (pounds)	5,000	5,500
Material unit price	$4	$5
Labor (hours)	3,000	2,500
Labor rate per hour	3,000	2,500
Power (kilowatt hours)	1,200	1,800
Price per kilowatt hour	$2.50	$3

19. The partial operational productivity measure for materials for 2004 is: (a) 0.625; (b) 1.60; (c) 1.67; (d) 1.10

20. The partial operational productivity measure for materials for 2005 is: (a) 1.82; (b) 1.87; (c) 2.0; (d) 1.55

21. From 2004 to 2005, productivity for materials: (a) increased; (b) decreased

22. The partial operational productivity measure for labor for 2004 is: (a) 2.67; (b) 4.00; (c) 0.375; (d) 1.20

23. The partial operational productivity measure for direct labor for 2005 is: (a) 2.5; (b) 2.8; (c) 4; (d) 4.2

24. From 2004 to 2005, productivity for labor: (a) increased; (b) decreased

25. The partial operational productivity measure for power for 2004 is: (a) 0.15; (b) 1.5; (c) 8.33; (d) 6.67

26. The partial operational productivity measure for power for 2005 is: (a) 5.52; (b) 5.56; (c) 7.24; (d) 16.67

27. From 2004 to 2005, power usage productivity: (a) increased; (b) decreased

→ **Compare your answers with those at the end of the chapter. Review any questions missed.**

PRACTICE TEST

PROBLEM 1

The following information pertains to Magic, Inc., for 2004:

Sales	$30,000,000
External failure costs	900,000
Internal failure costs	1,800,000
Prevention costs	400,000
Appraisal costs	600,000

Instructions:

1. Calculate each category of quality costs as a percentage of sales.

   External failure costs: ____________________

   Internal failure costs: ____________________

   Prevention costs: ____________________

   Appraisal costs: ____________________

2. Calculate total quality costs as a percentage of sales.

3. If quality costs were reduced to 2.5% of sales, determine the increase in profit that would result.

PROBLEM 2

At the beginning of the year, Westfall Company initiated a quality improvement program. The program was successful in reducing scrap and rework costs.

To help assess the impact of the quality improvement program, the following data was collected for the current and preceding year:

	Preceding Year	Current Year
Sales	$4,000,000	$4,000,000
Quality training	10,000	15,000
Materials inspection	25,000	35,000
Scrap	200,000	180,000
Rework	250,000	200,000
Product inspection	40,000	60,000
Product warranty	300,000	250,000

Instructions:

1. Classify each of the costs as one of the following:
   - prevention cost
   - appraisal cost
   - internal failure cost
   - external failure cost

   Quality training: ______________________

   Materials inspection: ______________________

   Scrap: ______________________

   Rework: ______________________

   Product inspection: ______________________

   Product warranty: ______________________

2. Compute each category of quality costs as a percentage of sales.

	Preceding Year	Current Year
Prevention costs	________	________
Appraisal costs	________	________
Internal failure costs	________	________
External failure costs	________	________

PROBLEM 2 *(Continued)*

3. **a.** How much has profit increased as a result of quality improvement?

b. If quality costs can be reduced to 2.5% of sales, how much additional profit would result?

PROBLEM 3

The following pertains to the last two years of operation of the Lowell Company:

	2004	2005
Output	15,000	18,000
Selling price per unit	$20	$20
Input quantities:		
Materials (pounds)	5,000	5,000
Labor (hours)	4,000	4,500
Input prices:		
Materials (per pound)	$4	$4.50
Labor (per hour)	$8	$8.10

Instructions:

1. **a.** Calculate the partial operational productivity ratios for materials and labor for each year.

	2004	2005
Material	__________	__________
Labor	__________	__________

b. Did material and labor productivity improve from 2004 to 2005?

PROBLEM 3 *(Continued)*

2. a. Compute the profit-linked productivity measure.

b. By how much did profits increase due to changes in productivity?

PROBLEM 4

The following information pertains to the Starr Company:

	2004	2005
Output	4,000	4,500
Output prices	$8	$8
Materials (pounds)	2,500	3,000
Material unit price	$2	$3
Labor (hours)	2,000	1,800
Labor rate per hour	$7	$7
Power (kilowatt hours)	800	900
Price per kilowatt hour	$1.50	$2

Instructions:

1. Compute the partial operational measures for each input for 2004 and 2005. Discuss productivity improvement.

	2004	2005
Material	__________	__________
Labor	__________	__________
Power	__________	__________

PROBLEM 4 *(Continued)*

2. Prepare an income statement for each year and calculate the total change in profits.

	2004	**2005**

3. Calculate the profit-linked productivity measure for 2005. Discuss the results.

4. Calculate the price-recovery component. Explain the results.

ANSWERS

KEY TERMS TEST

1. Zero defects
2. External failure costs
3. Internal failure costs
4. Appraisal costs
5. Prevention costs
6. Costs of quality
7. Operational productivity measures
8. financial productivity measure
9. Productivity
10. Total productive efficiency
11. Total productivity measurement
12. partial productivity measurement
13. Technical efficiency
14. Input trade-off efficiency
15. Profit-linked productivity measurement
16. Productivity measurement
17. acceptable quality level, AQL
18. price-recovery component
19. Quality of conformance
20. Control activities
21. Failure activities
22. Hidden quality costs
23. Observable quality costs
24. Gainsharing

CHAPTER QUIZ

1. 1. prevention costs
   2. appraisal costs
   3. internal failure costs
   4. external failure costs
2. sales
3. 1. acceptable
   2. total
4. efficiently
5. output, input
6. external failure cost
7. prevention cost
8. appraisal cost
9. internal failure cost
10. external failure cost
11. appraisal cost
12. internal failure cost
13. appraisal cost
14. external failure cost
15. internal failure cost
16. a True
17. b False As prevention and appraisal costs increase, internal and external failure costs are expected to decrease.
18. True
19. b 8,000/5,000 = 1.60
20. a 10,000/5,500 = 1.82
21. a
22. a 8,000/3,000 = 2.67
23. c 10,000/2,500 = 4
24. a
25. d 8,000/1,200 = 6.67
26. b 10,000/1,800 = 5.56
27. b

PRACTICE TEST

PROBLEM 1

1. External failure costs: $900,000/$30,000,000 = 3.0%
   Internal failure costs: $1,800,000/$30,000,000 = 6.0%
   Prevention costs: $400,000/$30,000,000 = 1.3%
   Appraisal costs: $600,000/$30,000,000 = 2.0%
2. Total quality costs: $3,700,000/$30,000,000 = 12.3%
3.

Current quality costs	$3,700,000
Goal (2.5% × $30,000,000)	750,000
Increase in profit	$2,950,000

PROBLEM 2

1.

Quality training:	prevention cost
Materials inspection:	appraisal cost
Scrap:	internal failure cost
Rework:	internal failure cost
Product inspection:	appraisal cost
Product warranty:	external failure cost

2.

	Preceding Year		Current Year	
Prevention costs:				
Quality training	$ 10,000	.25%	$ 15,000	.38%
Appraisal costs:				
Materials inspection	$ 25,000		$ 35,000	
Product inspection	40,000		60,000	
Total appraisal costs	$ 65,000	1.63%	$ 95,000	2.38%
Internal failure costs:				
Scrap	$200,000		$180,000	
Rework	250,000		200,000	
Total internal failure costs	$450,000	11.25%	$380,000	9.50%
External failure costs:				
Product warranty	$300,000	7.50%	$250,000	6.25%

3. a.

Total quality costs—preceding year	$825,000
Total quality costs—current year	740,000
Increase in profit	$ 85,000

b.

Total quality costs—current year	$740,000
Goal (2.5% × $4,000,000)	100,000
Increase in profit	$640,000

PROBLEM 3

1. a. Partial operational productivity ratios:

	2004	2005
Material	15,000/5,000 = 3.00	18,000/5,000 = 3.60
Labor	15,000/4,000 = 3.75	18,000/4,500 = 4.00

b. Yes. Both materials and labor productivity improved from 2004 to 2005.

2. a. Profit-linked productivity measure:

	(1) PQ^a	(2) $PQ \times P$	(3) AQ	(4) $AQ \times P$	(2) − (4) $(PQ \times P) - (AQ \times P)$
Materials	6,000	$27,000	5,000	$22,500	$4,500
Labor	4,800	38,880	4,500	36,450	2,430
		$65,880		$58,950	$6,930

[a]Materials: 18,000/3.00 = 6,000
Labor: 18,000/3.75 = 4,800

b. Profits increased by $6,930 due to improvements in productivity.

PROBLEM 4

1. Partial operational measures:

	2004	2005
Material	4,000/2,500 = 1.60	4,500/3,000 = 1.50
Labor	4,000/2,000 = 2.00	4,500/1,800 = 2.50
Power	4,000/800 = 5.00	4,500/900 = 5.00

Productive efficiency has decreased for materials, increased for labor, and remained the same for power. Overall productivity improvement can be evaluated by valuing the trade-off.

2.

	2004	2005
Sales		
(4,000 × $8)	$32,000	
(4,500 × $8)		$36,000
Cost of Inputs:		
Materials		
(2,500 × $2)	(5,000)	
(3,000 × $3)		(9,000)
Labor		
(2,000 × $7)	(14,000)	
(1,800 × $7)		(12,600)
Power		
(800 × $1.50)	(1,200)	
(900 × $2.00)		(1,800)
Income	$11,800	$12,600

Total change in profit = $12,600 – $11,800 = $800 increase

3. Profit-linked productivity measure:

	(1) *PQ*[a]	(2) *PQ* × *P*	(3) *AQ*	(4) *AQ* × *P*	(2) – (4) (*PQ* × *P*) – (*AQ* × *P*)
Materials	2,813	$ 8,439	3,000	$ 9,000	$ (561)
Labor	2,250	15,750	1,800	12,600	3,150
Power	900	1,800	900	1,800	–0–
		$25,989		$23,400	$2,589

[a]Materials: 4,500/1.60 = 2,813
Labor: 4,500/2 = 2,250
Power: 4,500/5 = 900

The value of the increase in efficiency for labor more than offsets the decrease in efficiency for materials. There was no change in value of the productivity efficiency of power usage.

4. Price-recovery component:

Price-recovery component = Profit change – Profit-linked productivity change
Price-recovery component = $800 – $2,589 = $(1,789)

Without the productivity improvement, profits would have declined by $1,789. The $4,000 increase in revenues would not have offset the increase in the cost of inputs. It is only because of the productivity increase that the firm showed an increase in profitability.

CHAPTER 12
Environmental Cost Management

CHAPTER REVIEW

MEASURING ENVIRONMENTAL COSTS

The Benefits of Ecoefficiency

- ❒ **Ecoefficiency** is the environmental management view that organizations can produce more useful goods and services while *simultaneously* reducing negative environmental impacts, resource consumption, and costs.
- ❒ Ecoefficiency is supportive of **sustainable development**, the development that meets the needs of the present without compromising the ability of future generations to meet their own needs.
- ❒ Environmental costs can be a significant percentage of total operating costs and should be reported as a separate classification so managers can assess their impact on firm profitability.

Environmental Quality Cost Model

- ❒ **Environmental costs** are costs incurred because poor environmental quality *exists* or because poor environmental quality *may* exist.
- ❒ Four categories of environmental costs are:
  1. **Environmental prevention costs**—costs incurred to prevent damage to the environment, such as the production of contaminants. Examples include designing processes and products to reduce contaminants.
  2. **Environmental detection costs**—costs incurred to detect if the firm is in compliance with environmental standards. Three types of environmental standards and procedures are:
     - governmental regulatory laws
     - voluntary standards (ISO 14001) developed by the International Standards Organization, and
     - environmental policies developed by management.

     An example of detection activities includes measuring contamination levels.
  3. **Environmental internal failure costs**—costs incurred after contaminants are produced but before they are introduced into the environment. Examples of internal failure costs include treating and disposing of toxic materials and recycling scrap.
  4. **Environmental external failure costs**—costs incurred after contaminants are introduced into the environment. **Realized external failure costs** are external costs the firm has to pay. **Unrealized external failure costs** (or **societal costs**) are external costs caused by the firm but paid for by society.
- ❒ An environmental cost report lists the environmental costs by category (prevention, detection, internal failure, and external failure) and as a percentage of operating costs.
- ❒ An environmental financial report lists environmental benefits (such as income from recycling) as well as environmental costs.

Reducing Environmental Costs

- Environmental failure costs can be reduced by investing more in prevention and detection activities. This is consistent with the concept that prevention is cheaper than the cure.

ASSIGNING ENVIRONMENTAL COSTS

- Environmental costs can be assigned using either of the following:
  1. **full private costing**—the assignment of only private environmental costs to products.
  2. **full environmental costing**—the assignment of all environmental costs, both private and societal, to products.
- In addition, environmental costs can be assigned using either of the following:
  1. functional-based environmental cost assignment—environmental costs are assigned to individual products using unit-level drivers such as direct labor hours and machine hours. Functional-based cost assignment can produce distortions if there is product diversity.
  2. activity-based environmental cost assignment—costs are assigned to environmental activities, activity rates are calculated, and then the rates are used to assign environmental costs to products.

LIFE-CYCLE COST ASSESSMENT

- **Life-cycle assessment** is the means for improving **product stewardship**, the practice of designing, manufacturing, maintaining, and recycling products to minimize adverse environmental impacts.
- **Life-cycle cost assessment** assigns costs and benefits to the environmental consequences and improvements.

Assessment Stages

- Three stages to life-cycle assessment are:
  1. **inventory analysis**—specifies the types and quantities of materials and energy inputs needed and the resulting environmental releases in the form of solid, liquid, and gaseous residues.
  2. **impact analysis**—compares and evaluates the environmental impacts of different product or process designs.
  3. **improvement analysis**—efforts to reduce the environmental impacts revealed by the inventory and impact steps.

STRATEGIC-BASED ENVIRONMENTAL RESPONSIBILITY ACCOUNTING

- A continuous improvement framework for environmental control can be achieved by adding a fifth perspective, an environmental perspective, to the Balanced Scorecard framework discussed in Chapter 10.
- Five core objectives for the environmental perspective are:
  1. Minimize the use of raw or virgin materials.
  2. Minimize the use of hazardous materials.
  3. Minimize energy requirements for production and use of the product.
  4. Minimize the release of solid, liquid, and gaseous residues.
  5. Maximize opportunities to recycle.

- Activity-based environmental costing can be used to:
  1. identify environmental costs and what products or processes are causing them, and
  2. classify environmental activities as value-added and nonvalue-added costs. Nonvalue-added activities are activities that would not be necessary if the firm operated in an optimal environmentally efficient state.

KEY TERMS TEST

Test your recall of the key terms as follows. Try to recall as many key terms as possible without assistance. If you need assistance, refer to the list of key terms at the end of this section.

1. ________________ ________ are costs incurred because poor environmental quality exists or may exist.
2. ________________ ______________ ________ are costs incurred to prevent damage to the environment.
3. ________________ ______________ ________ are costs incurred to detect poor environmental performance.
4. ______________ ____________ ____________ ________ are costs incurred after contaminants are produced but before they are introduced into the environment.
5. ______________ ____________ ____________ ________ are costs incurred after contaminants are introduced into the environment.
6. ________________ ____________ ____________ ________ are environmental costs caused by environmental degradation and paid for by the responsible organization.
7. ________________ ____________ ____________ ________ or ____________ ________ are environmental costs caused by an organization but paid for by society.
8. ____________ ________ are environmental costs that an organization has to pay.
9. ________ ____________ __________ is the assignment of only private costs to individual products.
10. ________ ________________ __________ is the assignment of all environmental costs, both private and societal, to products.
11. ________________ ____________ is a life-cycle assessment step where the quantities and types of materials, energy, and environmental releases are described.
12. ________________ ____________ is a life-cycle assessment step where the environmental impacts of different product or process designs are compared and evaluated.
13. ________________ ____________ is a life-cycle assessment step where efforts are made to reduce the environmental impacts revealed by the inventory and impact steps.
14. ________________ is a view of environmental management that maintains that organizations can produce more useful goods and services while simultaneously reducing negative environmental impacts, resource consumption, and costs.
15. ________________ ______________ meets the needs of the present without compromising future generations' ability to meet their needs.

KEY TERMS:

ecoefficiency
environmental costs
environmental detection costs
environmental external failure costs
environmental internal failure costs
environmental prevention costs
full environmental costing
full private costing
impact analysis
improvement analysis
inventory analysis
private costs
realized external failure costs
societal costs
sustainable development
unrealized external failure costs

→ **Compare your answers with those at the end of the chapter. Review any key terms missed.**

CHAPTER QUIZ

Circle the single best answer.

1. Incentives and causes for increased efficiency as a result of improved environmental performance (ecoefficiency) include: (a) lower insurance rates for environmentally responsible firms; (b) customer demand for cleaner products; (c) improved company image; (d) innovation and new opportunities for markets for formerly useless residues; (e) all of the above
2. Which of the following is an environmental prevention activity? (a) evaluating and selecting pollution control equipment; (b) losing a lake for recreational use; (c) testing for contamination; (d) maintaining pollution equipment
3. Which of the following is an environmental detection activity? (a) evaluating and selecting suppliers; (b) testing for contaminants; (c) restoring land to a natural state; (d) maintaining pollution equipment
4. Environmental internal failure activities include all of the following except: (a) recycling products; (b) operating pollution control equipment; (c) treating and disposing of toxic waste; (d) recycling scrap
5. External failure activities include all of the following except: (a) cleaning up a polluted lake; (b) receiving medical care due to polluted air; (c) obtaining ISO 140001 certification; (d) settling environmentally related personal injury claims
6. All environmental failure activities are nonvalue-added activities: (a) true; (b) false

Write your answers in the spaces provided.

7. List the five core objectives of the environmental perspective for the Balanced Scorecard:
   1. ______________________________
   2. ______________________________
   3. ______________________________
   4. ______________________________
   5. ______________________________

→ **Compare your answers with those at the end of the chapter. Review any questions missed.**

PRACTICE TEST

PROBLEM 1

The following information was provided for the year 2004 for Crystal Corporation:

Operating costs	$5,000,000
Cleaning up hazardous waste	200,000
Training employees (environmental)	30,000
Operating pollution equipment	150,000
Inspecting processes	120,000
Disposing of hazardous waste	300,000
Property damage claim	140,000
Maintaining pollution equipment	100,000
Selecting pollution control equipment	20,000
Measuring contamination levels	50,000

Instructions:

Prepare an environmental cost report for the year 2004 with costs classified as prevention, detection, internal failure, or external failure costs. In addition, express each category of cost as a percentage of operating costs.

Environmental Cost Report
Crystal Corporation
For the Year Ended December 31, 2004

PROBLEM 2

The Stiles Company would like to evaluate how environmental activities affect the cost of two products—Product X and Product Z. The following information was collected:

	Product X	Product Z
Pounds of product produced	200,000	100,000
Process design hours	9,000	3,000
Pounds of waste treated	20,000	60,000
Contamination testing (hours)	10,000	20,000
Waste cleanup (hours)	4,000	16,000

The following environmental activity costs were reported for the period:

Process design	$ 60,000
Waste treatment	240,000
Contamination testing	48,000
Waste cleanup	80,000

Instructions:

1. Calculate the activity rates for each activity.

Process design:	$_____	/ _____	= _____	per _____
Waste treatment:	$_____	/ _____	= _____	per _____
Contamination testing:	$_____	/ _____	= _____	per _____
Waste cleanup:	$_____	/ _____	= _____	per _____

2. Use the activity rates to assign environmental costs and calculate the environmental cost per pound for each product.

	Product X
Process design	$_____
Waste treatment	_____
Contamination testing	_____
Waste cleanup	_____
Total environmental cost	$_____
Divided by number of pounds	÷_____
Environmental unit cost	$_____

	Product Z
Process design	$_____
Waste treatment	_____
Contamination testing	_____
Waste cleanup	_____
Total environmental cost	$_____
Divided by number of pounds	÷_____
Environmental unit cost	$_____

3. Determine which product appears to be the most environmentally harmful.

ANSWERS

KEY TERMS TEST

1. Environmental costs
2. Environmental prevention costs
3. Environmental detection costs
4. Environmental internal failure costs
5. Environmental external failure costs
6. Realized external failure costs
7. Unrealized external failure costs, societal costs
8. Private costs
9. Full private costing
10. Full environmental costing
11. Inventory analysis
12. Impact analysis
13. Improvement analysis
14. Ecoefficiency
15. Sustainable development

CHAPTER QUIZ

1. e
2. a
3. b
4. a
5. c
6. a True Adopting more efficient environmental approaches can eliminate the need for environmental failure activities.
7. 1. Minimize the use of raw or virgin materials.
   2. Minimize the use of hazardous materials.
   3. Minimize energy requirements for production and use of the product.
   4. Minimize the release of solid, liquid, and gaseous residues.
   5. Maximize opportunities to recycle.

PRACTICE TEST

PROBLEM 1

Environmental Cost Report
Crystal Corporation
For the Year Ended December 31, 2004

Environmental Costs			Percentage of Operating Costs
Prevention Costs:			
Training employees (environmental)	$ 30,000		
Selecting pollution control equipment	20,000	$ 50,000	1.00%
Detection Costs:			
Inspecting processes	$120,000		
Measuring contamination levels	50,000	170,000	3.40%
Internal Failure Costs:			
Operating pollution equipment	$150,000		
Disposing of hazardous waste	300,000		
Maintaining pollution equipment	100,000	550,000	11.00%
External Failure Costs:			
Cleaning up hazardous waste	$200,000		
Property damage claim	140,000	340,000	6.80%
Totals		$1,110,000	22.20%

PROBLEM 2

1. Activity rates for each activity:

Process design:	$60,000/12,000 = $5.00 per design hour
Waste treatment:	$240,000/80,000 = $3.00 per pound of waste
Contamination testing:	$48,000/30,000 = $1.60 per hour of testing
Waste cleanup:	$80,000/20,000 = $4.00 per cleanup hour

2. Environmental costs and environmental cost per pound for each product:

	Product X
Process design ($5.00 × 9,000)	$ 45,000
Waste treatment ($3.00 × 20,000)	60,000
Contamination testing ($1.60 × 10,000)	16,000
Waste cleanup ($4.00 × 4,000)	16,000
Total environmental cost	$137,000
Divided by number of pounds	÷200,000
Environmental unit cost	$ 0.685

	Product Z
Process design ($5.00 × 3,000)	$ 15,000
Waste treatment ($3.00 × 60,000)	180,000
Contamination testing ($1.60 × 20,000)	32,000
Waste cleanup ($4.00 × 16,000)	64,000
Total environmental cost	$291,000
Divided by number of pounds	÷100,000
Environmental unit cost	$ 2.91

3. It appears that Product Z causes the most environmental harm with an environmental cost per pound of $2.91 versus $0.685 for Product X.

CHAPTER 13
Performance Evaluation in the Decentralized Firm

CHAPTER REVIEW

RESPONSIBILITY ACCOUNTING

- Responsibility accounting is a system that measures the results of responsibility centers according to the information managers need to operate their center.
- A **responsibility center** is a segment of a business whose manager is accountable for specified sets of activities. Four types of responsibility centers are:
  - **cost center**—the manager is responsible only for costs
  - **revenue center**—the manager is responsible only for sales (revenues)
  - **profit center**—the manager is responsible for both revenues and costs
  - **investment center**—the manager is responsible for revenues, costs, and investments

DECENTRALIZATION

- To manage diverse and complex activities, organizations usually choose one of two approaches:
  - **centralized decision making**—a system in which decisions are made at the top level of an organization and lower-level managers implement the decisions
  - **decentralized decision making**—a system in which decisions are made and implemented by lower-level managers
- **Decentralization** is the practice of delegating or decentralizing decision-making authority to lower levels.
- The majority of firms tend to be decentralized.

Reasons for Decentralization

- Reasons for using a decentralized organizational structure include:
  - *Gathering and using local information.* The quality of decisions is affected by the quality of information. Because lower-level managers have access to information about operating conditions, customers, and competition, they are often in a position to make better decisions.
  - *Focusing of central management.* Decentralization allows top management to concentrate on firmwide problems, strategic planning, and decision making.
  - *Training and motivating managers.* Divisional management is a source of personnel for promotion to top management positions. A decentralized organization provides better training for top management positions than a more centralized organization where managers simply carry out top management's orders. Also, greater responsibility can produce more job satisfaction and motivate the local manager to exert greater effort.

- *Enhanced competition.* In a highly centralized company, large overall profit margins can mask inefficiencies within the various subdivisions. More fully exposing a division to market forces can help reveal noncompetitive divisions and improve divisional performance.

The Units of Decentralization

- Decentralization is usually achieved by creating decentralized units called *divisions.*
- Divisions might be differentiated by:
  - types of goods or services produced
  - geographic regions
  - type of responsibility given to the divisional manager (cost center, revenue center, profit center, or investment center)

MEASURING THE PERFORMANCE OF INVESTMENT CENTERS

- Since it is possible for a division to perform well or poorly irrespective of the efforts of its manager, companies try to separate the evaluation of the segment from the evaluation of the segment manager.
- Two methods used to evaluate division performance of investment centers are:
  - return on investment (ROI)
  - economic value added (EVA)

Return on Investment

- **Return on investment (ROI)**, the most common measure of performance for an investment center, is calculated as follows:

$$\text{ROI} = \text{Operating income}/\text{Average operating assets}$$

- **Operating income** is earnings before interest and taxes.
- **Operating assets** are those assets used to generate operating income, usually including cash, receivables, inventories, property, plant, and equipment.

$$\text{Average operating assets} = \frac{(\text{Beginning net book value} + \text{Ending net book value})}{2}$$

Most firms use historical cost net book value when calculating average operating assets.

Margin and Turnover

- ROI can be broken into two components:

$$\text{ROI} = \text{Margin} \times \text{Turnover}$$

$$= \frac{\text{Operating income}}{\text{Sales}} \times \frac{\text{Sales}}{\text{Average operating assets}}$$

- **Margin** shows the amount of each dollar of net sales that is profit.
- **Turnover** compares a division's investment in operating assets with the ability of those assets to generate revenues.

- Firms with a low profit margin, such as discount stores, may rely upon a high turnover to generate profits. Conversely, a firm with a low turnover, such as a fine jeweler, may rely upon high profit margins.

Advantages of ROI

- Three positive results from using ROI are:
  - It encourages managers to focus on the relationship among sales, expenses, and investment.
  - It encourages managers to focus on cost efficiency.
  - It encourages managers to focus on operating asset efficiency.

Disadvantages of the ROI Measure

- Two disadvantages associated with ROI are:
  - It encourages managers to focus on the short run at the expense of the long run (myopic behavior). For example, a manager might cut research and development expenses in the short run to improve ROI, but the cuts may not be in the best long-term interests of the division.
  - It discourages managers from investing in projects that would decrease the division's ROI but would increase the profitability of the company as a whole. Generally, projects with an ROI less than a division's current ROI would be rejected by the division manager.
- Example: Assume a division is expected to have income of $100,000 with an investment base of $500,000.

  Expected ROI for the division excluding the proposed project is 20%, calculated as follows:

  Current ROI = Income/Investment
  = $100,000/$500,000
  = 20%

  A proposed project has been evaluated and found to be acceptable using discounted cash flow analysis. The project would increase divisional income by $24,000 and divisional investment by $160,000.

  ROI of the proposed project is 15%, calculated as follows:

  ROI of proposed project = Incremental income/Incremental investment
  = $24,000/$160,000
  = 15%

  Since the proposed project has a lower ROI than the expected ROI for the division, acceptance of the project will lower the division's ROI.

  ROI for the division including the proposed project is 18.8%, calculated as follows:

$$\textbf{ROI including proposed project} = \frac{\$100{,}000 + \$24{,}000}{\$500{,}000 + \$160{,}000} = 18.8\%$$

  If the division manager accepts the proposed project, it will lower his division's ROI from 20% to 18.8%. Thus, it is not in the manager's best interests to accept the project even if it might be in the best interests of the firm.

  In fact, the manager would not want to accept any project with a return of less than 20% since it would lower the division's ROI.

Economic Value Added

- **Economic value added (EVA)** is a performance measure calculated as after-tax operating profit minus the total annual cost of capital.
- EVA is calculated as follows:

  EVA = After-tax operating income – (Weighted average cost of capital × Total capital employed)

- Total capital employed includes:
  - amounts paid for buildings, land, and machinery
  - other expenditures meant to have a long-term payoff, such as research and development and employee training. These costs are included in total capital employed even if they are expensed as required by GAAP for financial accounting purposes.
- A positive EVA indicates that the company earned operating profit greater than the cost of the capital used. The company is creating wealth. If EVA is negative, then the company is destroying capital.
- Whereas ROI is a percentage rate of return, EVA is a dollar figure. EVA emphasizes *after-tax* operating profit and the *actual* cost of capital.
- Stock prices follow EVA better than earnings per share or return on equity.

Using EVA for Individual Projects

- EVA can be calculated for individual projects as follows:

  EVA = Project income – Cost of capital
  = Project income – (Cost of capital % × Assets employed)

- Using EVA encourages managers to accept any project that earns above the minimum rate.

Behavioral Aspects of EVA

- EVA encourages managers to consider the cost of financial investment (the cost of capital) when making decisions. Therefore, EVA helps to encourage desirable behavior from division managers that an emphasis on operating income alone cannot.

Multiple Measures of Performance

- In addition to the financial measures of ROI and EVA, firms may use nonfinancial operating measures such as:
  - market share
  - customer complaints
  - personnel turnover ratios, and
  - personnel development.

MEASURING AND REWARDING THE PERFORMANCE OF MANAGERS

Incentive Pay for Managers

- In a corporation, the stockholders (owners) are represented by the board of directors who hire a CEO to manage the corporation. The CEO hires division managers to operate their divisions on behalf of the owners.

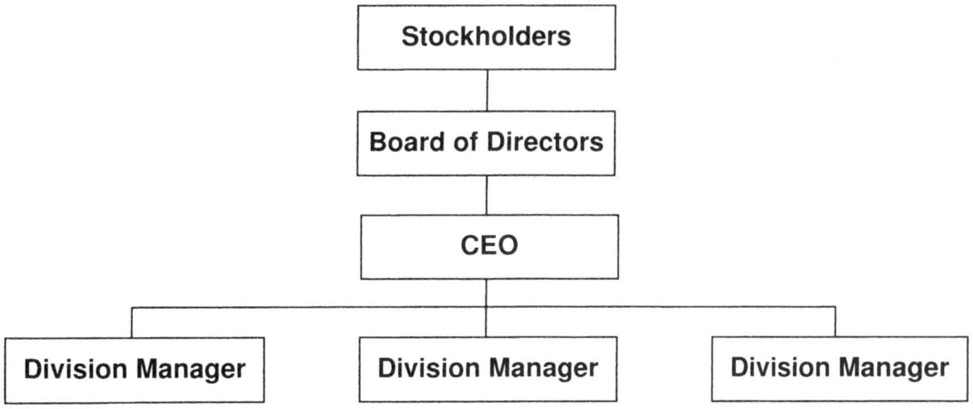

- There are three reasons why managers might not provide good service:
  1. They may have low ability.
  2. They may prefer to not work as hard as needed.
  3. They may prefer to spend company resources on perquisites. **Perquisites** are a type of fringe benefit received by managers over and above salary. Examples include use of a company car and expense accounts.
- The first reason requires owners to discover information about the manager before hiring him or her. The second and third reasons require the owner to monitor the manager or to arrange an incentive scheme that will closely ally the manager's goals with those of the owners.

Managerial Compensation: Encouraging Goal Congruence

- Firms may encourage goal congruence by using management compensation programs that reward managers for taking actions that benefit the firm.
- Managerial rewards include:
  - salary increases
  - bonuses based on reported income
  - stock options
  - noncash compensation

Cash Compensation

- Cash compensation includes salaries and bonuses.
- Bonuses give a company more flexibility than salary increases.
- Many companies use a combination of salary and bonus to reward performance, keeping salaries fairly stable and basing bonuses on divisional income or targeted increases in net income.
- Income-based compensation can encourage dysfunctional behavior, such as postponing research and development or maintenance.

Issues in Structuring Income-Based Compensation

- The underlying objective of the company that uses income-based compensation is goal congruence between owner and manager. However, single measures of performance, which are often the basis of bonuses, are often subject to gaming behavior. That is, managers may increase short-term measures at the expense of the long-term health of the firm.

- Cash bonuses can encourage a short-term orientation. To encourage a longer-term orientation, some companies are requiring top executives to purchase and hold a certain amount of company stock to retain employment.

Noncash Compensation

- Noncash compensation might consist of titles, office location, expense accounts, and other perquisites.

TRANSFER PRICING

- **Transfer prices** are prices charged for goods transferred between two divisions of the same firm. The output of the selling division is used as input of the buying division.

Impact on Performance Measures

- Transfer pricing affects the transferring divisions and the overall firm through its impact on:
  - divisional performance measures
  - firmwide profits, and
  - divisional autonomy.

Impact on Divisional Performance Measures

- The price charged for transferred goods is revenue to the selling division and cost of goods sold to the buying division.
- Thus, profits and profit-based performance measures (ROI and EVA) of both divisions are affected by the transfer price.

Impact on Firmwide Profits

- While the actual transfer price nets out for the company as a whole, transfer pricing affects profits earned by the company as a whole if it affects divisional behavior.
- Divisions, acting independently, may set transfer prices that maximize divisional profits but adversely affect firmwide profits.

Impact on Autonomy

- Because transfer pricing decisions can affect firmwide profitability, top management is often tempted to intervene and dictate desirable transfer prices.
- If such intervention becomes a frequent practice, however, the organization has effectively abandoned decentralization and all of its advantages.

The Transfer Pricing Problem

- The **transfer pricing problem** concerns finding a transfer pricing system that simultaneously satisfies the following three objectives:
  1. *Accurate performance evaluation.* No one divisional manager should benefit at the expense of another.
  2. *Goal congruence.* Divisional managers are motivated to select actions that maximize firm-wide profits.
  3. *Divisional autonomy.* Central management should not interfere with the decision-making freedom of divisional managers.

- Although direct intervention by central management to set specific transfer prices may not be advisable, general transfer pricing guidelines or policies may be useful.

The Opportunity Cost Approach as a Guide for Transfer Pricing

- The **opportunity cost approach** identifies:
  - the **minimum transfer price**, which is the transfer price that would leave the selling division indifferent between selling the goods to an outside party or transferring the goods to an internal division
  - the **maximum transfer price**, which is the transfer price that would leave the buying division indifferent between buying the goods from an outside party or purchasing from an internal division
- The transferred goods should be transferred internally whenever the opportunity cost (minimum price) of the selling division is less than the opportunity cost (maximum price) of the buying division.

Market Price

- If there is a perfectly competitive outside market for the transferred goods, the optimal transfer price is the market price. (In a perfectly competitive market, the selling division can sell all it wishes at the prevailing market price.)
- The opportunity cost approach also identifies the market price as the optimal transfer price.
- The minimum transfer price for the selling division is the market price, because the selling division receives the market price whether it sells the product internally or externally.
- The maximum transfer price for the buying division is the market price, because the buying division pays the market price whether it purchases the product internally or from an outside supplier.

Negotiated Transfer Prices

- If a perfectly competitive market for the transferred goods exists, the optimal transfer price is the market price.
- If a perfectly competitive market for the transferred goods does *not* exist, a negotiated transfer price may be a practical alternative.
- Opportunity costs for the buying division and selling division form the upper and lower boundaries for the transfer price.

Minimum Transfer Price	**Maximum Transfer Price**
Opportunity Cost for Selling Division	**Opportunity Cost for Buying Division**

- The selling division wants a high transfer price that will increase *its* income. The buying division wants a low transfer price that will increase *its* income.

Avoidable Distribution Costs

- If the selling division avoids costs such as distribution costs by selling internally, the opportunity cost to the selling division is the market price minus the avoidable cost.
- The opportunity cost to the buying division is the market price.

❒ The lower limit of the bargaining range is the market price minus avoidable costs, and the upper limit is the market price.

Minimum Transfer Price	**Maximum Transfer Price**
Market Price Less Selling Division's Avoidable Costs	**Market Price**

Excess Capacity

❒ When the selling division has excess capacity, a bargaining range exists.

❒ The lower limit of the bargaining range is the selling division's incremental costs. This is the minimum the selling division would be willing to accept.

❒ The upper limit of the range is the lower of:

- the buying division's outside purchase price, or
- the transfer price that results in a zero contribution margin on the goods for the buying division.

This is the maximum amount the buying division would be willing to pay.

❒ At the lower limit of the range, the entire profit goes to the buying division.

❒ At the upper limit of the range, the entire profit goes to the selling division.

Disadvantages of Negotiated Transfer Prices

❒ Three disadvantages of negotiated transfer prices are as follows:

1. One divisional manager who has private information may take advantage of another divisional manager.
2. Performance measures may be distorted by the negotiating skills of managers.
3. Negotiation can consume considerable time and resources.

Advantages of Negotiated Transfer Prices

❒ Negotiated transfer prices can help achieve the three objectives of:

- goal congruence
- autonomy, and
- accurate performance evaluation.

❒ If negotiation helps insure goal congruence, top management is not as likely to intervene and divisional autonomy is not diminished.

❒ If the negotiating skills of managers are comparable or if the firm views negotiating skills as an important part of being a manager, concerns about accurate performance evaluation are avoided.

Cost-Based Transfer Prices

❒ Three types of cost-based transfer prices are:

- full cost
- full cost plus markup, and
- variable cost plus fixed fee.

- If cost-based transfer prices are used, *standard costs* should be used in order to avoid passing on the inefficiencies of one division to another.

Full-Cost Transfer Pricing

- Transfer prices should be determined based upon the opportunity costs of the buying and selling divisions.
- Full cost rarely provides accurate information about opportunity costs; therefore, using full-cost transfer prices can result in dysfunctional manager behavior.
- If the selling division transfers products at the standard full cost, the selling division will not recognize any profit on the transfer.

Full Cost Plus Markup

- Using standard full cost plus a markup for profit for transfer prices can lead to decisions that are not in the best interests of the entire firm.
- In addition, if the profit markup is determined by formula (such as 20 percent of cost), the transfer price is of limited usefulness in evaluating the division's performance.
- If the markup is negotiated, then it is negotiated transfer pricing.

Variable Cost Plus Fixed Fee

- If the fixed fee is negotiable, the variable-cost-plus-fixed-fee approach is equivalent to negotiated transfer pricing.

Propriety of Use

- Reasons for using cost-based transfer prices include:
  - Cost-based transfer prices are objective and simple to apply.
  - If the transfers between divisions have a small impact on the profit of either division, it may be cost-beneficial to use a cost-based formula rather than spending valuable resources on negotiations.
  - The use of the full-cost plus markup formula may be the agreed-upon result of negotiations.

KEY TERMS TEST

Test your recall of the key terms as follows. Try to recall as many key terms as possible without assistance. If you need assistance, refer to the list of key terms at the end of this section.

1. ________________ ______________ ____________ is a system in which decisions are made at the top level of an organization and local managers are given the charge to implement these decisions.
2. _____________________ is the granting of decision-making freedom to lower operating levels.
3. ________________ ______________ ____________ is a system in which decisions are made and implemented by lower-level managers.
4. ______________ __________ __________ is a performance measure calculated by taking the after-tax operating profit minus the total annual cost of capital.
5. __________ ______ ________________ or _______ is the ratio of operating net income to operating assets.
6. _____________ is the ratio of net operating income to sales.
7. _____________ is the ratio of sales to average operating assets.
8. ______________ _________ are assets used to generate operating income, consisting of cash, inventories, receivables, property, plant, and equipment.
9. ______________ _________ is earnings before interest and taxes.
10. The price charged for goods transferred from one division to another is called the ____________ _________.
11. The _____________ ___________ ___________ is the problem of finding a transfer pricing system that simultaneously satisfies the three objectives of accurate performance evaluation, goal congruence, and autonomy.
12. The _____________ _____________ ________ is the transfer price that will make the buying division no worse off if an input is acquired internally.
13. The _____________ _____________ ________ is the transfer price that will make the selling division no worse off if the intermediate product is sold internally.
14. _________________ _______ _____________ is a transfer pricing system that identifies the minimum price a selling division is willing to accept and the maximum price a buying division is willing to pay.
15. _________________ are a type of fringe benefit over and above salary that is received by managers.
16. A(n) ________________ ___________ is a segment of the business whose manager is accountable for specified sets of activities.
17. A(n) ________________ ___________ is a division of a company that is evaluated on the basis of cost.
18. A(n) ________________ ___________ is a segment of the business that is evaluated on the basis of sales.
19. A(n) ________________ ___________ is a division of a company that is evaluated on the basis of operating income or profit.
20. A(n) ________________ ___________ is a division of a company that is evaluated on the basis of return on investment.

KEY TERMS:

centralized decision making
cost center
decentralization
decentralized decision making
economic value added
investment center
margin
maximum transfer price
minimum transfer price
operating assets
operating income
opportunity cost approach
perquisites
profit center
responsibility center
return on investment (ROI)
revenue center
transfer price
transfer pricing problem
turnover

→ **Compare your answers with those at the end of the chapter. Review any key terms missed.**

CHAPTER QUIZ

Write your answers in the spaces provided.

1. Four types of responsibility centers are:

1. ______________________________

2. ______________________________

3. ______________________________

4. ______________________________

2. Two methods used to evaluate investment center performance are:

1. ______________________________

2. ______________________________

3. In order for decentralization to be effective, performance must be evaluated for control purposes. The measures used to evaluate performance can affect a manager's behavior; therefore, the performance measures used should encourage ________ ________________.

4. Return on investment is calculated as follows:

ROI = ______________________ /______________________________

5. A disadvantage of ROI as a performance measure is that it may encourage ________________ ____________.

6. Economic value added is calculated as follows:

EVA = ____________________ – (____________________ × ____________________)

7. Nonfinancial operating measures of performance include:

1. ______________________________

2. ______________________________

3. ______________________________

4. ______________________________

8. Three objectives of a transfer pricing system should be:

   1. ______________________________

   2. ______________________________

   3. ______________________________

9. Under conditions of perfect competition, when the selling division has no excess capacity, the optimal transfer price is the __________ __________.

10. The opportunity cost approach to transfer pricing identifies a minimum transfer price and a maximum transfer price. If a perfectly competitive market for the transferred goods does *not* exist, a negotiated transfer price can be used. The lower boundary for the transfer price is ______________________________. The upper boundary for the transfer price is ______________________________.

11. With regard to transfer prices, if the selling division has excess capacity, a bargaining range exists. The floor of the bargaining range is the selling division's __________ __________. The ceiling of the bargaining range is the maximum amount the buying division is willing to pay, which is the lower of ______________________________ or ______________________________ ______________________________.

12. Transfer prices based on __________ __________ do not encourage the selling division to be efficient.

Circle the single best answer.

Use the following information to answer Questions 13 and 14:

The following results for the year pertain to the Russell Division of TADD Corporation:

Revenues	$500,000
Variable expenses	250,000
Fixed expenses	100,000
After-tax operating profit	130,000

Total capital employed is $800,000. The firm's weighted average cost of capital is 10%.

13. EVA for the Russell Division is: (a) $50,000; (b) $70,000; (c) $150,000; (d) $170,000

14. Return on investment for the Russell Division is: (a) 5.34%; (b) 10%; (c) 12.5%; (d) 18.75%

→ **Compare your answers with those at the end of the chapter. Review any questions missed.**

PRACTICE TEST

PROBLEM 1

The Kendall Division of Stephens Enterprises expects the following results for 2004:

Revenues	$500,000
Variable expenses	200,000
Contribution margin	$300,000
Fixed expenses	180,000
Operating income	$120,000

Total divisional assets are $1,000,000.

Instructions:

Calculate profit margin, asset turnover, and ROI for the division.

PROBLEM 2

The following information pertains to Roger Corporation:

After-tax operating profit	$ 100,000
Financing:	
Bonds (10% interest)	600,000
Common stock (average risk)	400,000
Total capital employed	1,200,000
Marginal tax rate	40%

Instructions:

1. Calculate the weighted average cost of capital for the company.

PROBLEM 2 *(Continued)*

2. Calculate economic value added for the company.

3. Discuss the significance of Roger's EVA.

PROBLEM 3

Colby, Incorporated, has just formed a new division, and the following four investment opportunities are available to the division:

Investment Opportunity	Income	Investment
1	$ 80,000	$200,000
2	120,000	600,000
3	80,000	500,000
4	50,000	200,000

The firm requires a minimum return of 20%.

Instructions:

1. If you were the division manager and your evaluation was based on ROI, which investment opportunities would you accept?

PROBLEM 3 *(Continued)*

2. If you were president of Colby, Incorporated, which projects would you want the division to accept?

PROBLEM 4

Goldwasser Industries has two divisions, the Lauren Division and the Lindsey Division. Information about a component that the Lauren Division produces is as follows:

Revenue	$100 per unit
Variable manufacturing costs	$25 per unit
Fixed manufacturing overhead	$15 per unit
Expected sales in units	7,000 units

The Lauren Division can produce up to 8,000 components per year. The Lindsey Division needs 500 units of the component for a product it manufactures.

Instructions:

1. Determine the minimum transfer price that the Lauren Division would accept.

2. Determine the maximum transfer price that the manager of the Lindsey Division would pay.

3. How would your answers to Requirements 1 and 2 change if the Lauren Division did not have excess capacity?

PROBLEM 5

Alexander Industries is a decentralized company that evaluates its divisions based on ROI.

Division K has the capacity to make 10,000 units of a product. Division K's variable costs are $60 per unit.

Division N can use the product as a component in one of its products. Division N would incur $40 of variable costs to convert the component into its own product, which sells for $200.

Instructions:

The following requirements are independent of each other.

1. Division K can sell all that it produces for $120 each. Division N needs 1,000 units. What is the correct transfer price?

2. Division K can sell 8,000 units at $150 each. Any excess capacity will be unused unless the units are purchased by the N division, which could use up to 1,000 units. Determine the floor and ceiling of the bargaining range.

ANSWERS

KEY TERMS TEST

1. Centralized decision making
2. Decentralization
3. Decentralized decision making
4. Economic value added
5. Return on investment, ROI
6. Margin
7. Turnover
8. Operating assets
9. Operating income
10. transfer price
11. transfer pricing problem
12. maximum transfer price
13. minimum transfer price
14. Opportunity cost approach
15. Perquisites
16. responsibility center
17. cost center
18. revenue center
19. profit center
20. investment center

CHAPTER QUIZ

1. 1. cost centers
   2. revenue centers
   3. profit centers
   4. investment centers
2. 1. return on investment
   2. economic value added
3. goal congruence
4. Operating income/Average operating assets
5. dysfunctional behavior (or myopic behavior)
6. After-tax operating income – (Weighted average cost of capital × Total capital employed)
7. 1. market share
   2. customer complaints
   3. personnel turnover ratios
   4. personnel development
8. 1. accurate performance evaluation
   2. goal congruence
   3. divisional autonomy
9. market price
10. the opportunity cost for the selling division, the opportunity cost for the buying division
11. incremental costs, the buying division's outside purchase price, the transfer price that results in a zero contribution margin on the goods for the buying division
12. actual costs
13. a $130,000 – (10% × $800,000) = $50,000
14. d $500,000 – $250,000 – $100,000 = $150,000; $150,000/$800,000 = 18.75%

PRACTICE TEST

PROBLEM 1

ROI = Operating income/Average operating assets
= $120,000/$1,000,000
= 12%

ROI = Margin × Turnover
= (Operating income/Sales) × (Sales/Average operating assets)
= ($120,000/$500,000) × ($500,000/$1,000,000)
= .24 × .50 = .12 or 12%

PROBLEM 2

1. After-tax cost of bonds = (.10 × .60) = .06 or 6%

   Cost of common stock = Return on long-term treasury bonds + Average premium
   = 6% + 6% = 12%

   Weighted average cost of capital:

	Amount	Percent	×	After-Tax Cost	=	Weighted Cost
Bonds	$600,000	.60	×	.06	=	.036
Common stock	400,000	.40	×	.12	=	.048
Weighted average cost of capital						.084

2. Cost of capital = $1,200,000 × .084 = $100,800

   Economic value added:

After-tax profit	$100,000
Less: Weighted average cost of capital	100,800
EVA	$ (800)

3. Roger's EVA was a negative $800, indicating that capital was destroyed. If the EVA had been positive, this would indicate that wealth had been created.

PROBLEM 3

1.

Investment Opportunity	Income	Investment	ROI
1	$ 80,000	$200,000	40%
2	120,000	600,000	20%
3	80,000	500,000	16%
4	50,000	200,000	25%

If the division manager accepts only Project 1, his ROI will be 40%. Accepting any of the other projects would lower his ROI. For example, if the divisional manager accepts Project 1 and Project 4, his ROI would drop from 40% to 32.5%.

ROI = ($80,000 + $50,000)/($200,000 + $200,000) = 32.5%

2. The president of the firm would want the division to accept any project with a return in excess of the firm's required return of 20%.

PROBLEM 4

1. The lower boundary of the bargaining range would be the selling division's variable cost of $25. This would be the minimum amount the selling division would accept.

2. The upper boundary of the range would be $100 (the amount the buying division would pay an outside supplier).

3. If the Lauren Division could sell 8,000 units to outside customers for $100 each, the Lauren Division would have to receive $100 per unit from the Lindsey Division.

   If the Lauren Division sells to the Lindsey Division, it foregoes $100 per unit from outside customers. Therefore to be as well off, the Lauren Division must receive $100 per unit from the Lindsey Division.

PROBLEM 5

1. The transfer price would be the market price of $120 each.

   If Division K sells to Division N, it would forego $120 per unit; therefore to be as well off, Division K must receive $120 per unit from Division N. Division N would pay the market price of $120 whether it purchased the component from Division K or from an outside supplier.

2. The floor of the bargaining range is $60 per unit (Division K's variable cost to produce the component).

   The ceiling of the range would be the lower of:

   a. the buying division's outside purchase price ($150), or
   b. the transfer price that results in a zero contribution margin on the goods for the buying division ($200 – $40 variable cost = $160).

   The ceiling would be $150 (the amount Division N would pay to acquire the component from an outside supplier).

CHAPTER 14

International Issues in Management Accounting

CHAPTER REVIEW

MANAGEMENT ACCOUNTING IN THE INTERNATIONAL ENVIRONMENT

❒ The management accountant in an international firm must stay current in a variety of business areas, from information systems, to marketing, to management, to politics, and to economics, as well as be familiar with the financial accounting rules of the countries in which the firm operates.

LEVELS OF INVOLVEMENT IN INTERNATIONAL TRADE

❒ A **multinational corporation (MNC)** is a corporation for which a significant amount of business is done in more than one country.

❒ Companies involved in international business may structure their activities in the following ways:

- They may engage in import/export activities.
- They may use wholly owned subsidiaries.
- They may participate in joint ventures.

Importing and Exporting

❒ The multinational corporation may import raw materials and/or export finished products.

Importing

❒ An imported part may have a tariff (or duty). A **tariff** is a tax on imports levied by the federal government. The tariff is considered a cost of materials.

❒ In order to reduce tariffs, companies may:

- restrict the amount of imported materials
- alter the materials by adding U.S. resources (to increase the domestic content and gain more favorable tariff status), or
- utilize foreign trade zones. **Foreign trade zones** are areas that are physically on U.S. soil but considered to be outside U.S. commerce. Goods imported into a foreign trade zone are duty-free until they leave the zone.

  Since tariffs are not paid until the imported materials leave the zone as part of a finished product, the company can postpone payment of the duty and the associated loss of working capital.

Exporting

❒ Exporting is the sale of a company's products in foreign countries.

- Foreign countries have a variety of import and tariff regulations, and the job of complying with the foreign rules and regulations often falls to the controller's office.

Treaties and Tariffs

- The North American Free Trade Agreement (NAFTA) allows importers in the United States, Mexico, and Canada to pay reduced tariffs on goods produced in the three countries. Management accountants must be aware of the customs regulations and ensure internal control procedures are in place to ensure compliance.

Wholly Owned Subsidiaries

- A company may choose to purchase an existing foreign company, making the purchased company a wholly owned subsidiary of the parent.
- **Outsourcing** is the payment by a company for a business function that was formerly done in-house. For example, some domestic companies outsource their legal needs to outside law firms rather than hire corporate attorneys. For a multinational corporation, outsourcing refers to moving a business function to another country.
- The costs and benefits of outsourcing are affected by:
  - tax structures
  - incentives of local authorities
  - overall educational level of the country
  - infrastructure

Joint Ventures

- A **joint venture** is a type of partnership in which investors co-own the enterprise.
- Sometimes a joint venture is required because of restrictive laws. For example, India and Thailand require local ownership.
- The **maquiladora** is a special type of joint venture with manufacturing plants located in Mexico that process imported materials and reexport them to the United States.
- Mexico grants maquiladora an exemption from Mexican laws governing foreign ownership, and the United States grants exemptions from or reductions in custom duties levied on reexported goods.

FOREIGN CURRENCY EXCHANGE

- When a company begins to operate in the international arena, it must use foreign currencies.
- The **exchange rate** is the rate at which foreign currency can be exchanged for domestic currency. Exchange rates change, often on a daily basis.
- **Currency risk management** refers to the company's management of its transaction, economic, and translation exposure due to exchange rate fluctuations.
- **Transaction risk** refers to the possibility that future cash transactions will be affected by changing exchange rates.
- **Economic risk** refers to the possibility that a firm's present value of future cash flows will be affected by exchange fluctuations.
- **Translation (or accounting) risk** is the degree to which a firm's financial statements are exposed to exchange rate fluctuation.

Managing Transaction Risk

- Currencies may be traded for one another depending on the exchange rate in effect at the time of the trade.
- **The spot rate** is the exchange rate of one currency for another for immediate delivery (i.e., today). Changes in the spot rates can affect the value of a company's future cash transactions, posing transaction risk. For example, if an account receivable of $100,000 is to be received in a foreign currency that must be exchanged for dollars, there is a transaction risk that could result in an exchange gain or loss.

Currency Appreciation and Depreciation

- **Currency appreciation** occurs when a country's currency becomes stronger and can purchase more units of another country's currency.
- **Currency depreciation** occurs when a country's currency becomes weaker and can purchase fewer units of another country's currency.

Exchange Gains and Losses

- An **exchange gain** is the gain on exchange of one currency for another due to appreciation of the home currency.
- An **exchange loss** is a loss on the exchange of one currency for another due to depreciation of the home currency.

Hedging

- **Hedging** is one way of insuring against gains and losses on foreign currency exchanges.
- The **forward contract** is an agreement that requires the buyer to exchange a specified amount of a currency at a specified rate (the forward rate) on a specified future date.

Managing Economic Risk

- Economic risk is the impact of exchange rate fluctuations on the present value of a firm's future cash flows.
- For example, currency fluctuations can result in a weaker dollar, making U.S. exports relatively cheaper to foreign customers.

Managing Translation Risk

- If a parent company restates all subsidiaries' income into the home currency, a gain or loss on the revaluation of foreign currencies can impact a subsidiary's financial statements and the related return on investment and economic value added computations.

DECENTRALIZATION

Advantages of Decentralization in the MNC

- Advantages of decentralization include:
  - Local managers are often in a position to make better decisions.
  - Local managers in the MNC are capable of a more timely response in decision making as they can respond quickly to customer discount demands, local government demands, and changes in the political climate.

- Decentralization for large, diversified companies is necessary because of cognitive limitations—it is impossible for any one central manager to be fully knowledgeable of all products and markets.
- Decentralization provides an opportunity to train and motivate local managers.
- Decentralization frees up top management from day-to-day operating conditions so that they can spend time on more long-range activities, such as strategic planning.

Creation of Divisions

❒ The MNC can create divisions along geographic lines, product lines, or functional management lines.

❒ The presence of divisions in more than one country creates the need for performance evaluation that can take into account differences in divisional environments.

MEASURING PERFORMANCE IN THE MULTINATIONAL FIRM

❒ It is important for the MNC to separate the evaluation of the *manager* of a division from the evaluation of the *division*.

❒ In a multinational corporation, a manager's performance evaluation should not include factors over which he or she exercises no control, such as currency fluctuations and taxes.

❒ Environmental factors that differ from country to country include:

- economic factors, such as inflation, foreign exchange rates, and transfer prices
- legal factors, such as prohibitions against cash being taken out of a country
- political factors
- social and cultural factors
- educational factors

❒ Because managers cannot control environmental factors, the corporation must consider the differing environmental factors when assessing managerial performance.

Multiple Measures of Performance

❒ Because both EVA and ROI are short-run measures of performance, the temptation exists for managers to trade off short-run benefits at the expense of the long-run well-being of the company.

❒ One way to discourage myopic behavior is to use additional measures of performance that relate more closely to the long-run health of the division. For example, in addition to ROI and EVA, top management might look at such factors as:

- market share
- customer complaints
- personnel turnover ratios, and
- personnel development.

TRANSFER PRICING AND THE MULTINATIONAL FIRM

❒ For the multinational firm, transfer pricing must accomplish two objectives:

1. Performance evaluation
2. Optimal determination of income taxes

Performance Evaluation

- Divisions are frequently evaluated on the basis of net income and return on investment; therefore, the selling division wants a high transfer price that will raise *its* income, and the buying division wants a low transfer price that will raise *its* income.
- Transfer prices in MNCs are frequently set by the parent company; therefore, the use of mandated transfer prices makes the use of ROI and income suspect, as they are not under the control of divisional managers and no longer serve as indicators of management performance.

Income Taxes and Transfer Pricing

- MNCs with subsidiaries in both high-tax and low-tax countries may use transfer pricing to shift costs to the high-tax countries (where their deductibility will lower tax payments) and to shift revenues to low-tax countries.
- Reinvoicing centers may be used to lower tax payments. A reinvoicing center takes title to the goods but does not physically receive them. The primary objective of a reinvoicing center is to shift profits to divisions in low-tax countries.
- U.S.-based multinationals are subject to Internal Revenue Code Section 482 on the pricing of intercompany transactions. Basically, Section 482 requires that sales between divisions be made at "arm's length."
- The IRS allows three pricing methods that approximate arm's-length pricing. In order of preference, these are:
  - the **comparable uncontrolled price method**, which is essentially market price
  - the **resale price method**, which is equal to the sales price received by the reseller less an appropriate markup
  - the **cost-plus method**, which is the cost-based transfer price
- The IRS will permit a fourth method—a transfer price negotiated between the company and the IRS. However, this type of negotiation occurs after income tax returns have been submitted and the company is being audited.
- Recently, the IRS has authorized the use of **advance pricing agreements**. An advance pricing agreement is an agreement between the IRS and a taxpayer on the transfer price to be used in an international transaction.
- A survey of transfer pricing methods used by Fortune 500 companies in 1977 and 1990 shows that MNCs have reduced their reliance on cost-based transfer prices in favor of market-based transfer prices. The most important environmental variable considered by MNCs in setting a transfer pricing policy is overall profit to the company, including the income tax impact of intracompany transfers.

ETHICS IN THE INTERNATIONAL ENVIRONMENT

- MNCs face ethical issues that do not arise for domestic companies. Foreign countries may have business customs and laws that differ from those of the home country. For example, in some countries, bribes are considered a necessary part of doing business. Another example is insider trading, which is not illegal in Europe but is illegal in the United States.
- The MNC must determine whether a particular custom is merely a different way of doing business or is a violation of its own code of ethics.
- When a MNC is faced with conflicting sets of ethics, two questions that might be asked are:
  - Is the action right legally?
  - Is the action right morally?

KEY TERMS TEST

Test your recall of the key terms as follows. Try to recall as many key terms as possible without assistance. If you need assistance, refer to the list of key terms at the end of this section.

1. A(n) __________ is the tax on imports levied by the federal government.

2. ________________ is the payment by a company for a business function that was formerly done in-house.

3. A type of partnership in which investors co-own the enterprise is a(n) ________ ________.

4. __________________ are manufacturing plants located in Mexico that process imported materials and reexport them to the United States.

5. The rate at which a foreign currency can be exchanged for the domestic currency is the ____________ ________.

6. A loss on the exchange of one currency for another due to depreciation in the home currency is a(n) ____________ ________.

7. A gain on the exchange of one currency for another due to appreciation in the home currency is a(n) ____________ ________.

8. ____________ ________ ________________ refers to the company's management of its transaction, economic, and translation exposure due to exchange rate fluctuations.

9. ______________ ________ refers to the possibility that future cash transactions will be affected by changing exchange rates.

10. ______________ ________ refers to the possibility that a firm's present value of future cash flows can be affected by exchange fluctuations.

11. ______________ ________ is the degree to which a firm's financial statements are exposed to exchange rate fluctuations.

12. The exchange rate of one currency for another for immediate delivery is the __________ ________.

13. ____________ ______________ occurs when a country's currency becomes stronger and can purchase more units of another country's currency.

14. ____________ ______________ occurs when a country's currency becomes weaker and can purchase fewer units of another country's currency.

15. __________ is one way of insuring against gains and losses on foreign currency exchange.

16. An agreement that requires the buyer to exchange a specified amount of a currency at a specified rate (the forward rate) on a specified future date is a(n) __________ __________.

17. The __________ ______________ ______ _________ is the pricing method most preferred by the Internal Revenue Service under Section 482 in which the transfer price is essentially equal to the market price.

18. The ________ ________ __________ is a pricing method acceptable to the Internal Revenue Service under Section 482 in which the transfer price equals the sales price received by the reseller less an appropriate markup.

19. The ________-________ __________ is a pricing method acceptable to the Internal Revenue Service under Section 482 which uses simply a cost-based transfer price.

20. A(n) ___________ __________ ____________ is an agreement between the Internal Revenue Service and a taxpayer on the acceptability of a transfer price. The agreement is private and is binding on both parties for a specified period of time.

21. _________ ________ ________ are areas that are physically on U.S. soil but considered to be outside U.S. commerce. Goods imported into these areas are duty-free until they leave the area.

22. A(n) _________________ _____________ or _______ is a corporation for which a significant amount of business is done in more than one country.

KEY TERMS:

advance pricing agreement
comparable uncontrolled price method
cost-plus method
currency appreciation
currency depreciation
currency risk management
economic risk
exchange gain
exchange loss
exchange rate
foreign trade zones
forward contract
hedging
joint venture
maquiladoras
multinational corporation (MNC)
outsourcing
resale price method
spot rate
tariff
transaction risk
translation (or accounting) risk

→ **Compare your answers with those at the end of the chapter. Review any key terms missed.**

CHAPTER QUIZ

Write your answers in the spaces provided.

1. List three different ways that companies involved in international business might structure their activities.

1. ______________________________

2. ______________________________

3. ______________________________

2. Two advantages of locating in foreign trade zones are:

1. ______________________________

____

2. ______________________________

____

3. A(n) _______________ __________ takes title to goods but does not physically receive them. Its primary objective is to shift profits to low-tax countries.

4. A survey of transfer pricing methods used by Fortune 500 companies found that the most important environmental variable considered by MNCs in setting a transfer pricing policy is ______________________________, including the ________________ impact of intracompany transfers.

Circle the single best answer.

5. A stronger dollar makes U.S. exports relatively cheaper to foreign customers: (a) true; (b) false

6. The gain or loss that results from restating foreign subsidiaries' financial statements in the home currency is an example of transaction risk: (a) true; (b) false

7. A $200,000 account receivable that is to be paid in yen two months from now would be an example of translation risk: (a) true; (b) false

8. When evaluating manager performance, in addition to ROI and EVA, other performance measures, such as market share and customer satisfaction, can be used in order to discourage myopic behavior: (a) true; (b) false

9. The comparable uncontrolled price method is the IRS transfer pricing method that uses a transfer price equal to the sales price received by the reseller minus an appropriate markup: (a) true; (b) false

10. The cost-plus method is the IRS transfer pricing method that uses a cost-based transfer price: (a) true; (b) false

11. The comparable uncontrolled price method is the transfer pricing method preferred by the IRS: (a) true; (b) false

12. A multinational corporation has two divisions, B Division and S Division. B Division is located in a country with a high income tax rate, while S Division is located in a country with a low income tax rate. S Division sells to B Division and wants to charge a transfer price of $200 per unit. B Division prefers a transfer price of $150 per unit. Assuming the resale price is $280, which transfer price would result in lower total income tax liability for the multinational corporation? (a) $200; (b) $150

Use the following information to answer Questions 13 through 16:

(Round numbers to two decimal places.)

On June 1, Barkley, Inc., received an order from a Japanese customer for 2,500,000 yen to be paid upon receipt of the goods, scheduled for August 1.

The rates for $1 U.S. are as follows:

	Exchange Rates for $1 for Yen
Spot rate, June 1	125
Forward rate, August 1	126
Spot rate, August 1	130

13. The amount that Barkley would receive from the Japanese customer in U.S. dollars using the spot rate at the time of the order would be: (a) $312,500,000.00; (b) $20,000.00; (c) $19,230.77; (d) $325,000,000.00

14. The amount that Barkley would receive from the Japanese customer in U.S. dollars using the spot rate at the time of payment would be: (a) $325,000,000.00; (b) $312,500,000.00; (c) $19,230.77; (d) $20,000.00

15. If Barkley receives payment from the Japanese customer using the spot rate at the time of payment, Barkley's exchange gain or loss would be: (a) $12,500 loss; (b) $12,500.00 gain; (c) $769.23 gain; (d) $769.23 loss

16. If Barkley's policy is to hedge foreign currency transactions, the amount that Barkley expects to receive on August 1 would be: (a) $19,841.27; (b) $315,000,000.00; (c) $20,000.00; (d) $19,230.77

→ **Compare your answers with those at the end of the chapter. Review any questions missed.**

PRACTICE TEST

PROBLEM 1

The Orient Express, Inc., imports wicker and porcelain products that it resells in the United States. The company's warehouse, located in a foreign trade zone, houses imported merchandise. The average shipment has a cost of $500,000, and on average, the inventory is stored for three months before it is moved from the warehouse in the foreign trade zone. Inventory shrinkage at the warehouse due to breakage is about 10% of the total. The average tariff rate on the imports is 12%. The company's carrying cost is 8%.

Instructions:

Determine the cost savings per year to Orient Express from locating its warehouse in a foreign trade zone.

PROBLEM 2

Seelbach, Inc., imports French cheeses for distribution in the United States. On April 1, the company purchased cheese costing 400,000 francs. Payment is due in francs on July 1. The spot rate on April 1 was $0.20 per franc, and on July 1, it was $0.25 per franc.

Instructions:

1. How much would Seelbach have to pay for the purchase (in dollars) if it paid on April 1?

2. How much would Seelbach have to pay for the purchase (in dollars) if it paid on July 1?

3. If Seelbach paid for the purchase using the July 1 spot rate, what would be the exchange gain or loss?

PROBLEM 3

On August 1, Jordan, Inc., received an order from a British customer for 1,000,000 pounds to be paid on receipt of the goods, scheduled for November 1. The rates for $1 U.S. are as follows:

	Exchange Rates for $1 for British Pound
Spot rate, August 1	.65
Forward rate, November 1	.64
Spot rate, November 1	.60

Instructions:

1. How much does Jordan expect to receive from the British customer in U.S. dollars using the spot rate at the time of the order?

2. a. How much does Jordan expect to receive from the British customer in U.S. dollars using the spot rate at the time of payment?

   b. If Jordan receives payment from the British customer using the spot rate at the time of payment, what would be Jordan's exchange gain or loss?

3. If Jordan's policy is to hedge foreign currency transactions, what is the amount Jordan expects to receive on November 1 in U.S. dollars?

ANSWERS

KEY TERMS TEST

1. tariff
2. Outsourcing
3. joint venture
4. Maquiladoras
5. exchange rate
6. exchange loss
7. exchange gain
8. Currency risk management
9. Transaction risk
10. Economic risk
11. Translation risk (or Accounting risk)
12. spot rate
13. Currency appreciation
14. Currency depreciation
15. Hedging
16. forward contract
17. comparable uncontrolled price method
18. resale price method
19. cost-plus method
20. advance pricing agreement
21. Foreign trade zones
22. multinational corporation, MNC

CHAPTER QUIZ

1. 1. MNCs might engage in import/export activities.
   2. MNCs might purchase wholly owned subsidiaries.
   3. MNCs might participate in joint ventures.
2. 1. Companies can postpone payment of duties until the imported materials leave the foreign trade zone. Since money has a time value, postponing the payment results in a cost savings.
   2. Duties are not paid on damaged or evaporated goods that never leave the foreign trade zone.
3. reinvoicing center
4. overall profit to the company, income tax
5. b False A stronger dollar makes U.S. exports relatively more expensive to foreign customers.
6. b False It is an example of *translation* risk.
7. b False It is an example of *transaction* risk.
8. a True
9. b False It is the resale price method.
10. a True
11. a True
12. a $200 A $200 transfer price would result in more profit for S Division, which would be taxed at a lower rate than if the profit were recorded by B Division.
13. b $20,000.00 (2,500,000 yen/125) = $20,000.00
14. c $19,230.77 (2,500,000 yen/130) = $19,230.77
15. d $769.23 loss ($20,000.00 – $19,230.77) = $769.23
16. a $19,841.27 (2,500,000 yen/126) = $19,841.27

PRACTICE TEST

PROBLEM 1

	Foreign Trade Zone	No Foreign Trade Zone
Tariff paid at purchase ($500,000 × 12%)		$ 60,000
Carrying cost of tariff ($500,000 × 12% × 8% × 3/12)		1,200
Tariff paid ($500,000 × 90% × 12%)	$ 54,000	
Total tariff and tariff-related cost per shipment	$ 54,000	$ 61,200
Total tariff and tariff-related cost per year (Cost per shipment × 4)	$216,000	$244,800

Cost savings per year = $244,800 – $216,000 = $28,800

PROBLEM 2

1. 400,000 francs × $0.20 dollars per franc = $80,000
2. 400,000 francs × $0.25 dollars per franc = $100,000
3.

Liability in dollars, 4/1	$ 80,000
Paid in dollars, 7/1	100,000
Exchange loss	$ 20,000

PROBLEM 3

1. 1,000,000 pounds/.65 = $1,538,461.54
2. a. 1,000,000 pounds/.60 = $1,666,666.67
   b.

Receivable in dollars, 8/1	$1,538,461.54
Received in dollars, 11/1	1,666,666.67
Exchange gain	$ 128,205.13

3. 1,000,000 pounds/.64 = $1,562,500

CHAPTER 15

Segmented Reporting and Performance Evaluation

CHAPTER REVIEW

VARIABLE COSTING AND ABSORPTION COSTING: AN ANALYSIS AND COMPARISON

- Two methods for calculating a product's cost are:
  1. absorption costing
  2. variable costing
- **Absorption costing** is required for *external* financial reporting and income tax purposes.
- **Variable costing** is used for *internal* reporting to management because it provides information that is useful for planning, control, and decision making.
- The main difference between the two methods relates to how fixed manufacturing overhead is recorded.
  - When using absorption costing, fixed manufacturing overhead is considered a product cost, included in inventory and expensed when the inventory is sold.
  - When using variable costing, fixed manufacturing overhead is *not* included in inventory but is expensed in the period it is incurred.
- The ending finished goods inventory values for absorption and variable costing will differ by the amount of fixed manufacturing costs included in ending inventory.
- Product and period costs under absorption and variable costing are summarized below:

	Absorption Costing	Variable Costing
Product costs:	direct materials (DM) direct labor (DL) variable overhead (VOH) fixed overhead (FOH)	direct materials (DM) direct labor (DL) variable overhead (VOH)
Period costs:	variable selling expenses fixed selling expenses variable administrative expenses fixed administrative expenses	fixed overhead (FOH) variable selling expenses fixed selling expenses variable administrative expenses fixed administrative expenses

❒ The following diagram illustrates the flow of manufacturing costs using absorption costing:

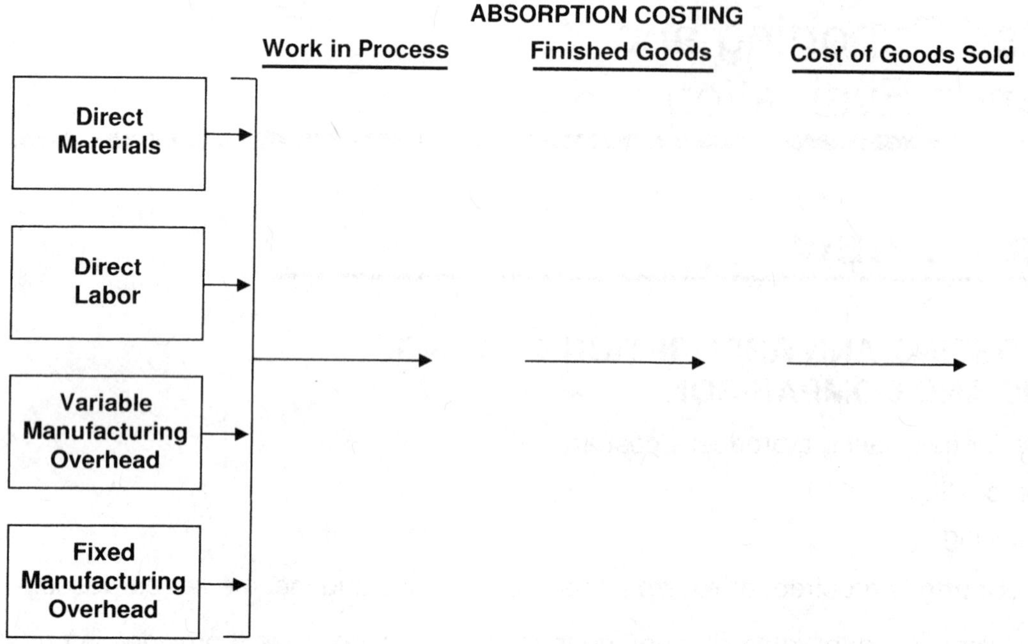

❒ The following diagram illustrates the flow of manufacturing costs using variable costing:

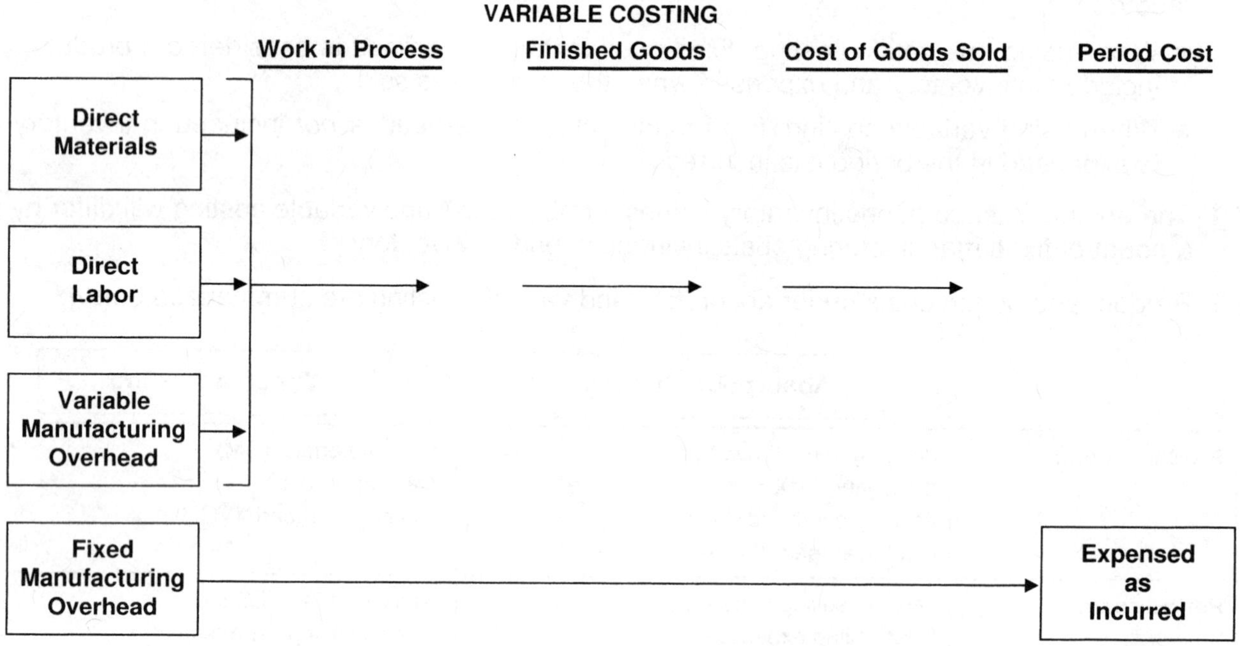

Income Statements: Analysis and Reconciliation

❒ Under absorption costing, costs are classified by *function* as:

1. manufacturing costs (both fixed and variable)
2. selling and administrative costs (both fixed and variable)

- The format used when costs are classified by function for absorption costing is:

Sales
– Cost of goods sold (Manufacturing costs)
= Gross margin
– Selling and administrative expenses
= Net income

- When variable costing is used, costs are classified by *behavior* as:
  1. variable costs
     - variable manufacturing
     - variable selling and administrative
  2. fixed costs
     - fixed manufacturing
     - fixed selling and administrative

- The format used for a variable-costing income statement follows:

Sales
– Variable expenses:
Variable cost of goods sold
Variable selling and administrative
= Contribution margin
– Fixed expenses:
Fixed overhead
Fixed selling and administrative
= Net income

Production, Sales, and Income Relationships

- When sales equal production, income is the same under variable and absorption costing.
- When production exceeds sales, absorption-costing income will generally exceed variable-costing income. This occurs because under variable costing, all fixed manufacturing costs are expensed, while under absorption costing, the part of *fixed manufacturing costs associated with unsold units are deferred in inventory.*
- When sales exceed production, variable-costing income will generally exceed absorption-costing income. This occurs because as the unit balance in ending absorption inventory decreases, *fixed manufacturing costs deferred from prior years are now expensed.*
- Production, sales, and income relationships are summarized below:

If	***Then***
Production > Sales	**Absorption net income > Variable net income**
Production < Sales	**Absorption net income < Variable net income**
Production = Sales	**Absorption net income = Variable net income**

- The difference between absorption-costing income and variable-costing income results from differences in the *timing* of the recognition of fixed manufacturing overhead costs as an expense. Variable costing always recognizes the period's fixed overhead as an expense.
- Absorption costing recognizes as an expense only the fixed overhead *attached* to the units sold.

- The difference in incomes can be calculated as the change in the number of units in inventory multiplied by the fixed overhead rate per unit.

$$\text{Absorption-costing income} - \text{Variable-costing income} = \text{Fixed overhead rate} \times \text{Change in total units in inventory}$$

$$\text{Absorption-costing income} - \text{Variable-costing income} = \text{Fixed overhead rate} \times (\text{Units produced} - \text{Units sold})$$

The Treatment of Fixed Factory Overhead in Absorption Costing

- Under absorption costing, fixed factory overhead is:
  1. assigned to units produced, and
  2. expensed when the units to which it is attached are sold.
- Applied fixed overhead is the fixed manufacturing overhead assigned to production using a predetermined fixed overhead rate.
- The difference between applied fixed overhead and actual fixed overhead equals over- or underapplied fixed overhead.

Over- or underapplied fixed overhead = Applied fixed overhead – Actual fixed overhead

- If applied fixed overhead exceeds actual fixed overhead, fixed overhead is overapplied.
- If applied fixed overhead is less than actual fixed overhead, fixed overhead is underapplied.
- If over- or underapplied fixed overhead is immaterial in amount, it is closed to Cost of Goods Sold.
- Over- or underapplied variable overhead is treated in the same fashion.

VARIABLE COSTING AND PERFORMANCE EVALUATION OF MANAGERS

- A manager's performance is often evaluated based on the profit of the organizational units he or she controls. In general, if a manager's performance is evaluated based on income, then managers have the right to expect the following (assuming all other things are equal):
  1. If sales revenue *increases*, income should *increase*.
  2. If sales revenue *decreases*, income should *decrease*.
  3. If sales revenue remains the *same*, income should remain the *same*.
- Variable costing always results in the expected association between sales and income.
- Absorption income is affected by the level of inventory and does not always result in the expected association between sales and income.

VARIABLE COSTING AND SEGMENTED REPORTING

- A **segment** is a subunit of an organization and can be a division, product line, sales territory, or plant.
- **Segmented reporting** is the process of preparing financial performance reports for segments within a firm.
- Segment reports can be prepared for any level of the organization: division, product line, plants within a division, and so on.
- Segmented reports prepared using variable costing produce better evaluations and decisions than those prepared on an absorption-costing basis.

Segmented Reporting: Variable-Costing Basis

❒ A comparison of the formats for a variable-costing income statement and a segmented income statement using variable costing follows:

Variable-Costing Income Statement	Variable-Costing Segmented Income Statement
Sales	**Sales**
– **Variable expenses:**	– **Variable expenses:**
Variable cost of goods sold	Variable cost of goods sold
Variable selling and administrative	Variable selling and administrative
= **Contribution margin**	= **Contribution margin**
	– **Direct fixed expenses:**
	Direct fixed overhead
– **Fixed expenses:**	Direct selling and administrative
Fixed overhead	= **Segment margin (or Product margin)**
Fixed selling and administrative	– **Common fixed expenses:**
	Common fixed overhead
	Common selling and administrative
= **Net income**	= **Net income**

❒ **Direct fixed expenses** are fixed costs that are *directly traceable to a particular segment* and arise because of the existence of that segment.

❒ Direct fixed expenses are *avoidable* because they would be eliminated or avoided if the segment is eliminated.

❒ **Common fixed expenses** are fixed costs that *benefit more than one segment* and are not directly traceable to a particular segment. An example of a common fixed cost would be the corporate president's salary.

❒ Common fixed costs continue to be incurred even if one of the segments is eliminated.

❒ The segment contribution margin (sales less variable costs) provides information useful in making short-run operating decisions such as accepting or rejecting orders at special prices.

❒ **Segment margin** is the segment contribution margin remaining after covering the direct fixed costs of the segment. Segment margin is the amount the segment contributes toward covering the firm's common fixed costs and generating profit. Thus, variable costing enables management to evaluate each segment's contribution to overall firm performance.

❒ The segment margin (sales less variable costs less direct fixed costs) provides information useful in assessing the long-run profitability of a segment.

❒ If a segment does not affect the sales of other segments, the segment margin is the amount by which the firm's profits would change if the segment were eliminated.

Customer Profitability

❒ Customer profitability can be assessed by treating each customer group as a segment and determining activities associated with each group.

❒ Steps in determining customer profitability include:

- Identify the customer.
- Determine which customer groups are most profitable (considering product, marketing, and administrative activities used to serve each class of customer).
- Eliminate the unprofitable customers.
- Retain and add to the base of profitable customers.

VARIABLE COSTING FOR PLANNING AND CONTROL

- ❒ Management may wish to look at several different levels of sales in order to assess the possibilities facing the firm. Because fixed costs do not vary with volume changes, a distinction between fixed and variable costs is critical for planning costs at different sales and production volumes.
- ❒ Management controls operations by comparing actual performance with plans. When controlling operations, a knowledge of cost behavior is important.

KEY TERMS TEST

Test your recall of the key terms as follows. Try to recall as many key terms as possible without assistance. If you need assistance, refer to the list of key terms at the end of this section.

1. ____________ ____________ is calculated as revenue less variable costs and direct fixed costs.

2. ______________ ___________ is the product-costing method that assigns only variable manufacturing costs to a product: direct materials, direct labor, and variable overhead. Fixed overhead is treated as a period cost.

3. ______________ ___________ is the product-costing method that assigns all manufacturing costs to a product: direct materials, direct labor, variable overhead, and fixed overhead.

4. ____________ _________ _____________ are directly traceable to a given segment and would be avoided if the segment is eliminated.

5. ____________ _________ _____________ are not directly traceable to a particular segment and are unaffected by the elimination of any one segment.

6. _____________ _____________ is the process of preparing financial performance reports for segments within a firm.

KEY TERMS:

absorption costing
common fixed expenses
direct fixed expenses
segment margin
segmented reporting
variable costing

→ **Compare your answers with those at the end of the chapter. Review any key terms missed.**

CHAPTER QUIZ

Write your answers in the spaces provided.

1. Two product costing methods are absorption costing and variable costing. _______________ costing is used for internal reporting to management because it provides information that is useful for planning, control, and decision making. _______________ costing is required for external financial reporting and income tax purposes.

2. The main difference between absorption costing and variable costing relates to how ________ _____________ is treated.

3. When absorption costing is used, the costs considered product costs are:

   1. ____
   2. ____
   3. ____
   4. ____

4. When absorption costing is used, the costs considered period costs are:

   1. ______________________________
   2. ______________________________
   3. ______________________________
   4. ______________________________

5. When variable costing is used, the costs considered product costs are:

   1. ______________________________
   2. ______________________________
   3. ______________________________

6. When variable costing is used, the costs considered period costs are:

   1. ______________________________
   2. ______________________________
   3. ______________________________
   4. ______________________________
   5. ______________________________

7. The income statement used for absorption costing classifies costs by ____________.

8. A variable-costing income statement classifies costs by ___________ as either ___________ costs or ___________ costs.

Circle the single best answer.

9. Variable costing may be used for internal or external reporting: (a) true; (b) false

10. When using absorption costing, all manufacturing costs (direct materials, direct labor, variable overhead, and fixed overhead) are considered product costs: (a) true; (b) false

11. The income statement used for variable costing usually classifies costs by function (manufacturing costs vs. selling and administrative costs): (a) true; (b) false

12. Contribution margin equals sales minus variable manufacturing costs: (a) true; (b) false

13. When sales equal production, net income is the same under the two methods: (a) true; (b) false

14. When sales exceed production, absorption-costing income will generally exceed variable-costing income: (a) true; (b) false

15. The difference between absorption-costing income and variable-costing income can be calculated as the change in the number of units in inventory multiplied by the fixed overhead rate per unit: (a) true; (b) false

16. The segment margin provides information useful in assessing the long-run profitability of a segment: (a) true; (b) false

Use the following information to answer Questions 17 through 24:

Selected data for the Christie Company's past year of operations are presented below:

	Product A	Product B
Production (units)	160,000	300,000
Sales (units)	100,000	250,000
Selling price	$6.00	$5.00
Direct labor hours	60,000	90,000
Manufacturing costs:		
Direct materials	$ 80,000	$270,000
Direct labor	240,000	540,000
Variable overhead	24,000	30,000
Fixed overhead:		
Direct	80,000	50,000
Common[a]	25,000	25,000
Nonmanufacturing costs:		
Variable selling	$ 40,000	$ 75,000
Direct fixed selling	50,000	65,000
Common fixed selling[b]	30,000	30,000

[a]Common overhead totals $50,000 and is divided equally between the two products.
[b]Common fixed selling totals $60,000 and is divided equally between the two products.

Budgeted fixed overhead for the year of $180,000 equaled actual fixed overhead. Fixed overhead is assigned to products using a plantwide rate based on expected direct labor hours, which were 150,000. The company had 5,000 of Product B in inventory at the beginning of the year. These units had the same unit cost as the units produced during the year. (Round amounts to two decimal places.)

17. The unit product cost for Product A using variable costing is: (a) $2.00; (b) $2.15; (c) $2.45; (d) $2.60

18. The unit product cost for Product A using absorption costing is: (a) $2.15; (b) $2.45; (c) $2.60; (d) $2.80

19. The unit product cost for Product B using variable costing is: (a) $2.15; (b) $2.45; (c) $2.80; (d) $3.04

20. The unit product cost for Product B using absorption costing is: (a) $3.16; (b) $2.80; (c) $2.60; (d) $2.45

21. Variable cost of goods sold for the year is: (a) $700,000; (b) $915,000; (c) $1,025,000; (d) $1,072,000

22. Variable-costing net income for the year is: (a) $938,000; (b) $763,000; (c) $648,000; (d) $465,000

23. Using absorption costing, cost of goods sold for the year is: (a) $1,050,000; (b) $912,000; (c) $797,000; (d) $760,000

24. Absorption-costing net income for the year is: (a) $840,000; (b) $648,000; (c) $510,000; (d) $488,000

25. Complete the following:

Product Costing Methods

	Absorption Costing	Variable Costing
Product costs:		
Period costs:		

→ **Compare your answers with those at the end of the chapter. Review any questions missed.**

PRACTICE TEST

PROBLEM 1

Barth Industries began operations on January 1, 2004. The company sells a single product for $10 per unit. During 2004, 60,000 units were produced and 50,000 units were sold. There was no work-in-process inventory at December 31, 2004.

Barth uses an actual cost system for product costing and actual costs for 2004 were as follows:

	Fixed Costs	Variable Costs
Direct materials	–0–	$2.00 per unit produced
Direct labor	–0–	$1.00 per unit produced
Manufacturing overhead	$60,000	$0.50 per unit produced
Selling and administrative expense	$40,000	$0.80 per unit sold

PROBLEM 1 *(Continued)*

Instructions:

1. What is the product cost per unit under each of the following?
   a. variable costing

   b. absorption costing

2. What is the finished goods inventory cost at December 31, 2004 under each of the following?
   a. variable costing

   b. absorption costing

PROBLEM 1 *(Continued)*

3. Prepare income statements for 2004 under each of the following:

a. variable costing

b. absorption costing

PROBLEM 1 *(Continued)*

4. Reconcile the difference between variable-costing income and absorption-costing income.

PROBLEM 2

Griffiths Manufacturing uses an actual cost system for product costing. The company's income statement for 2004 is presented below:

Griffiths Manufacturing
Income Statement
For the Year Ending December 31, 2004

Sales (10,000 units @ $20)		$200,000
Cost of goods sold:		
Finished goods inventory, January 1	$ –0–	
Cost of goods manufactured (12,000 units @ $15)	180,000	
Goods available for sale	$180,000	
Finished goods inventory, December 31 (2,000 units @ $15)	30,000	
Cost of goods sold		150,000
Gross margin		$ 50,000
Operating expenses:		
Selling	$ 20,000	
Administrative	20,000	
Total selling and administrative		40,000
Net income		$ 10,000

The following additional information is available:

Variable costs per unit:	
Direct materials	$4
Direct labor	5
Manufacturing overhead	2
Selling expense	1
Fixed costs for the period:	
Manufacturing overhead	$48,000
Selling	10,000
Administrative	20,000

PROBLEM 2 *(Continued)*

Instructions:

1. When absorption costing was used, how much fixed manufacturing overhead was deferred in finished goods inventory?

2. Recast the income statement for 2004 using variable costing.

PROBLEM 2 *(Continued)*

3. Reconcile variable-costing income and absorption-costing income.

PROBLEM 3

The Snow Company began the year 2004 with no inventories of work in process or finished goods. The company produces a single product, and cost data for the product are given below:

Variable costs:		
Direct materials	$10	per unit
Direct labor	15	per unit
Manufacturing overhead	6	per unit
Selling expenses	4	per unit
Fixed costs:		
Manufacturing overhead	$50,000	per month
Selling and administrative	20,000	per month

During the first three months of 2004, production and sales in units were as follows:

	Production	Sales
January	10,000	10,000
February	10,000	8,000
March	10,000	12,000
Total	30,000	30,000

The company uses an actual cost system. The selling price of the product is $50 per unit. There were no work-in-process inventories at the end of each month.

Instructions:

1. Determine the unit cost of production each month under each of the following:

a. variable costing

	January	February	March

PROBLEM 3 *(Continued)*

b. absorption costing

	January	February	March

2. Prepare income statements for the three months for each of the following:

a. variable costing

	January	February	March	Total

PROBLEM 3 *(Continued)*

b. absorption costing

	January	February	March	Total

3. If selling prices and costs do not change significantly, what can be said about the relationship of income under absorption costing and variable costing for each of the following?

a. Sales equal production.

b. Sales are less than production.

c. Sales are greater than production.

PROBLEM 4

Belmont, Inc., has just completed its first year of operations. The unit costs on a normal costing basis are as follows:

Manufacturing costs:	
Direct materials (3 lbs. @ $2)	$ 6.00 per unit
Direct labor (2 hrs. @ $8)	16.00 per unit
Variable overhead (2 hrs. @ $1.75)	3.50 per unit
Fixed overhead	?
Total	$?
Selling and administrative costs:	
Variable	$4.00 per unit
Fixed	$100,000

During the year, the company had the following activity:

Units produced	20,000
Units sold	16,000
Unit selling price	$50
Direct labor hours worked	40,000

Actual fixed overhead was $170,000 for the year, and actual variable overhead was $72,000. Budgeted fixed overhead was $180,000, and the company used an expected activity level of 40,000 direct labor hours to compute the predetermined overhead rates. Any overhead variances are closed to Cost of Goods Sold.

Instructions:

1. Compute the unit cost using each of the following:

   a. absorption costing

   b. variable costing

PROBLEM 4 *(Continued)*

2. Prepare an absorption-costing income statement.

PROBLEM 4 *(Continued)*

3. Prepare a variable-costing income statement.

4. Reconcile the difference between the two income statements.

PROBLEM 5

Lawson Industries produces two products, Product X and Product Y. Information relating to the products for 2004 is as follows:

	Product X	Product Y
Units produced and sold	20,000	50,000
Selling price per unit	$15	$10
Variable expenses per unit	$8	$4

Lawson's fixed costs totaled $350,000, of which $60,000 can be avoided if Product X is dropped and $120,000 can be avoided if Product Y is dropped.

PROBLEM 5 *(Continued)*

Instructions:

1. Prepare a segmented income statement using variable costing and segregating direct and common fixed costs.

2. What would be the effect on Lawson's profit if Product X is dropped?

3. What would be the effect on Lawson's profit if Product Y is dropped?

4. Would you recommend that Lawson drop Product X or Product Y? Why or why not?

ANSWERS

KEY TERMS TEST

1. Segment margin
2. Variable costing
3. Absorption costing
4. Direct fixed expenses
5. Common fixed expenses
6. Segmented reporting

CHAPTER QUIZ

1. Variable, Absorption
2. fixed overhead
3. 1. direct materials
   2. direct labor
   3. variable manufacturing overhead
   4. fixed manufacturing overhead
4. 1. variable selling expenses
   2. fixed selling expenses
   3. variable administrative expenses
   4. fixed administrative expenses
5. 1. direct materials
   2. direct labor
   3. variable manufacturing overhead
6. 1. fixed manufacturing overhead
   2. variable selling expenses
   3. fixed selling expenses
   4. variable administrative expenses
   5. fixed administrative expenses
7. function (manufacturing, selling and administrative)
8. behavior, variable, fixed
9. b False Absorption costing is required for external financial reporting and income tax purposes.
10. a True
11. b False When variable costing is used, a contribution margin format is usually used. The contribution margin format classifies costs by behavior (variable costs vs. fixed costs).
12. b False Contribution margin equals sales minus all variable costs (variable manufacturing and variable selling and administrative costs).
13. a True
14. b False
15. a True
16. a True
17. b

Direct materials ($80,000/160,000)	$0.50
Direct labor ($240,000/160,000)	1.50
Variable overhead ($24,000/160,000)	0.15
Variable cost per unit	$2.15

18. c

Direct materials ($80,000/160,000)	$0.50
Direct labor ($240,000/160,000)	1.50
Variable overhead ($24,000/160,000)	0.15
Variable cost per unit	$2.15
Fixed overhead	
[(60,000 DLH × $1.20[a])/160,000]	0.45
Absorption cost per unit	$2.60

[a]Fixed overhead rate = $180,000/150,000 = $1.20

19. c

Direct materials ($270,000/300,000)	$0.90
Direct labor ($540,000/300,000)	1.80
Variable overhead ($30,000/300,000)	0.10
Variable cost per unit	$2.80

20. a

Direct materials ($270,000/300,000)	$0.90
Direct labor ($540,000/300,000)	1.80
Variable overhead ($30,000/300,000)	0.10
Variable cost per unit	$2.80
Fixed overhead	
[(90,000 DLH × $1.20)/300,000]	0.36
Absorption cost per unit	$3.16

21. b (100,000 × $2.15) + (250,000 × $2.80) = $915,000

22. d

Sales (100,000 × $6) + (250,000 × $5)	$1,850,000
Variable cost of goods sold	(915,000)
Variable selling ($40,000 + $75,000)	(115,000)
Fixed overhead	(180,000)
Fixed selling	(175,000)
Net income	$ 465,000

23. a (100,000 × $2.60) + (250,000 × $3.16) = $1,050,000

24. c

Sales	$ 1,850,000
Cost of goods sold	(1,050,000)
Selling expenses	(290,000)
Net income	$ 510,000

25. See page 271.

PRACTICE TEST

PROBLEM 1

1. a. Cost per unit using variable costing:

Direct materials	$2.00
Direct labor	1.00
Variable manufacturing overhead	0.50
Cost per unit	$3.50

b. Cost per unit using absorption costing:

Direct materials	$2.00
Direct labor	1.00
Variable manufacturing overhead	0.50
Fixed manufacturing overhead ($60,000/60,000 units)	1.00
Cost per unit	$4.50

2. a. Finished goods inventory cost at December 31, 2004 under variable costing: 10,000 units × $3.50 = $35,000

b. Finished goods inventory cost at December 31, 2004 under absorption costing: 10,000 units × $4.50 = $45,000

3. a.

Barth Industries
Income Statements
For the Year Ending December 31, 2004

Variable Costing

Sales (50,000 × $10)		$500,000
Less variable expenses:		
Variable cost of goods sold (50,000 × $3.50)	$175,000	
Variable selling (50,000 × $0.80)	40,000	
Total variable expenses		215,000
Contribution margin		$285,000
Less fixed expenses:		
Fixed overhead	$ 60,000	
Fixed selling and administrative	40,000	
Total fixed expenses		$100,000
Net income		$185,000

b.

Absorption Costing

Sales (50,000 × $10)		$500,000
Cost of goods sold[a]		225,000
Gross profit		$275,000
Selling and administrative expenses:		
Fixed	$ 40,000	
Variable	40,000	
Total selling and administrative expenses		80,000
Net income		$195,000

[a]Beginning inventory	$ –0–
Cost of goods manufactured (60,000 × $4.50)	270,000
Goods available for sale	$270,000
Ending inventory (10,000 × $4.50)	45,000
Cost of goods sold	$225,000

4. The difference in incomes results from the difference in the treatment of fixed manufacturing overhead costs.

Difference in income = Absorption-costing income – Variable-costing income
= $195,000 – $185,000
= $10,000

Difference in income = Change in inventory in units × Fixed overhead rate per unit
= 10,000 × $1
= $10,000

When absorption costing is used, $10,000 of fixed overhead costs are deferred in finished goods inventory, resulting in a $10,000 higher income.

PROBLEM 2

1. Fixed overhead cost per unit = $48,000/12,000 units = $4 per unit

   Fixed overhead deferred in finished goods inventory = 2,000 units × $4 per unit = $8,000

2. **Variable Costing**

Sales (10,000 × $20)		$200,000
Less variable expenses:		
Variable cost of goods sold[a]	$110,000	
Variable selling (10,000 × $1)	10,000	
Total variable expenses		120,000
Contribution margin		$ 80,000
Less fixed expenses:		
Fixed overhead	$ 48,000	
Fixed selling	10,000	
Fixed administrative	20,000	
Total fixed expenses		$ 78,000
Net income		$ 2,000

[a]Beginning inventory	$ –0–
Cost of production (12,000 × $11)	132,000
Goods available for sale	$132,000
Ending inventory (2,000 × $11)	22,000
Variable cost of goods sold	$110,000

3. Difference in income = Absorption-costing income – Variable-costing income
   = $10,000 – $2,000
   = $8,000

   Difference in income = Change in inventory in units × Fixed overhead rate per unit
   = 2,000 × $4
   = $8,000

PROBLEM 3

1. a. Unit cost of production under variable costing:

	January	February	March
Direct materials	$10	$10	$10
Direct labor	15	15	15
Variable manufacturing overhead	6	6	6
Total manufacturing cost per unit	$31	$31	$31

b. Unit cost of production under absorption costing:

	January	February	March
Direct materials	$10	$10	$10
Direct labor	15	15	15
Variable manufacturing overhead	6	6	6
Fixed manufacturing overhead ($50,000/10,000)	5	5	5
Total manufacturing cost per unit	$36	$36	$36

Basic unit information:

	January	February	March	Total
Beginning inventory in units	–0–	–0–	2,000	–0–
Units produced	10,000	10,000	10,000	30,000
Units sold	10,000	8,000	12,000	30,000
Ending inventory in units	–0–	2,000	–0–	–0–

2\. a.

Variable-Costing Income Statements

	January	February	March	Total
Sales	$500,000	$400,000	$600,000	$1,500,000
Less variable expenses:				
Beginning inventory	–0–	–0–	62,000	–0–
Cost of production (10,000 × $31)	310,000	310,000	310,000	930,000
Goods available for sale	$310,000	$310,000	$372,000	$ 930,000
Ending inventory	–0–	62,000	–0–	–0–
Cost of goods sold	$310,000	$248,000	$372,000	$ 930,000
Selling expenses ($4 per unit)	40,000	32,000	48,000	120,000
Total variable expenses	$350,000	$280,000	$420,000	$1,050,000
Contribution margin	$150,000	$120,000	$180,000	$ 450,000
Less fixed expenses:				
Fixed manufacturing	$ 50,000	$ 50,000	$ 50,000	$ 150,000
Fixed selling and administrative	20,000	20,000	20,000	60,000
Total fixed expenses	$ 70,000	$ 70,000	$ 70,000	$ 210,000
Net income	$ 80,000	$ 50,000	$110,000	$ 240,000

b.

Absorption-Costing Income Statements

	January	February	March	Total
Sales	$500,000	$400,000	$600,000	$1,500,000
Cost of goods sold:				
Beginning inventory	–0–	–0–	72,000	–0–
Cost of production (10,000 × $36)	360,000	360,000	360,000	1,080,000
Goods available for sale	$360,000	$360,000	$432,000	$1,080,000
Ending inventory	–0–	72,000	–0–	–0–
Cost of goods sold	$360,000	$288,000	$432,000	$1,080,000
Gross profit	$140,000	$112,000	$168,000	$ 420,000
Selling and administrative	60,000	52,000	68,000	180,000
Net income	$ 80,000	$ 60,000	$100,000	$ 240,000

3\. a. If sales equal production, income under the two methods should be the same.

b. If sales are less than production, absorption-costing income will be greater than variable-costing income because some fixed manufacturing overhead will be deferred in ending inventory.

c. If sales are greater than production, absorption-costing income will be less than variable-costing income because some fixed manufacturing overhead deferred from a prior period will be expensed in the current period when the units are sold.

PROBLEM 4

Note that Problems 1, 2, and 3 of this chapter used an actual cost system while this problem uses a normal cost system. Recall that a normal cost system uses actual costs for direct materials and direct labor and predetermined overhead rates to apply overhead. Because applied overhead and actual overhead usually differ, overapplied or underapplied overhead often exists when a normal cost system is used.

1\. a. Unit cost using absorption costing:

Direct materials (3 lbs. @ $2)	$ 6.00
Direct labor (2 hrs. @ $8)	16.00
Variable overhead (2 hrs. @ $1.75)	3.50
Fixed overhead (2 hrs. @ $4.50[a])	9.00
Total	$34.50

[a] Predetermined fixed overhead rate = $\frac{\text{Budgeted fixed overhead}}{\text{Budgeted activity}}$

= $180,000/40,000 direct labor hours = $4.50/direct labor hour

b. Unit cost using variable costing:

Direct materials (3 lbs. @ $2)	$ 6.00
Direct labor (2 hrs. @ $8)	16.00
Variable overhead (2 hrs. @ $1.75)	3.50
Total	$25.50

2. Both variable and fixed overhead were applied on the basis of direct labor hours. Since 40,000 hours were worked, total applied fixed overhead amounts to $180,000. Actual fixed overhead was $170,000.

Fixed Overhead

Applied fixed overhead (40,000 hours worked × $4.50/DLH)	$180,000
Actual fixed overhead	170,000
Overapplied fixed overhead	$ 10,000

Variable Overhead

Applied variable overhead (40,000 hours worked × $1.75/DLH)	$70,000
Actual variable overhead	72,000
Underapplied variable overhead	$ (2,000)

Belmont, Inc.
Absorption-Costing Income Statement

Sales (16,000 @ $50)		$800,000
Cost of goods sold (16,000 @ $34.50)	$552,000	
Less: Overapplied overhead ($10,000 – $2,000)	8,000	544,000
Gross margin		$256,000
Less: Selling and administrative expenses [$100,000 + (16,000 × $4)]		164,000
Net income		$ 92,000

3. **Belmont, Inc.**
Variable-Costing Income Statement

Sales (16,000 @ $50)		$800,000
Variable cost of goods sold (16,000 @ $25.50)	$408,000	
Add: Underapplied variable overhead	2,000	(410,000)
Variable selling expense (16,000 @ $4)		(64,000)
Contribution margin		$326,000
Less fixed expenses:		
Fixed factory overhead	$170,000	
Fixed selling and administrative	100,000	270,000
Net income		$ 56,000

Note that *actual* fixed factory overhead, not applied fixed factory overhead, is expensed on the income statement.

4. Absorption income – Variable income = Fixed overhead rate per unit × (Production – Sales)
$92,000 – $56,000 = $9 × (20,000 – 16,000)
$36,000 = $9 × 4,000
$36,000 = $36,000

PROBLEM 5

1. **Lawson Industries**
Segmented Income Statement
For the Year Ended December 31, 2004

	Product X	Product Y	Total
Sales	$300,000	$500,000	$800,000
Less: Variable expenses	160,000	200,000	360,000
Contribution margin	$140,000	$300,000	$440,000
Less: Direct fixed expenses	60,000	120,000	180,000
Product margin	$ 80,000	$180,000	$260,000
Less: Common fixed expenses			170,000
Net income			$ 90,000

2. If Product X is dropped, Lawson's profit would decrease by $80,000, the amount of Product X's product margin.

3. If Product Y is dropped, Lawson's profit would decrease by $180,000, the amount of Product Y's product margin.

4. Based on the information presented, Lawson should not drop Product X nor Product Y because dropping either product would reduce total profit.

CHAPTER 16

Cost-Volume-Profit Analysis: A Managerial Planning Tool

CHAPTER REVIEW

- Cost-volume-profit analysis enables a firm to determine the sales (in units or dollars) necessary to attain a desired level of profit. CVP analysis is useful in assessing the effect of operating changes (such as changes in selling price or operating costs) upon profit.

BREAK-EVEN POINT IN UNITS

- The **break-even point** is the point where total revenues equal total expenses, the point where profit equals zero. This can be expressed as:

$$\textbf{Total revenue} - \textbf{Total variable cost} - \textbf{Total fixed cost} = \$0$$

or

$$\textbf{Total revenue} = \textbf{Total variable cost} + \textbf{Total fixed cost}$$

Shortcut to Calculating Break-Even Units

- To determine how many units must be sold in order to break even, solve for *X* (the number of units) in the following equation:

$$\text{Total revenue} = \text{Variable cost} + \text{Fixed cost}$$

$$(\text{Selling price per unit})(X) = (\text{Variable cost per unit})(X) + \text{Fixed cost}$$

$$X = \frac{\text{Fixed cost}}{\text{Selling price per unit} - \text{Variable cost per unit}}$$

$$X = \frac{\text{Fixed cost}}{\text{Contribution margin per unit}}$$

- **Contribution margin** per unit is calculated as:

$$\text{Contribution margin per unit} = \text{Selling price per unit} - \text{Variable cost per unit}$$

- **Operating income** is income or profit *before* income taxes.

Unit Sales Needed to Achieve Targeted Profit

- In order to earn a desired profit, total revenues must equal variable costs, fixed costs *and* desired profit.

$$\text{Total revenue} = \text{Total variable cost} + \text{Total fixed cost} + \text{Desired profit}$$

- To determine how many units must be sold in order to earn a desired profit, solve for X (the number of units) in the following equation:

Total revenue = Total variable cost + Total fixed cost + Desired profit

(Selling price per unit)(X) = (Variable cost per unit)(X) + Total fixed cost + Desired profit

$$X = \frac{\text{Fixed cost} + \text{Desired profit}}{\text{Selling price per unit} - \text{Variable cost per unit}}$$

$$X = \frac{\text{Fixed cost} + \text{Desired profit}}{\text{Contribution margin per unit}}$$

- After fixed costs are covered, the contribution margin per unit above break-even volume is profit per unit.

After-Tax Profit Targets

- If a firm knows desired after-tax profit, desired before-tax profit can be calculated as follows:

Before-tax desired profit × (1 – Tax rate) = After-tax desired profit

$$\text{Before-tax desired profit} = \frac{\text{After-tax desired profit}}{1 - \text{Tax rate}}$$

- By substituting [(After-tax profit)/(1 – Tax rate)] for before-tax profit into the equation for CVP analysis, the equation becomes:

$$X = \frac{\text{Fixed cost} + [(\text{After-tax profit})/(1 - \text{Tax rate})]}{\text{Contribution margin per unit}}$$

BREAK-EVEN POINT IN SALES DOLLARS

- Instead of using units sold, managers might prefer to use sales revenue as the measure of sales activity.
- Break-even in units can be converted to break-even in sales revenue as follows:

Break-even sales = (Selling price per unit × Unit sales at break-even)

- Also, break-even in sales dollars can be calculated using the following equation:

$$\text{Break-even sales} = \frac{\text{Fixed cost}}{\text{Contribution margin ratio}}$$

- **The contribution margin ratio** is the proportion of each sales dollar available to cover fixed costs and provide for profit.
- The contribution margin ratio can be calculated in three different ways:

1. **Contribution margin ratio = Total contribution margin/Total revenue**
2. **Contribution margin ratio = Contribution margin per unit/Selling price per unit**
3. **Contribution margin ratio = 1 – Variable cost ratio**

- The **variable cost ratio** is the proportion of each sales dollar that must be used to cover variable costs.

Variable cost ratio = Variable cost/Sales revenue

Profit Targets and Sales Revenue

- Sales dollars necessary to earn a desired profit can be calculated as:

$$\textbf{Sales revenue} = \frac{\textbf{Fixed cost + Desired profit}}{\textbf{Contribution margin ratio}}$$

MULTIPLE-PRODUCT ANALYSIS

Break-Even Point in Units

Sales Mix and CVP Analysis

- When CVP analysis is used by firms that manufacture more than one product, the sales mix (the proportion in which the various products are expected to be sold) must be considered.
- When CVP analysis is used for a multiple-product firm, the product is defined as a package of products. For example, if the sales mix is 3:1 for Products A and B, the package would consist of 3 units of Product A and 1 unit of Product B.
- The contribution margin per package is calculated as:

(Contribution margin per unit of A × Sales mix for A)
+ (Contribution margin per unit of B × Sales mix for B)
= Package contribution margin

- Break-even in packages for a multiple-product firm is then calculated as:

$$\textbf{Break-even packages} = \frac{\textbf{Fixed cost}}{\textbf{Package contribution margin}}$$

Sales Dollars Approach

- Break-even in sales dollars for a multiple-product firm is calculated as:

$$\textbf{Break-even sales} = \frac{\textbf{Fixed cost}}{\textbf{Contribution margin ration}}$$

- The contribution margin ratio is calculated as:

Contribution margin ratio = Total contribution margin/Total sales

GRAPHICAL REPRESENTATION OF CVP RELATIONSHIPS

The Profit-Volume Graph

- The **profit-volume graph** portrays the relationship between profits and sales volume.
- The profit-volume graph is the graph of the operating income equation:

Operating income = (Price × Units) – (Unit variable cost × Units) – Fixed cost

The Cost-Volume-Profit Graph

❒ The **cost-volume-profit graph** depicts the relationships among cost, volume, and profits.

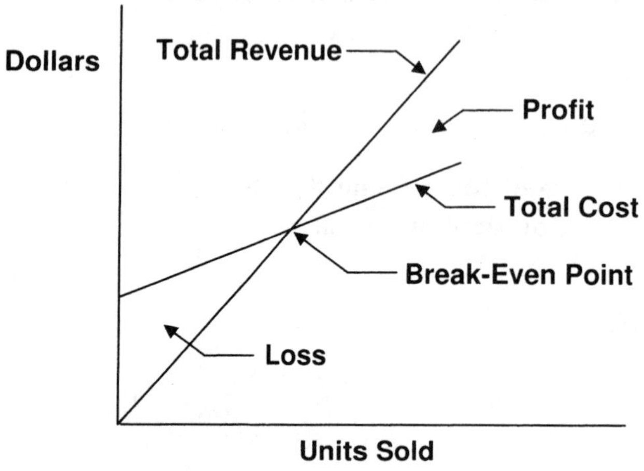

❒ The point where the total revenue line and the total cost line intersect is the break-even point.

Assumptions of Cost-Volume-Profit Analysis

❒ Limitations of CVP analysis include:

- The analysis assumes a linear revenue function and a linear cost function.
- The analysis assumes that price, total fixed costs, and unit variable costs can be accurately identified and remain constant over the relevant range.
- The analysis assumes that units produced are sold.
- For multiple-product analysis, the sales mix is assumed to be known.
- The selling prices and costs are assumed to be known with certainty.

CHANGES IN THE CVP VARIABLES

Introducing Risk and Uncertainty

Margin of Safety

❒ The **margin of safety** is a measure of how far sales can drop until the break-even point is reached.

❒ The margin of safety expressed in dollars is the difference between budgeted sales and break-even sales.

Margin of safety = Expected sales – Sales at break-even

❒ The margin of safety can be viewed as a crude measure of risk.

Operating Leverage

❒ **Operating leverage** is concerned with the mix of fixed costs and variable costs.

❒ For example, if a firm chooses to automate its operations, fixed costs increase, variable costs (direct labor) decrease, and operating leverage increases.

- The **degree of operating leverage (DOL)** is a measure of the sensitivity of profit changes to changes in sales volume. DOL measures the percentage of change in profit that results from a percentage of change in sales.

Degree of operating leverage = Contribution margin/Profit

- The higher the degree of operating leverage, the greater the change in profit when sales change.

Percentage change in profit = DOL × Percentage change in sales

Sensitivity Analysis and CVP

- **Sensitivity analysis** is a "what if" technique that examines the impact of changes on an answer. For example, computer spreadsheets are used to analyze changes in prices, variable costs, and fixed costs on expected profits.

CVP ANALYSIS AND ACTIVITY-BASED COSTING

- Conventional cost-volume-profit analysis assumes that costs can be classified as:
  1. variable costs—costs that vary, in total, with sales volume, and
  2. fixed costs—costs that do not vary, in total, with sales volume.
- There are many costs that do not vary with volume but vary with changes in other cost drivers.
- In an activity-based costing system, CVP analysis divides costs into:
  - unit-based costs
  - nonunit-based costs (batch-level and product-level costs)
  - fixed costs

CVP Analysis and JIT

- JIT manufacturing reduces volume-driven costs (variable costs) and increases fixed costs.
- Because cell workers are trained in different skills, many costs traditionally classified as variable, such as direct labor and maintenance, are viewed as fixed. When the cell workers are not involved in production of the product, the idle time may be used to do preventive maintenance on the production equipment. Thus, the cell workers' labor cost would not vary with production.
- With JIT manufacturing, the major variable cost remaining is direct materials.
- Under JIT, the number and magnitude of direct fixed costs increase.
- Batch-level costs are eliminated because with JIT the batch is one unit.

KEY TERMS TEST

Test your recall of the key terms as follows. Try to recall as many key terms as possible without assistance. If you need assistance, refer to the list of key terms at the end of this section.

1. The __________ __________ __________ is calculated as variable costs divided by sales revenue.
2. The __________ __________ __________ is a measure of how far sales can drop until break-even is reached.
3. The __________ __________ __________ is calculated as contribution margin divided by sales revenue.
4. The point where total sales revenue equals total costs is called the __________-__________ __________. It is the point of zero profits.
5. __________ __________ __________ __________ measures the percentage change in profits resulting from a percentage change in sales.
6. The relative combination of products (or services) sold by an organization is called __________ __________.
7. __________ __________ is achieved by increasing fixed costs while lowering variable costs.
8. A(n) __________-__________-__________ __________ depicts the relationships among costs, volume, and profits.
9. __________ __________ is sales revenue minus total variable cost.
10. __________ __________ is income or profit before taxes.
11. The __________ __________ is the range of volume for which the linear cost and revenue relationships are valid.
12. __________ __________ is a "what if" technique that examines the impact of changes in underlying assumptions on an answer.

KEY TERMS:

break-even point
contribution margin
contribution margin ratio
cost-volume-profit graph
degree of operating leverage
margin of safety
operating income
operating leverage
relevant range
sales mix
sensitivity analysis
variable cost ratio

→ **Compare your answers with those at the end of the chapter. Review any key terms missed.**

CHAPTER QUIZ

Write your answers in the spaces provided.

1. Cost-volume-profit analysis enables a firm to determine __________ necessary to attain a desired level of __________.

2. Variable-costing income is calculated as follows:

   Sales
   − Variable costs
   = ______________________________
   − ______________________________
   = Operating income

3. Break-even in units = ________________/____

4. Sales revenue at break-even = ________________/________________________________

5. Before-tax profit = ______________________/____________________

6. The margin of safety, a crude measure of risk, indicates how far sales can drop until break-even is reached. The margin of safety is calculated as follows:

   Margin of safety = ____________________ − ______________________________

7. Operating leverage magnifies increases in profit as sales increase and magnifies reductions in profit as sales decrease. The degree of operating leverage is calculated as follows:

   Degree of operating leverage = ____________________________/____________

8. The higher the degree of operating leverage, the greater the change in profit when sales change. The percentage change in profit is calculated as follows:

   Percentage change in profit = ________________________ × ________________________

Circle the single best answer.

9. Break-even is the point where: (a) revenue equals variable manufacturing costs; (b) revenue equals variable manufacturing and variable selling and administrative costs; (c) revenue equals variable and fixed manufacturing costs; (d) revenue equals all variable and fixed costs

10. The contribution margin ratio equals: (a) revenue minus variable costs; (b) variable costs divided by revenue; (c) contribution margin divided by revenue; (d) variable costs divided by contribution margin

11. Limitations of CVP analysis include all of the following except: (a) a nonlinear revenue function and a nonlinear cost function; (b) what is produced is sold; (c) selling prices and costs are known with certainty; (d) costs can be separated into fixed and variable components

Use the following information to answer Questions 12 through 17:

Selling price per unit	$100
Variable manufacturing costs per unit	$20
Fixed manufacturing costs per unit	$30
Variable selling costs per unit	$25
Fixed selling costs per unit	$10
Expected production and sales	1,000 units

12. Contribution margin per unit is: (a) $15; (b) $50; (c) $55; (d) $80

13. The contribution margin ratio is: (a) 15%; (b) 45%; (c) 50%; (d) 55%

14. Break-even for the product (rounded to the nearest whole unit) is: (a) 727 units; (b) 888 units; (c) 1,000 units; (d) 1,500 units

15. If the firm wants to earn $70,000 in before-tax profit, sales revenue must equal: (a) $60,500; (b) $110,000; (c) $200,000; (d) $244,444

16. If the firm wants to earn $70,000 in before-tax profit, contribution margin must equal: (a) $98,000; (b) $110,000; (c) $125,000; (d) $155,000

17. If the tax rate is 40 percent, how many units must be sold to earn an after-tax profit of $60,000? (a) 4,000 units; (b) 1,500 units; (c) 2,640 units; (d) 2,546 units

→ **Compare your answers with those at the end of the chapter. Review any questions missed.**

PRACTICE TEST

PROBLEM 1

AAH, Inc., manufactures a product that sells for $50. The variable costs per unit are:

Direct materials	$15
Direct labor	5
Variable manufacturing overhead	4

During 2004, the budgeted fixed manufacturing overhead is estimated to be $500,000, and budgeted fixed selling, general, and administrative costs are expected to be $300,000. Variable selling costs are $6 per unit.

Instructions:

1. Determine the break-even point in units.

2. Determine the number of units that must be sold to earn $100,000 in profit before taxes.

PROBLEM 1 *(Continued)*

3. What dollar amount of sales must be attained in order to earn $300,000 in profit before taxes?

4. If there is a 40% tax rate, determine the sales level in dollars that must be attained in order to generate an after-tax profit of $300,000.

PROBLEM 2

The Anton Company has developed the following income statement using a contribution margin format:

Anton Company
Projected Income Statement
For the Year Ending December 31, 2004

Revenues		$200,000
Less variable costs:		
Variable manufacturing	$60,000	
Variable selling	20,000	
Total variable costs		80,000
Contribution margin		$120,000
Less fixed costs:		
Fixed manufacturing	$80,000	
Fixed selling, general, and administrative	25,000	
Total fixed costs		105,000
Net income		$ 15,000

The projected income statement was based upon sales of 10,000 units. Anton has the capacity to produce 15,000 units during the year.

Instructions:

Each of the following questions is independent of the others.

1. Determine the break-even point in units.

PROBLEM 2 *(Continued)*

2. Calculate the margin of safety in dollars.

3. The sales manager believes the company could increase sales by 1,000 units if advertising expenditures are increased by $16,000. Should the company increase advertising expenditures?

PROBLEM 2 *(Continued)*

4. What is the maximum amount the company could pay for advertising if the advertising would increase sales by 1,000 units?

5. Management believes that by lowering the selling price to $17 per unit, the company can increase sales by 2,000 units. Based upon these estimates, would it be profitable for the company to lower its selling price?

PROBLEM 3

The Laurel Company produces two types of food processors. Information about the two product lines for 2004 is as follows:

	Regular	Deluxe
Selling price per unit	$75	$100
Variable costs per unit	50	50
Contribution margin per unit	$25	$ 50

The company expects fixed costs to be $150,000 in 2004. The firm expects 80% of its sales (in units) to be Regular model food processors.

Instructions:

1. Determine the break-even point in units.

2. Determine sales in units of Regular and Deluxe models necessary to generate a before-tax profit of $90,000.

PROBLEM 3 *(Continued)*

3. Determine sales in units of Regular and Deluxe models necessary to generate an after-tax profit of $90,000 if the tax rate is 40%.

PROBLEM 4

The Matt Company produces two models of garage door openers, Standard and Supreme.

The company expects to sell 900 units of the Standard model and 300 units of the Supreme model (a sales mix of 3:1).

A projected income statement for the firm as a whole for 2004 follows:

The Matt Company
Projected Income Statement
For the Year Ending December 31, 2004

Revenues	$300,000
Less: Variable costs	120,000
Contribution margin	$180,000
Less: Total fixed costs	60,000
Profit	$120,000

Instructions:

1. Determine the break-even point in sales dollars for 2004.

2. Determine sales revenue necessary to generate a before-tax profit of $150,000.

3. Determine sales revenue necessary to generate an after-tax profit of $210,000 if the tax rate is 30%.

PROBLEM 5

Using a conventional cost system, the cost formula for one of a company's products is as follows:

$$Y = \$37{,}000 + \$15X_1$$

where X_1 = units sold

Using an ABC system, the cost formula for the same product is as follows:

$$Y = \$20{,}000 + \$15X_1 + \$3{,}000X_2 + \$400X_3$$

where X_1 = units sold
X_2 = number of batches
X_3 = number of engineering change orders

The unit selling price is $40. The company plans to produce and sell 4,000 units. For up to 4,000 units, the company expects to produce 5 batches and use 5 engineering change orders.

Instructions:

1. Using the conventional cost system data, calculate the break-even point in units.

2. Using the ABC system data, calculate the break-even point in units.

3. Using the ABC system data, calculate profit if 4,000 units are produced and sold.

4. Based on revised estimates, the company now expects to sell 7,000 units, which would require the production of 7 batches and the use of 6 engineering change orders. Using the ABC system data, calculate profit if 7,000 units are sold.

ANSWERS

KEY TERMS TEST

1. variable cost ratio
2. margin of safety
3. contribution margin ratio
4. break-even point
5. Degree of operating leverage
6. sales mix
7. Operating leverage
8. cost-volume-profit graph
9. Contribution margin
10. Operating income
11. relevant range
12. Sensitivity analysis

CHAPTER QUIZ

1. sales, profit
2. Contribution margin, Fixed costs
3. Fixed costs, Contribution margin per unit
4. Fixed costs, Contribution margin ratio
5. After-tax profit, (1 – Tax rate)
6. Expected sales, Sales at break-even
7. Contribution margin, Profit
8. Degree of operating leverage (DOL), Percentage change in sales
9. d
10. c
11. a
12. c $100 – ($20 + $25) = $55
13. d $55/$100 = 55%
14. a ($30 + $10) × 1,000 units = $40,000; $40,000/$55 = 727 units
15. c ($40,000 + $70,000)/55% = $200,000
16. b ($30 × 1,000) +($10 × 1,000) + $70,000 = $110,000
17. d {$40,000 + [$60,000/(1 – .40)]}/$55 = 2,546 units

PRACTICE TEST

PROBLEM 1

1. $$\text{Break-even in units} = \frac{\text{Fixed cost}}{\text{Contribution margin per unit}} = \frac{\$800{,}000^{*}}{\$20^{**}} = 40{,}000 \text{ units}$$

*Total fixed costs:

Budgeted fixed manufacturing overhead		$500,000
Budgeted fixed selling, general, and administrative		300,000
Total fixed costs		$800,000

**Contribution margin per unit:

Selling price per unit		$50
Variable cost per unit:		
Direct materials	$15	
Direct labor	5	
Variable manufacturing overhead	4	
Variable selling costs	6	
Total variable cost per unit		30
Contribution margin per unit		$20

2. Unit sales necessary to earn $100,000 in before-tax profit:

$$\text{Units} = \frac{\text{Fixed cost} + \text{Desired profit}}{\text{Contribution margin per unit}} = \frac{\$800{,}000 + \$100{,}000}{\$20} = 45{,}000 \text{ units}$$

3. Sales dollars necessary to earn a before-tax profit of $300,000:

$$\text{Sales dollars} = \frac{\text{Fixed cost} + \text{Desired profit}}{\text{Contribution margin ratio}}$$

$$= \frac{\$800{,}000 + \$300{,}000}{0.4^*} = \$2{,}750{,}000$$

*Contribution margin ratio = $20/$50 = 0.4

4. Sales dollars necessary to earn an after-tax profit of $300,000:

$$\text{Sales dollars} = \frac{\text{Fixed cost} + [\text{After-tax profit} / (1 - \text{Tax rate})]}{\text{Contribution margin ratio}}$$

$$= \frac{\$800{,}000 + (\$300{,}000/.60)}{0.4}$$

$$= \frac{\$800{,}000 + \$500{,}000}{0.4} = \$3{,}250{,}000$$

PROBLEM 2

1. Break-even in units

$$\text{Break-even in units} = \frac{\text{Fixed cost}}{\text{Contribution margin per unit}}$$

$$= \frac{\$105{,}000}{\$12^*}$$

$$= 8{,}750 \text{ units}$$

*Contribution margin per unit:

Selling price per unit ($200,000/10,000)		$20
Variable cost per unit:		
Variable manufacturing costs ($60,000/10,000)	$6	
Variable selling costs ($20,000/10,000)	2	
Total variable cost per unit		8
Contribution margin per unit		$12

2. Margin of safety in dollars:

Margin of safety = Expected sales – Sales at break-even
= $200,000 – (8,750 units × $20)
= $200,000 – $175,000
= $25,000

Sales could decrease by $25,000 from the expected sales level before the company would reach break-even.

3. For this alternative to be profitable, the contribution margin from the additional sales of 1,000 units must at least cover the additional advertising expenditure.

Incremental contribution margin from 1,000 units ($12 × 1,000 units)	$12,000
Less: Incremental advertising expenditures	16,000
Decrease in income	$ (4,000)

A new income statement that considers the effect on sales and costs could be prepared to verify the effect on income.

Anton Company
Projected Income Statement
For the Year Ending December 31, 2004

Revenues (11,000 × $20)		$220,000
Less variable costs:		
Variable manufacturing (11,000 × $6)	$66,000	
Variable selling (11,000 × $2)	22,000	
Total variable costs		88,000
Contribution margin		$132,000
Less fixed costs:		
Fixed manufacturing	$80,000	
Fixed selling, general, and administrative ($25,000 + $16,000)	41,000	
Total fixed costs		121,000
Net income		$ 11,000

The Anton Company's income would decrease from $15,000 to $11,000 if the advertising expenditures were made.

4. The maximum amount the company could pay for additional advertising in order to sell 1,000 more units would be $12,000.

Additional contribution margin from 1,000 units	$12,000
Less: Additional advertising expenditures	12,000
Effect on income	$ –0–

The company also might want to consider the reliability of the estimates and the effect the advertising might have on sales in later periods.

5. A projected income statement based upon a $17 selling price and sales of 12,000 units follows:

Anton Company
Projected Income Statement
For the Year Ending December 31, 2004

Revenues (12,000 × $17)		$204,000
Less variable costs:		
Variable manufacturing (12,000 × $6)	$72,000	
Variable selling (12,000 × $2)	24,000	
Total variable costs		96,000
Contribution margin		$108,000
Less fixed costs:		
Fixed manufacturing	$80,000	
Fixed selling, general, and administrative	25,000	
Total fixed costs		105,000
Net income		$ 3,000

No, Anton Company should not lower the sales price because income drops from $15,000 to $3,000.

PROBLEM 3

1.

	Selling Price	–	Variable Cost	=	Contribution Margin	×	Mix		
Regular	$ 75	–	$50	=	$25	×	8	=	$200
Deluxe	100	–	50	=	50	×	2	=	100
Contribution margin per package									$300

$$\text{Break-even packages} = \frac{\text{Fixed cost}}{\text{Package contribution margin}}$$

$$= \frac{\$150{,}000}{\$300}$$

$$= 500 \text{ packages}$$

The 500 packages would be divided as follows:

Regular (500 packages × 8 units)	4,000 units
Deluxe (500 packages × 2 units)	1,000 units
Total	5,000 units

2. Unit sales necessary to generate a before-tax profit of $90,000:

$$\text{Sales packages} = \frac{\text{Fixed cost} + \text{Desired profit}}{\text{Package contribution margin}}$$

$$= \frac{\$150{,}000 + \$90{,}000}{\$300}$$

$$= 800 \text{ packages}$$

The 800 packages would be divided as follows:

Regular (800 packages × 8 units)	6,400 units
Deluxe (800 packages × 2 units)	1,600 units
Total	8,000 units

3. Unit sales necessary to generate an after-tax profit of $90,000:

$$\text{Sales packages} = \frac{\text{Fixed cost} + [\text{After-tax profit} / (1 - \text{Tax rate})]}{\text{Package contribution margin}}$$

$$= \frac{\$150,000 + (\$90,000/.60)}{\$300}$$

$$= 1,000 \text{ packages}$$

The 1,000 packages would be divided as follows:

Regular (1,000 packages × 8 units)	8,000 units
Deluxe (1,000 packages × 2 units)	2,000 units
Total	10,000 units

PROBLEM 4

1. Contribution margin ratio = $180,000/$300,000 = 0.6
Break-even sales = $60,000/0.6 = $100,000

2. ($60,000 + $150,000)/0.6 = $350,000

3. {$60,000 + [$210,000/(1 – .30)]}/0.6 = $600,000

PROBLEM 5

1. $X = F/(P - V)$
$= \$37,000/(\$40 - \$15)$
$= 1,480$ units

2. $X_1 = (F + V_2X_2 + V_3X_3)/(P - V_1)$
= [$20,000 + ($3,000 × 5) + ($400 × 5)]/$25
= ($20,000 + $15,000 + $2,000)/$25
= $37,000/$25
= 1,480 units

3.

Revenues (4,000 × $40)	$160,000
Variable costs (4,000 × $15)	60,000
Contribution margin	$100,000
Nonunit-based costs:	
($3,000 × 5 batches)	(15,000)
($400 × 5 engineering change orders)	(2,000)
Fixed costs	(20,000)
Net income	$ 63,000

4.

Revenues (7,000 × $40)	$280,000
Variable costs (7,000 × $15)	105,000
Contribution margin	$175,000
Nonunit-based costs:	
($3,000 × 7 batches)	(21,000)
($400 × 6 engineering change orders)	(2,400)
Fixed costs	(20,000)
Net income	$131,600

CHAPTER 17
Tactical Decision Making

CHAPTER REVIEW

TACTICAL DECISION MAKING

- **Tactical decision making** involves choosing among alternatives and tends to be short-run in nature with an immediate end in view.
- **Strategic decision making** involves selecting among alternative strategies so a long-term competitive advantage is achieved.
- Sound tactical decision making results in decisions that achieve an immediate objective *and* serve the overall strategic goals of the organization.

Model for Making Tactical Decisions

- The six steps in the decision making process are as follows:
  1. Define the problem.
  2. Identify alternatives as possible solutions to the problem; eliminate alternatives that are not feasible.
  3. Identify the relevant costs and benefits associated with each feasible alternative; eliminate irrelevant costs and benefits from consideration.
  4. Total the relevant costs and benefits for each alternative.
  5. Assess qualitative factors.
  6. Select the alternative with the greatest overall benefit.

Relevant Costs Defined

- **Relevant costs:**
  - are future costs, and
  - differ among the alternatives.
- An irrelevant cost can be:
  - a past cost, or
  - a future cost that does not differ among the alternatives being considered.
- A **sunk cost** is a cost for which the outlay has already been made. Sunk costs are the result of past decisions and cannot be changed by current or future action. After sunk costs are incurred, they are unavoidable.
- Since sunk costs are past costs that do not differ among the alternatives, sunk costs are irrelevant costs.
- The acquisition cost of equipment purchased in the past is a sunk cost.

- Depreciation of equipment acquired in the past is an allocation of a past cost; therefore, depreciation of equipment already purchased is irrelevant.
- Allocations of common fixed costs are irrelevant if *total* common fixed costs do not differ among the alternatives.

Ethics in Tactical Decision Making

- In tactical decision making, ethical concerns relate to the way in which decisions are implemented and the possible sacrifice of long-run objectives for short-run gain.
- Objectives should be attained within an ethical framework and be consistent with the company's missions and goals.

RELEVANCY, COST BEHAVIOR, AND THE ACTIVITY RESOURCE USAGE MODEL

- The activity resource usage model includes:
  - flexible resources (resources acquired as used and needed)
  - committed resources (resources acquired in advance of usage)

Flexible Resources

- Flexible resources can be easily purchased in the amount needed and at the time of use. For example, electricity to operate production equipment is acquired as needed at the time of use.
- Flexible resource costs are typically referred to as variable costs.
- If the demand for an activity changes across alternatives, then resource spending will change and the cost of the activity is relevant to the decision.
- The amount of resource demanded by the firm equals the amount of resource supplied.

Committed Resources

- Committed resources are purchased before they are used; therefore, there may be unused capacity.
- Two types of committed resources are:
  1. those that can be altered in the short run, and
  2. those that provide capacity for multiple periods.

Committed Resources for the Short Run

- Some committed resources are acquired in advance of usage through implicit contracting, such as with salaried and hourly employees. These resources are usually acquired in lumpy amounts, such as step-variable or step-fixed costs.
- If there is unused capacity available, an increase in demand for an activity across alternatives may not mean that the activity cost will increase.
- A change in resource spending can occur in one of two ways:
  1. The demand for the resource exceeds the supply (increasing resource spending).
  2. The demand for the resource drops permanently and supply exceeds demand enough so that activity capacity can be reduced (decreasing resource spending).

Committed Resources for Multiple Periods

- Often resources are acquired in advance for multiple periods before the resource demands are known. Leasing or buying a building is an example.
- Decisions involving multiperiod capabilities are called *capital investment decisions* and are discussed in Chapter 18.
- Changes in activity demands across alternatives rarely affect resource spending and are therefore not usually relevant for tactical decision making.

ILLUSTRATIVE EXAMPLES OF RELEVANT COST APPLICATIONS

Make-or-Buy Decisions

- A **make-or-buy decision** involves deciding whether to manufacture a product or component or buy it from another firm.
- The relevant costs of a make-or-buy analysis consist of the following avoidable costs:
  - variable costs associated with producing the product: direct materials, direct labor, and variable overhead
  - avoidable fixed overhead
- The relevant (avoidable) costs of manufacturing the product are then compared to the outside supplier's price. The firm cannot afford to pay more to an outside supplier than it saves (avoids) by not manufacturing the component.
- If the firm buys the component from an outside supplier, other uses of the manufacturing facilities may be possible, such as producing a different product.
- If the firm continues to produce the original component instead of buying it from an outside supplier, there is an opportunity cost associated with this choice: the firm foregoes the opportunity to produce a new product. The cost of foregoing this opportunity is the contribution margin lost by not producing the new product.
- If the firm can eliminate machinery and equipment as a result of buying a component from a supplier, there is an opportunity cost involved. If the firm continues to manufacture the component, the firm foregoes the opportunity to sell the machinery and equipment, invest the proceeds, and earn a return.
- If the alternative of making a component requires the acquisition of machinery and equipment, then it is a long-run investment decision rather than a short-run decision.

Qualitative Factors

- Qualitative factors are factors that cannot be quantified.
- Qualitative factors that should be considered are:
  - How does the quality of the supplier's component compare to the quality of the component manufactured by the firm?
  - Is the supplier reliable in terms of providing the needed quantities of the component on a timely basis?

Keep-or-Drop Decisions

- **Keep-or-drop decisions** concern whether to discontinue segments of an organization, such as the shoe department in a clothing store. Segments can be a product line or a territory.

- The analysis of dropping a segment relies upon the concept of relevant or avoidable costs.
- Based solely on quantitative factors, the segment should be kept if it contributes incremental profit.
- Incremental profit is determined by comparing the segment's revenues with avoidable costs associated with the segment.
- The loss in sales of other segments as a result of closing down a complementary segment should also be considered.

Keep-or-Drop Decisions with Alternative Use of Facilities

- If the space and resources used by the current segment could be used by another segment, an opportunity cost is involved.
- If the firm keeps the current segment, it foregoes the incremental profit generated by the other segment.
- If the incremental profit generated by the other segment exceeds the incremental profit generated by the current segment, then the current segment should be dropped (assuming all other factors are equal).

Special-Order Decisions

- A **special-order decision** focuses on whether a specially priced order should be accepted. Generally, the product is the same or similar to the firm's regular products.
- If there is excess capacity, the minimum acceptable price must cover the incremental costs associated with the special order:
  - variable costs
    - direct materials
    - direct labor
    - variable overhead
  - incremental fixed costs (out-of-pocket costs)
- If the firm is operating at full capacity, no additional production can occur without eliminating something that is currently being produced. Thus, if the firm accepts the special order, it foregoes the opportunity to produce and sell some of its regular products.
- When the firm is at full capacity, the minimum acceptable special order price must cover the following:
  - variable costs
  - incremental fixed costs
  - contribution margin foregone on the regular units not produced
- A firm may not want to produce a special order that is in direct competition with its regular products.

Decisions to Sell or Process Further

- **Joint products** have common processes and costs of production up to a split-off point. The **split-off point** is the point of separation where the products become distinguishable.
- Joint product decisions concern whether the product should be sold at split-off or processed further.

- Any joint costs that have been allocated to a joint product are sunk and irrelevant for decision making.
- In general, the product should be processed further if incremental revenues from further processing exceed the incremental costs of further processing.
- The relevant costs to be compared are:
  - the market value of the product at split-off, and
  - the revenues resulting from further processing minus the incremental costs of further processing.

PRODUCT MIX DECISIONS

- In some cases product resources, such as materials, labor, or equipment, may be limited.
- **Constraints** are limitations due to limited resources or limited product demand. A manager must choose the optimal mix given the firm's constraints.

One Constrained Resource

- When there is one scarce resource, determine which product results in the *highest contribution margin per unit of the scarce resource.*
- For example, if the scarce resource is machine hours, for each product calculate the contribution margin per machine hour as follows:

$$\text{Contribution margin per machine hour} = \frac{\text{Contribution margin per unit of product}}{\text{Machine time required per unit}}$$

- The quantity needed of the product with the highest contribution margin per machine hour should be produced before producing the other products.

Multiple Constrained Resources

- When more than one resource is limited, *linear programming* can be used to determine the optimal solution.

PRICING

- Cost-based pricing uses a **markup**, or percentage applied to the base price, to determine the selling price.
- **Target costing** determines the cost of a product or service based on the price (target price) that customers are willing to pay. The marketing department determines what characteristics and price for the product are acceptable to customers, then engineers design and develop the product so that cost and profit can be covered by that price.
- **Predatory pricing** is the practice of setting prices below cost, attempting to injure competitors and eliminate competition. **Dumping** is predatory pricing on the international market.
- **Price discrimination** refers to charging different prices to different customers for essentially the same product. The Robinson-Patman Act regulates price discrimination for manufacturers and wholesalers.
- **Price gouging** refers to the practice of setting an "excessively high price" by firms with market power.

APPENDIX: LINEAR PROGRAMMING

- **Linear programming** is a method that searches among possible solutions until it finds the optimal solution.
- In linear programming, the relationship between the variables must be linear; that is, the relationship can be represented by a straight line.
- Linear programming problems can be solved using:
  - the graphical approach
  - the simplex method
- There are four basic steps in the solution of a linear programming problem:
  1. Determine the **objective function**.
  2. Identify and express the constraints in equation form.
  3. Determine the feasible alternatives considering the constraints.
  4. Determine which alternative results in the optimal solution to the objective function. The **optimal solution** is the one that maximizes total contribution margin.
- The graphical approach can be used as long as only two products are involved.
- The four steps in the graphical approach are:
  1. Graph each constraint.
  2. Identify the **feasible set of solutions**.
  3. Identify all corner-point values in the feasible set.
  4. Select the corner point that yields the largest value for the objective function.
- The **simplex method** is a mathematical technique that is useful when a large number of variables and constraints are present in a linear programming problem. Computer programs are available to solve such linear programming problems.

KEY TERMS TEST

Test your recall of the key terms as follows. Try to recall as many key terms as possible without assistance. If you need assistance, refer to the list of key terms at the end of this section.

1. Relevant costing analysis that focuses on whether a component should be made internally or purchased externally is a(n) _______-_____-_______ ___________.
2. Relevant costing analysis that focuses on whether a product should be processed beyond the split-off point is a decision to _______ _____ ___________ ___________.
3. The _______-_____ ________ is the point where products become distinguishable after passing through a common process.
4. A relevant costing analysis that focuses on keeping or dropping a segment of a business is a(n) _______-_____-_______ ___________.
5. ____________ ________ are future costs that differ among alternatives.
6. A(n) _________ ________ is a cost for which the outlay has already been made and that cannot be affected by a future decision.
7. Relevant costing analysis that focuses on whether a specially priced order should be accepted or rejected is a(n) _________-_______ ___________.
8. ___________ ___________ ___________ involves choosing among alternatives with an immediate or limited end in view.
9. ___________ ___________ ___________ involves selecting strategies that yield a long-term competitive advantage.
10. _________ __________ is a method of determining the cost of a product or service based on the price (target price) that customers are willing to pay.
11. ___________ is the percentage applied to a base cost and includes desired profit and any costs not included in the base cost.
12. ____________ __________ is the practice of setting prices below cost for the purpose of injuring competitors and eliminating competition.
13. ___________ is predatory pricing in the international market.
14. ________ _________________ refers to the practice of setting an "excessively" high price.
15. ________ _________________ is charging different prices to different customers for essentially the same product.

KEY TERMS:

dumping
keep-or-drop decision
make-or-buy decision
markup
predatory pricing
price discrimination
price gouging
relevant costs
sell or process further
special-order decision
split-off point
strategic decision making
sunk cost
tactical decision making
target costing

→ **Compare your answers with those at the end of the chapter. Review any key terms missed.**

CHAPTER QUIZ

Write your answers in the spaces provided.

1. ________________ ________ are the result of past decisions and cannot be changed by current or future actions.
2. ________________ ________ is the sacrifice that results from pursuing one alternative and foregoing another alternative.
3. For a cost or revenue to be relevant to a particular decision, it must
   1. ____, and
   2. ____.
4. Avoidable costs in a make-or-buy decision consist of two types of costs:
   1. ____
   2. ____
5. List two qualitative factors that should be considered when evaluating a make-or-buy decision:
   1. ____
      ____
   2. ____
      ____
6. When deciding whether to keep or drop a segment, if the decision is based solely on quantitative factors, the segment should be kept if it contributes ________________ ________.
7. When there is a scarce resource, the product with the highest contribution margin per ________ ________________ should be produced first.
8. List two sunk costs:
   1. ____
   2. ____
9. If there is excess capacity, the minimum acceptable price for a special order must cover:
   1. ____
   2. ____
10. If the firm is at full capacity, the minimum acceptable price for a special order must cover:
    1. ____
    2. ____
    3. ____
11. In general when considering a sell-or-process-further decision, the product should be processed further if ____
    ____.
12. Linear programming problems can be solved using:
    1. ________________________, and
    2. ________________________.

Circle the single best answer.

Use the following information to answer Questions 13 through 15:

Liza Company produces a product with the following unit cost:

Direct materials	$ 2.75
Direct labor	1.25
Variable overhead	4.00
Fixed overhead	2.50
Unit cost	$10.50

Fixed selling costs are $600,000 per year, and variable selling costs are $1.50 per unit sold.

Production capacity is 500,000 units per year. However, the company expects to produce only 300,000 units next year. The product normally sells for $15 each. A customer has offered to buy 150,000 units for $10 each. The units would be sold in an area outside the market area currently served.

13. The incremental cost per unit associated with the special order is: (a) $8.00; (b) $9.25; (c) $9.50; (d) $10.00

14. Total incremental cost associated with the special order is: (a) $1,237,500; (b) $1,342,000; (c) $1,387,500; (d) $1,425,000

15. If the firm produces the special order, the effect on income would be a: (a) $75,000 increase; (b) $90,000 increase; (c) $2,500 decrease; (d) $12,500 decrease

→ **Compare your answers with those at the end of the chapter. Review any questions missed.**

PRACTICE TEST

PROBLEM 1

The management of Garvin Industries is evaluating whether the company should continue manufacturing a component or buy it from an outside supplier. Based upon its accounting records, it appears that it costs the company $80 per unit to make the component. The $80 cost per component was determined as follows:

Direct materials	$16
Direct labor	30
Variable manufacturing overhead	12
Fixed manufacturing overhead	22
Unit cost	$80

Garvin Industries uses 10,000 components per year. After Stinson, Inc., submitted a bid of $70 per component, some members of management felt they could reduce costs by buying from outside and discontinuing production of the component.

If the component is obtained from Stinson, Inc., $5 of fixed manufacturing overhead per unit would be avoided and Garvin's unused production facilities could be leased to another company for $30,000 per year.

PROBLEM 1 *(Continued)*

Instructions:

1. Based upon relevant cost differences, should Garvin Industries make or buy the component? Include your supporting calculations.

   Supporting calculations:

2. Prepare a memorandum to Garvin management with your recommendation.

MEMORANDUM

DATE:

TO: Garvin Industries Management

FROM:

SUBJECT:

PROBLEM 2

The Critchfield Company has annual productive capacity of 60,000 units per year. Budgeted operating results for 2004 are as follows:

Revenues (50,000 units @ $10)		$500,000
Variable costs:		
Manufacturing (50,000 @ $3.20)	$160,000	
Selling (50,000 @ $0.80)	40,000	200,000
Contribution margin		$300,000
Fixed costs:		
Manufacturing	$100,000	
Selling and administrative	80,000	180,000
Operating income		$120,000

A wholesaler from another country wants to buy 5,000 units at a price of $8 per unit. All fixed costs would remain within the relevant range. Variable manufacturing costs would be the same per unit, but variable selling costs would increase by $2 per unit on the special order only.

Instructions:

1. Determine whether the company should produce the special order.

2. Assuming Critchfield's objective is to maximize profit, if the customer wants a special order of 20,000 units, should Critchfield accept or reject the special order?

PROBLEM 3

The Ahler Company manufactures three joint products: X, Y, and Z.

The cost of the joint process is $100,000.

Information about the three products follows:

Product	Anticipated Production	Selling Price per Pound at Split-Off	Additional Processing Costs per Pound after Split-Off (All Variable)	Selling Price per Pound after Further Processing	Allocated Joint Costs
X	10,000 lbs.	$10	$2	$20	$24,000
Y	30,000 lbs.	5	6	10	36,000
Z	20,000 lbs.	8	4	16	40,000

Instructions:

Determine whether each product should be sold at split-off or processed further.

PROBLEM 4

The operations of the Schmollinger Corporation are divided into the Perry Division and the Nicholas Division.

Projections for the next year are as follows:

	Perry Division	Nicholas Division	Total
Sales	$250,000	$100,000	$350,000
Variable costs	80,000	40,000	120,000
Contribution margin	$170,000	$ 60,000	$230,000
Direct fixed costs	60,000	40,000	100,000
Segment margin	$110,000	$ 20,000	$130,000
Allocated common costs	70,000	30,000	100,000
Operating income (loss)	$ 40,000	$ (10,000)	$ 30,000

Instructions:

1. Determine operating income for the Schmollinger Corporation as a whole if the Nicholas Division were dropped.

2. Should the Nicholas Division be eliminated?

PROBLEM 5

The Royer Company manufactures two products, 12-07 and 19-01. Contribution margin per unit is determined as follows:

	12-07	19-01
Revenue	$25	$20
Variable costs	15	12
Contribution margin	$10	$ 8

Total demand for Product 12-07 is 5,000 units, and for Product 19-01 it is 10,000 units.

Direct labor is a scarce resource. During the year, 40,000 direct labor hours are available. Product 12-07 requires 5 direct labor hours per unit, while Product 19-01 requires 2 direct labor hours per unit.

Instructions:

How many units of Product 12-07 and Product 19-01 should the Royer Company produce?

PROBLEM 6

Nance Manufacturing has idle capacity. A customer has offered to purchase 1,000 units of one of Nance's products for $5 each. The product normally sells for $7.50. The customer is located in a state not previously serviced by Nance Manufacturing. The activity-based accounting system provided the following information:

	Cost Driver	Unused Capacity	Quantity Demanded*	Activity Rate Fixed	Activity Rate Variable
Direct materials	Units	0	1,000		$1.50
Direct labor	Direct labor hours	0	200		3.50
Setups	Setup hours	10	20	$25.00	4.00
Machining	Machining hours	3,000	2,000	2.00	0.50

*This only represents the amount of resources demanded by the special order being considered.

Any expansion of the setup resource must be acquired in lumpy amounts. Each "lumpy" amount provides an additional 50 hours of setup servicing and is priced at the fixed activity rate.

Instructions:

1. Compute the change in income for Nance Manufacturing if the order is accepted.

2. If the setup activity had 30 hours of unused capacity, how would this affect the analysis?

PROBLEM 6 *(Continued)*

3. Prepare a memorandum to management stating your recommendation regarding whether the order should be accepted or rejected. Include a discussion of the strategic issues affecting the decision.

MEMORANDUM

DATE:

TO:

FROM:

SUBJECT:

PROBLEM 7 (Appendix)

Hediger, Inc., manufactures two products, X and Y. Information for the two products is as follows:

	Product X	Product Y
Selling price per unit	$50	$30
Variable cost per unit	$30	$15
Direct labor hours per unit.....................	2	4
Machine hours per unit.........................	10	5

During each month, 1,000 direct labor hours and 2,000 machine hours are available.

Instructions:

1. Formulate the linear programming objective function and constraint equations.

2. Using the graphical approach, determine the optimal solution.

ANSWERS

KEY TERMS TEST

1. make-or-buy decision
2. sell or process further
3. split-off point
4. keep-or-drop decision
5. Relevant costs
6. sunk cost
7. special-order decision
8. Tactical decision making
9. Strategic decision making
10. Target costing
11. Markup
12. Predatory pricing
13. Dumping
14. Price gouging
15. Price discrimination

CHAPTER QUIZ

1. Sunk costs
2. Opportunity cost
3. 1. differ between the alternatives being considered
   2. be a future cost
4. 1. the variable costs associated with producing the product: direct materials, direct labor, and variable overhead
   2. avoidable fixed overhead
5. 1. How does the quality of the supplier's component compare to the quality of the component manufactured by the firm?
   2. Is the supplier reliable in terms of providing the needed quantities of the component on a timely basis?
6. incremental profit
7. unit of scarce resource
8. 1. acquisition cost of equipment purchased in the past
   2. depreciation of equipment purchased in the past
9. 1. variable costs
   2. incremental fixed costs
10. 1. variable costs
    2. incremental fixed costs
    3. contribution margin foregone on the regular units not produced
11. the incremental revenues from further processing exceed the incremental costs of further processing
12. 1. the graphical approach
    2. the simplex method
13. c ($2.75 + $1.25 + $4.00 + $1.50) = $9.50
14. d ($9.50 × 150,000) = $1,425,000
15. a ($10.00 – $9.50) × 150,000 = $75,000 increase

PRACTICE TEST

PROBLEM 1

1.

	Buy	Make
Outside supplier's price (10,000 × $70)	$(700,000)	
Direct materials (10,000 × $16)		$(160,000)
Direct labor (10,000 × $30)		(300,000)
Variable manufacturing overhead (10,000 × $12)		(120,000)
Fixed manufacturing overhead:		
(10,000 × $22)		(220,000)
(10,000 × $17)	(170,000)	
Rental revenue	30,000	
Totals	$(840,000)	$(800,000)

There is a $40,000 difference in favor of manufacturing the component rather than buying it from the outside supplier.

The make-or-buy alternatives could also be analyzed as follows:

	Buy	Make
Outside supplier's price	$(700,000)	
Direct materials		$(160,000)
Direct labor		(300,000)
Variable manufacturing overhead		(120,000)
Avoidable fixed manufacturing overhead (10,000 × $5)		(50,000)
Rental revenue	30,000	
Totals	$(670,000)	$(630,000)

Notice that instead of including total fixed manufacturing overhead under each alternative, only the avoidable manufacturing overhead is included under the alternative of making the component. The difference in income is still $40,000 in favor of manufacturing the component.

2.

MEMORANDUM

DATE: *(insert current date here)*
TO: Garvin Industries Management
FROM: Management Consulting, Inc.
SUBJECT: Make-or-Buy Decision

This memo regards whether Garvin Industries should continue manufacturing one of its components or buy the component from an outside supplier.

Based on the attached calculations, I recommend that Garvin Industries continue manufacturing the component. There is a $40,000 difference in favor of manufacturing the component rather than buying it from an outside supplier. The net total cost of buying the component is $840,000. Fixed manufacturing overhead of $170,000 will be incurred even if the component is purchased. The net total cost of manufacturing the component is $800,000. Therefore, there is a cost difference of $40,000 in favor of manufacturing the component.

In addition, if we manufacture the component, we have control over the production scheduling and availability of the component. Another qualitative factor to consider is quality. Again, if the component is manufactured, we have control over the quality of the component produced.

If you have any questions concerning the analysis, please contact me at Extension 2531.

PROBLEM 2

1.

Incremental revenue (5,000 × $8)	$40,000
Incremental costs:	
Variable manufacturing (5,000 × $3.20)	(16,000)
Variable selling [5,000 × ($0.80 + $2.00)]	(14,000)
Incremental contribution margin	$10,000

Since the company would still be operating within the relevant range, fixed costs would remain the same.

If the company produces the special order, contribution margin and operating income would increase by $10,000.

2.

	Without Special Order	With Special Order
Revenues:		
(50,000 × $10)	$500,000	
(40,000 × $10)		$400,000
(20,000 × $8)		160,000
Less variable costs:		
Manufacturing:		
(50,000 × $3.20)	(160,000)	
(60,000 × $3.20)		(192,000)
Selling:		
(50,000 × $0.80)	(40,000)	
(40,000 × $0.80)		(32,000)
(20,000 × $2.80)		(56,000)
Contribution margin	$300,000	$280,000
Less fixed costs:		
Manufacturing	(100,000)	(100,000)
Selling and administrative	(80,000)	(80,000)
Operating income	$120,000	$100,000

If Critchfield accepts the 20,000 unit special order, it would have to forego 10,000 units in regular sales because of capacity constraints. This would result in a $20,000 decrease in contribution margin and operating income. Critchfield should reject the special order.

PROBLEM 3

Product	Sell at Split-Off	Process Further, Then Sell	Decision
X	$100,000	$200,000	
		(20,000)	Process Further
		$180,000	
Y	$150,000	$300,000	
		(180,000)	Sell at Split-Off
		$120,000	
Z	$160,000	$320,000	
		(80,000)	Process Further
		$240,000	

Notice that since the joint costs are incurred regardless of which action is taken, the joint costs are not relevant to the decision.

PROBLEM 4

1. If the Nicholas Division were dropped, the company's operating income would drop from $30,000 to $10,000.

Sales	$250,000
Less: Variable costs	80,000
Contribution margin	$170,000
Less: Direct fixed costs	60,000
Segment margin	$110,000
Less: Allocated common costs ($70,000 + $30,000)	100,000
Operating income (loss)	$ 10,000

The $30,000 of common costs allocated to the Nicholas Division will be incurred even if the Nicholas Division is dropped.

2. The Nicholas Division should not be dropped since it contributes $20,000 toward covering common corporate costs.

PROBLEM 5

Since direct labor hours are limited, the company should first produce the product that has the highest contribution margin per direct labor hour.

	12-07	19-01
Contribution margin per unit	$10	$8
Divided by:		
Direct labor hours required per unit	5	2
Contribution margin per direct labor hour	$ 2	$4

To maximize contribution margin, the Royer Company should produce 10,000 units of 19-01 and 4,000 units of 12-07.

Product	Units	DLH per Unit	DLH
19-01	10,000	2	20,000
12-07	4,000	5	20,000
Totals	14,000		40,000

PROBLEM 6

1. The relevant costs are those that change if the order is accepted. These costs would consist of the variable activity costs (resources acquired as needed) plus any cost of acquiring additional activity capacity (resources acquired in advance of usage). Income will change by the following amount:

Revenue ($5 × 1,000 units)	$5,000
Less increase in resource spending:	
Direct materials ($1.50 × 1,000 units)	(1,500)
Direct labor ($3.50 × 200 direct labor hours)	(700)
Setups [($25 × 50 hours) + ($4 × 20 hours)]	(1,330)
Machining ($0.50 × 2,000 machine hours)	(1,000)
Increase in income	$ 470

2. If 30 additional hours of excess setup capacity exists, then no additional resource spending for additional capacity would be required. Thus, the profitability of the special order would be increased by $1,250 ($25 × 50 hours—the increase in resource spending that would have been required). Total income would increase by $1,720 instead of only $470 if the order is accepted.

3. Your memorandum should contain discussion similar to the following:

   The special order would increase income by $470, but it requires expansion of the setup activity capacity. If a long-term expansion is required, the special order should be rejected. Even if the expansion is short-run in nature, it is questionable whether the firm should undertake the special order.

   If the expansion is a long-term commitment, the company would be exchanging a one-year benefit of $470 for an annual commitment of $1,250 (the cost of the expansion of setup activity capacity). Thus, the special order should be rejected if the expansion is a long-term commitment.

   Even if the expansion is short-run in nature, is it worth $470 in additional profits? Strategic factors that affect this decision include:

   - Will the special order affect any regular sales?
   - Is there the possibility the customer might resell the merchandise to regular customers at the regular sales price, thus reducing Nance's regular sales?
   - Will any regular customers learn of the price reduction and expect the same special price?
   - Is this an opportunity for Nance "to get its foot in the door" in a new sales territory? Can Nance build on this business in the future?
   - Is Nance searching for a permanent solution to its idle capacity?
   - Is it attempting to reduce unused capacity or find additional regular sales to make use of the unused capacity?

PROBLEM 7 (APPENDIX)

1. Contribution margin per unit:

	X	Y
Selling price	$50	$30
Less: Variable costs	30	15
Contribution margin per unit	$20	$15

Objective function: Maximize contribution margin: $\$20X + \$15Y$

Constraints:

Labor hour constraint: $2X + 4Y \leq 1{,}000$ hours

Machine hour constraint: $10X + 5Y \leq 2{,}000$ hours

Nonnegativity constraints: $X \geq 0$, $Y \geq 0$

2. **a.** Graph the labor hour constraint as follows:

Determine the value of Product Y if none of Product X is produced:

$$(2)(0) + 4Y = 1{,}000$$
$$4Y = 1{,}000$$
$$Y = 250$$
$$(X = 0,\ Y = 250)$$

Determine the value of Product X if none of Product Y is produced:

$$2X + (4)(0) = 1{,}000$$
$$2X = 1{,}000$$
$$X = 500$$
$$(X = 500,\ Y = 0)$$

Locate these two points on the graph: $(X = 0,\ Y = 250)$ $(X = 500,\ Y = 0)$

Draw a line on the graph connecting these two points.

b. Graph the machine hour constraint as follows:

Determine the value of Product Y if none of Product X is produced:

$$(10)(0) + 5Y = 2{,}000$$
$$5Y = 2{,}000$$
$$Y = 400$$
$$(X = 0,\ Y = 400)$$

Determine the value of Product X if none of Product Y is produced:

$$10X + (5)(0) = 2{,}000$$
$$10X = 2{,}000$$
$$X = 200$$
$$(X = 200,\ Y = 0)$$

Locate these two points on the graph: $(X = 0,\ Y = 400)$
$(X = 200,\ Y = 0)$

Draw a line on the graph connecting these two points.

Graph:

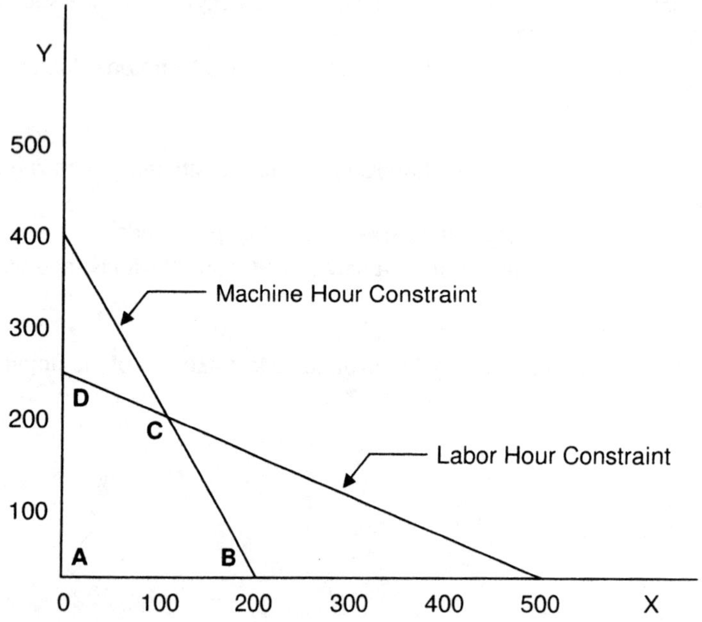

c. Compute the value of each corner point as follows:

Corner Point	***X*-Value**	***Y*-Value**	**$Z = \$20X + \$15Y$**
A	0	0	0
B	200	0	4,000
C	100	200	5,000*
D	0	250	3,750

*The optimal solution calls for producing and selling 100 units of Product X and 200 units of Product Y, resulting in a contribution margin of $5,000.

CHAPTER 18

Capital Investment Decisions

CHAPTER REVIEW

TYPES OF CAPITAL INVESTMENT DECISIONS

- **Capital investment decisions** involve planning, setting goals and priorities, arranging financing, and identifying criteria for making long-term investments.
- **Capital budgeting** is the process of determining which long-term capital assets to acquire.
- There are two types of capital investment projects:
  - **independent projects** that do not affect the cash flows of other projects
  - **mutually exclusive projects** that, if accepted, preclude the acceptance of all other competing projects

NONDISCOUNTING MODELS

- Capital budgeting decision models can be classified as:
  - nondiscounting models, or
  - discounting models.
- **Nondiscounting models** do *not* consider the time value of money. Two nondiscounting cash flow models are:
  - payback period
  - accounting rate of return (ARR)
- **Discounting models** consider the time value of money. Two discounting cash flow models are:
  - net present value (NPV)
  - internal rate of return (IRR)

Payback Period

- The **payback period** is the time required for a firm to recover its original investment.
- When the cash flows of a project are the same amount each period, payback is calculated as follows:

Payback period = Original investment/Annual cash flow

- If the cash flows are not the same amount each period, payback is calculated by adding the annual cash flows until the original investment is recovered.
- Firms may set a maximum payback period for all projects and reject projects that exceed the maximum payback period allowed.

❐ Reasons why the payback period may be used to screen projects are as follows:

- The payback period may be used as a rough measure of risk. (The longer the payback period, the riskier the project may be.)
- Firms with liquidity problems may want to select projects with quick paybacks.
- Firms in industries where the risk of obsolescence is high may want to recover invested funds rapidly.
- If a division manager's performance is based on short-run measures, such as net income, the manager may select projects with short paybacks in order to affect net income as quickly as possible.

❐ Two weaknesses of the payback period method are as follows:

- Payback ignores the time value of money.
- Payback ignores the profitability of investments beyond the payback period.

❐ Although payback should not be used as the sole evaluator for project selection, it may be used in conjunction with discounted cash flow methods that consider the time value of money.

Accounting Rate of Return

❐ The **accounting rate of return** measures a project's return in terms of accounting *income* instead of cash flows. Income differs from cash flows because of accruals and deferrals.

❐ The accounting rate of return is calculated as follows:

$$\textbf{Accounting rate of return} = \frac{\textbf{Average income}}{\textbf{Investment}}$$

$$\textbf{Accounting rate of return} = \frac{\textbf{Average annual net cash inflows} - \textbf{Average annual depreciation}}{\textbf{Investment}^{*}}$$

*Either original investment or average investment can be used. Average investment is calculated as follows:

$$\textbf{Average investment} = \frac{\textbf{(Original investment + Salvage value)}}{\textbf{2}}$$

❐ The accounting rate of return may be used:

1. as a screening measure to ensure that a new investment will not adversely affect accounting income, and
2. because bonuses of managers are often based on accounting income and managers may want to insure that a new investment has a favorable effect on net income (and the manager's bonus).

❐ The disadvantage of the accounting rate of return is that it does not consider the time value of money.

DISCOUNTING MODELS: THE NET PRESENT VALUE METHOD

❐ Discounting models consider the time value of money.

❐ Two discounting models are:

- net present value (NPV)
- internal rate of return (IRR)

❐ When using the net present value method:

- the cash flows for each year are identified

- all cash flows are stated in terms of their present value (discounted), and
- the present values are added together to find the **net present value**.

- The present values are determined using the required rate of return as the discount rate.
- The **required rate of return** is the minimum return that a project must earn in order to be acceptable.
- The cost of capital is often used as the minimum required rate of return. The **cost of capital** is the cost of investment funds, usually viewed as a weighted average of the costs of funds from all sources.
- If net present value is positive, the project's return is greater than the required rate of return or discount rate.

DISCOUNTING MODELS: THE INTERNAL RATE OF RETURN METHOD

- The **internal rate of return** is the interest rate (discount rate) that results in a net present value of zero.
- When net present value equals zero, the present value of the project's cash inflows exactly equals the investment outlay. Therefore, the internal rate of return is the interest rate that equates the present value of the *future* cash flows to the investment.
- If the cash flows are an annuity, the internal rate of return can be determined as follows:
  1. Use the following equation to solve for the discount factor:

     Investment = Annual cash flow × Annuity discount factor

     Annuity discount factor = Investment/Annual cash flow
  2. Find the discount factor under the appropriate number of periods using Exhibit 18B–2 on page 782 of the text and determine the interest rate that corresponds with the discount factor. This is the internal rate of return.
  3. If the discount factor computed falls between two discount factors listed in Exhibit 18B–2, the interest rate can be approximated using interpolation.
- If the cash flows are uneven, the internal rate of return can be determined using trial and error to find the net present value that equals zero or by using a computer program.
- The internal rate of return method assumes that the cash inflows from the project are reinvested to earn a return equal to the internal rate of return for the remaining life of the project.
- The investment should be rejected if the internal rate of return is less than the required rate of return.

POSTAUDIT OF CAPITAL PROJECTS

- A **postaudit** of a capital project compares the actual performance of the project with its expected performance.
- The postaudit might indicate:
  1. corrective action is needed to improve the performance of the project, or
  2. the project should be abandoned.
- Benefits of postaudits include the following:
  1. Postaudits ensure that resources are used wisely.
  2. If managers are held accountable for capital investment decisions, they are more likely to make such decisions in the best interests of the firm.
  3. Postaudits supply feedback to managers that should help improve future decision making.

- Limitations of postaudits include the following:
  1. They are costly to perform.
  2. The original analysis might have been based on assumptions that have been invalidated by changes in the actual operating environment.

MUTUALLY EXCLUSIVE PROJECTS

NPV Compared with IRR

- When NPV and IRR produce different rankings for mutually exclusive projects, the NPV method correctly identifies the best investment alternative.
- Two major differences between NPV and IRR are as follows:
  1. The NPV method assumes that cash flows from the project are reinvested at the *discount rate*. The IRR method assumes that cash flows are reinvested at the *internal rate of return* of the project.
  2. The NPV method measures the profitability of a project in absolute terms (in dollars), whereas the IRR method measures the profitability of a project in relative terms (as a percentage).
- Since the wealth of firm owners are maximized by total dollars of profit earned, not relative profits, NPV should be used when choosing among competing, mutually exclusive projects.
- When evaluating independent projects, a project is acceptable if the NPV is positive.
- When evaluating mutually exclusive projects, the project with the largest NPV is selected.
- The three steps in selecting the best project are as follows:
  1. Determine the cash-flow pattern for each project.
  2. Calculate the NPV of each project.
  3. Identify the project with the greatest NPV.

COMPUTATION AND ADJUSTMENT OF CASH FLOWS

- Two steps in computing the cash flows for capital budgeting are:
  1. forecasting revenues, expenses, and capital outlays, and
  2. converting the pre-tax cash flows to after-tax cash flows.

Adjusting Forecasts for Inflation

- The effects of inflation are considered in NPV analysis by:
  - using a cost of capital that consists of the real rate plus an inflation premium to compensate for the loss in general purchasing power of the dollar.
  - adjusting the operating cash flows for the effects of inflation. For example, revenues might be expected to increase by 8 percent, while costs are expected to increase by 5 percent. Since depreciation is based on actual (historical) costs, it is not affected by inflation.

Conversion of Gross Cash Flows to After-Tax Cash Flows

- After gross cash flows are estimated, they are adjusted for tax effects to determine after-tax cash flows.

After-Tax Cash Flows: Year 0

- The net cash outflow in Year 0 is the difference between the initial cost of the project and any cash inflows associated with the project in Year 0.

- The cost of the project includes:
  - the cost of land
  - the cost of equipment (including transportation and installation)
  - taxes on gains from the sale of old assets
  - increases in working capital
- Cash inflows occurring at the time of acquisition include:
  - tax savings from the sale of old assets
  - cash from the sale of old assets
  - tax benefits, such as investment tax credits
- The net investment can be computed as follows:

Total cost of new machine
– Net proceeds from old machine (net of tax effects)
= Net investment (cash outflow)

After-Tax Cash Flows from Operations: Life of the Project

- After-tax cash flow from operations can be calculated as follows:

After-tax cash flows = After-tax net income + Noncash expenses

Noncash expenses include depreciation and losses.

- The incremental cash flow from operations can be calculated as follows:

Incremental cash inflow from sales
– Incremental cash operating expenses
= Cash flow from operations before taxes
– Income taxes
= Net cash flow from operations after taxes

- After-tax cash flows from operations also can be calculated as follows:

After-tax cash flows = (Pre-tax cash flows)(1 – Tax rate)

Tax Savings from Depreciation

- Depreciation is *not* a cash outflow; however, since depreciation is deductible for tax purposes, it reduces the amount of income taxes a company must pay. For example, assume a company had cash inflows from operations of $100,000 and no deduction for depreciation. The company would pay $34,000 in taxes ($100,000 × 34%). If the company could deduct $10,000 of depreciation on their tax return, the company would pay only $30,600 in taxes.

	Without Depreciation Deduction	With Depreciation Deduction
Cash inflow from operations	$100,000	$100,000
Depreciation	–0–	10,000
Taxable income	$100,000	$ 90,000
Income taxes (34%)	$ 34,000	$ 30,600

$3,400 Tax savings

❒ Another way to calculate the tax savings from depreciation is to multiply the depreciation deduction by the tax rate.

Tax savings from depreciation = Depreciation deduction × Tax rate
= $10,000 × 34%
= $3,400

❒ The amount of depreciation allowed for tax purposes is determined by the tax laws.

❒ The Tax Act classifies personal property (all depreciable business assets other than real estate) into different classes.

Class	Types of Assets
3 years	Most small tools
5 years	Cars, light trucks, and computer equipment
7 years	Most equipment, machinery, and office equipment

❒ Depreciation is calculated using either:

- straight-line, or
- **MACRS (modified accelerated cost recovery system)**.

❒ Both methods produce the same total amount of depreciation over the life of the asset; however, the amount of depreciation claimed each year will differ under the two methods. Both methods use a **half-year convention**. The asset is assumed to be in service for one half of the taxable year it is acquired regardless of when the asset is actually placed in service.

❒ This means 5-year property is depreciated over 6 years and 7-year property is depreciated over 8 years.

❒ MACRS depreciation is calculated by multiplying the cost of the asset by prescribed percentages for each class of asset.

❒ The MACRS depreciation percentages are as follows:

Year	3-Year	5-Year	7-Year
1	33.33%	20.00%	14.29%
2	44.45	32.00	24.49
3	14.81	19.20	17.49
4	7.41	11.52	12.49
5		11.52	8.93
6		5.76	8.92
7			8.93
8			4.46
	100.00%	100.00%	100.00%

❒ Tax savings from depreciation can be calculated as follows:

Tax savings from depreciation = Depreciation deduction × Tax rate
= (Asset cost × MACRS%) × Tax rate

❒ For example, if a company acquires an asset classified as 5-year property for $200,000, the tax savings from depreciation would be calculated as follows:

	Cost	×	Depreciation %	=	Depreciation Deduction	×	Tax Rate[a]	=	Tax Savings
Year 1	$200,000	×	20.00%	=	$ 40,000	×	34%	=	$13,600.00
Year 2	200,000	×	32.00%	=	64,000	×	34%	=	21,760.00
Year 3	200,000	×	19.20%	=	38,400	×	34%	=	13,056.00
Year 4	200,000	×	11.52%	=	23,040	×	34%	=	7,833.60
Year 5	200,000	×	11.52%	=	23,040	×	34%	=	7,833.60
Year 6	200,000	×	5.76%	=	11,520	×	34%	=	3,916.80
					$200,000				

[a]Assume a tax rate of 34 percent.

- Straight-line depreciation per year is calculated as:

Straight-line depreciation = Cost of asset/Class life

- Because the half-year convention is used, only half of the straight-line amount is deducted in the first and the last year.
- For example, if the company acquires 5-year property for $200,000 and if straight-line depreciation is used, the tax savings from depreciation would be calculated as follows:

	Depreciation Deduction	×	Tax Rate	=	Tax Savings
Year 1	$ 20,000[a]	×	34%	=	$ 6,800
Year 2	40,000[b]	×	34%	=	13,600
Year 3	40,000	×	34%	=	13,600
Year 4	40,000	×	34%	=	13,600
Year 5	40,000	×	34%	=	13,600
Year 6	20,000	×	34%	=	6,800
	$200,000				

[a]($200,000/5)(1/2)
[b]($200,000/5)

- For the same investment, the present value of the tax savings from using MACRS is greater than the present value of the tax savings from using straight-line depreciation. Therefore, MACRS results in the higher NPV.

Cash Flow at Disposal

- Under current tax laws, one half of the usual depreciation deduction is allowed in the year of disposal. Using the information from the previous MACRS example, if 5-year property is disposed of in Year 5, the company can deduct $11,520 ($200,000 × 11.52% × 1/2) in the fifth year. If the property is disposed of in Year 6, the company can deduct $5,760 ($200,000 × 5.76% × 1/2) in Year 6.
- The tax basis or book value is the amount still undepreciated.
- If an asset is sold for *more* than its tax basis at the time of disposal, a *gain* results and the company will incur additional taxes.
- If an asset is sold for *less* than its tax basis, a *loss* and tax savings will result.
- For example, if the company in the previous MACRS example sold the 5-year property at the end of the third year for $150,000, the cash flows from the sale would be as follows:

	Calculations	Cash Flows
Selling price	$150,000	$150,000
Tax basis	76,800[a]	
Gain on sale	$ 73,200	
Taxes (34% × gain)		(24,888)
Net cash flow from disposal		$125,112

[a]Tax basis at disposal = Asset cost – Year 1 depreciation – Year 2 depreciation – 1/2 of Year 3 depreciation
= $200,000 – $40,000 – $64,000 – ($38,400 × 1/2)
= $76,800

The $150,000 received for the machine at disposal is a cash inflow.

The $24,888 paid in taxes is a cash outflow.

The net cash inflow at disposal after taxes is $125,112.

Working Capital Investment

- Working capital equals current assets minus current liabilities.
- Capital investment projects often require additional investments in inventories and accounts receivable (working capital accounts).
- The incremental working capital investment will be recovered at a later time.
- Investments in working capital represent an opportunity cost to the firm. The funds invested in working capital could have been used for other purposes.
- Working capital investments are considered in the capital budgeting format by including the investment and recovery amounts at the times when they occur.

CAPITAL INVESTMENT: THE ADVANCED MANUFACTURING ENVIRONMENT

- Companies can realize benefits by:
  - redesigning and simplifying the current manufacturing process
  - automating by adding robotics
  - automating by using flexible manufacturing systems
  - automating by using completely integrated manufacturing systems
  - automating by building *greenfield factories* (new factories designed and built from scratch with a commitment to automation)
- Capital budgeting in the advanced manufacturing environment differs from the traditional approach in the following ways:
  - *Investment.* For standard manufacturing equipment, the direct costs of acquisition represent virtually the entire investment. For automated manufacturing, the direct costs can be as low as 50 percent to 60 percent of the total investment. In addition, software, engineering, training, and implementation costs must be considered as part of the total investment cost.
  - *Estimates of Operating Cash Flows.* Typically, estimates of operating cash flows from investments in standard equipment were based on tangible benefits, such as direct savings from labor, power, and scrap. In the advanced manufacturing environment, it is important to consider intangible and indirect benefits, such as improved quality, greater reliability, improved customer satisfaction, and the ability to maintain or increase market share.

- *Salvage Value.* Because of the uncertainty involved in estimating salvage value, it has often been ignored or heavily discounted. However, salvage value could make the difference between investing and not investing; therefore, a better approach is to use **sensitivity analysis** (calculate the NPV using different salvage values). Being overly conservative with salvage values may result in the rejection of desirable projects.
- *Discount Rates.* In practice, future cash flows are uncertain and managers often compensate for this uncertainty by using a discount rate that is greater than the cost of capital. If the rate selected is excessively high, it biases the selection process toward short-term investments. Because the cash returns of an automated manufacturing system are received over a longer period of time, it is more difficult for automated manufacturing systems to appear acceptable. Being overly conservative with discount rates may result in the rejection of automated manufacturing systems.

KEY TERMS TEST

Test your recall of the key terms as follows. Try to recall as many key terms as possible without assistance. If you need assistance, refer to the list of key terms at the end of this section.

1. The process of determining which long-term capital assets to acquire is referred to as making ________ ________ ________.
2. There are two types of interest. Simple interest is paid each interest period. ________ ________ ________ is interest earned on interest.
3. Future cash flows expressed in present value terms are ________ ________ ________.
4. The factor used to convert a future cash flow to its present value is a(n) ________ ________.
5. ________ ________ is the value that will accumulate by the end of an investment's life if the investment earns a specified compounded return.
6. Projects that, if accepted or rejected, will not affect the cash flows of another project are ________ ________.
7. ________ ________ ________ is the difference between the present value of a project's cash inflows and the present value of its cash outflows.
8. ________ ________ are capital expenditure models that identify criteria for accepting or rejecting projects without considering the time value of money.
9. ________ ________ ________ ________ is the minimum rate of return that a project must earn in order to be acceptable.
10. The ________ ________ ________ ________ is calculated as income divided by the original or average investment.
11. A series of cash flows is a(n) ________.
12. The ________ ________ ________ is the cost of investment funds, usually viewed as a weighted cost of funds from all sources.
13. ________ is the act of finding the present value of future cash flows.
14. A(n) ________ ________ is any capital budgeting model that explicitly considers the time value of money in identifying criteria for accepting or rejecting proposed projects.
15. The ________ ________ is the rate of return used to compute the present value of future cash flows.
16. ________ ________ ________ ________ is the rate of return that equates the present value of a project's cash inflows with the present value of its cash outflows (the NPV equals zero).
17. Projects that, if accepted, preclude the acceptance of competing projects are ________ ________ ________.
18. The time required for a project to return its investment is called ________ ________.
19. ________ ________ is the current value of a future cash flow.

20. __________ is a method of accelerated depreciation permitted by tax law. The depreciation allowed is computed using a modified double-declining-balance method.

21. The _______-_______ ______________ is a tax rule that assumes a newly acquired asset is in service for one-half of the taxable year regardless of when it is actually placed in service.

22. A follow-up analysis of an investment decision is called a(n) _____________.

23. _____________ _____________ is the process of altering certain key variables to assess the effect on the original outcome.

KEY TERMS:

accounting rate of return
annuity
capital investment decisions
compounding of interest
cost of capital
discount factor
discount rate
discounted cash flows
discounting
discounting model
future value
half-year convention
independent projects
internal rate of return
MACRS
mutually exclusive projects
net present value
nondiscounting models
payback period
postaudit
present value
required rate of return
sensitivity analysis

→ **Compare your answers with those at the end of the chapter. Review any key terms missed.**

CHAPTER QUIZ

Write your answers in the spaces provided.

1. Capital expenditure decision models can be classified as nondiscounting models or discounting models. __________________ models consider the time value of money. __________________ models do not consider the time value of money.

2. Two nondiscounting cash flow models are:

   1. ______________________________

   2. ______________________________

3. Two discounting cash flow models are:

   1. ______________________________

   2. ______________________________

4. When the cash flows of a project are the same amount each period, payback is calculated as follows:

   Payback period = _______________________ /_______________________

5. Accounting rate of return is calculated as follows:

   ARR = (____________________ – ____________________)

   / ____________________

6. Present values can be calculated using discount factors and the following formula:

   Present value = ____________________ × ____________________

7. The present value of an annuity can be calculated using an annuity discount factor and the following formula:

   Present value of an annuity = ____________________ × ____________________

8. When NPV and IRR produce different rankings for mutually exclusive projects, the ________ method correctly identifies the best investment alternative.

9. The NPV method assumes that cash flows from a project are reinvested at the ____________________.

10. The IRR method assumes that cash flows from a project are reinvested at the ____________________.

11. The tax savings from depreciation can be calculated as follows:

    Tax savings from depreciation = ____________________ × ____________________

12. For tax purposes, depreciation is calculated using the straight-line method or MACRS. The depreciation deduction using MACRS is calculated as follows:

    MACRS depreciation deduction = ____________________ × ____________________

    Straight-line depreciation per year is calculated as follows:

    Straight-line depreciation = ____________________ / ____________________

Circle the single best answer.

13. Which of the following methods is used as a screening measure to insure that a new investment will not adversely affect income? (a) payback period; (b) accounting rate of return; (c) internal rate of return; (d) net present value

14. Which of the following methods determines the interest rate that equates the present value of the future cash flows with the investment outlay? (a) payback period; (b) accounting rate of return; (c) internal rate of return; (d) net present value

15. Which of the following methods considers the time value of money? (Circle two answers.) (a) payback period; (b) accounting rate of return; (c) internal rate of return; (d) net present value

16. The discount rate is: (a) the rate used to compute payback; (b) the rate used to compute the accounting rate of return; (c) the rate used to compute the internal rate of return; (d) the rate used to compute NPV

17. Discounting: (a) is the process of determining value at a future time; (b) is the process of converting future cash flows to their present value; (c) is a process that does not consider the time value of money; (d) is a process that can only be used for a single amount (not annuities); (e) all of the above

Note: Use the present value factor tables in the text.

18. The present value of $10,000 to be received 5 years from now and earning an annual return of 8% is: (a) $6,210; (b) $6,810; (c) $4,000; (d) $4,693

19. The present value of a 5-year annuity of $10,000, earning an annual return of 8% is: (a) $31,700; (b) $34,700; (c) $37,910; (d) $39,930

Use the following information to answer Questions 20 through 24:

Duane Flowers is considering the purchase of a small business that costs $500,000. The business is expected to generate annual cash inflows of $80,000. Duane plans to operate the business for 15 years and then turn it over to his son. The required rate of return is 10%. Ignore income taxes.

20. Payback for the project is: (a) 6.11 years; (b) 6.25 years; (c) 7.96 years; (d) 8.33 years

21. If depreciation is $25,000 per year, the accounting rate of return based on the initial investment is: (a) 11%; (b) 12%; (c) 16%; (d) 17.2%

22. Using the cost of capital as the discount rate, the net present value of the project is: (a) $89,360; (b) $108,480; (c) $114,680; (d) $228,180

23. The approximate internal rate of return of the project is: (a) 8%; (b) 12%; (c) 12.5%; (d) 14%

24. Based on quantitative factors, should the project be accepted or rejected? (a) accept; (b) reject

25. Depreciation is a cash outflow that should be considered when evaluating capital investments: (a) true; (b) false

26. If an asset is sold for less than its tax basis, a loss results and the company will incur additional taxes: (a) true; (b) false

27. If a company purchases 7-year property for $210,000, the depreciation deduction using the straight-line method would be $30,000 in the first year: (a) true; (b) false

28. If a company had a depreciation deduction of $20,000 and a tax rate of 40%, the company would save $8,000 in taxes: (a) true; (b) false

29. If a company had pre-tax cash inflows from operations of $50,000 and a tax rate of 40%, after-tax cash inflows from operations would be $20,000: (a) true; (b) false

30. Under the Tax Act, cars and light-duty trucks are classified as 3-year property: (a) true; (b) false

31. Most manufacturing equipment is considered 7-year property under the Tax Act: (a) true; (b) false

32. If a company disposes of 5-year property in the fifth year, the company cannot deduct depreciation on the asset in the fifth year: (a) true; (b) false

33. If an asset is sold for more than its tax basis, a gain results and the company will incur additional taxes: (a) true; (b) false

34. For tax purposes, 5-year property is fully depreciated after 5 years: (a) true; (b) false

35. Assuming a tax rate of 34%, if a company sells an asset with a tax basis of $30,000 for $20,000, the net cash flow at disposal would be $10,000: (a) true; (b) false

Use the following information to answer Questions 36 through 40:

The Reelitz Company is considering the purchase of the following production equipment:

Acquisition cost	$400,000
Annual cash inflow from operations	$90,000
Annual operating costs	$30,000
Expected salvage value	$50,000
Cost of capital	14%
Tax rate	34%
Depreciation method	MACRS

The company plans to keep the production equipment for 10 years and then sell it for its salvage value. (Round amounts to dollars.)

36. The MACRS deduction in Year 1 would be: (a) $57,160; (b) $30,600; (c) $17,000; (d) $13,600

37. The tax savings from depreciation in Year 1 would be: (a) $13,600; (b) $19,434; (c) $30,600; (d) $57,160

38. The annual after-tax cash flow from operations would be: (a) $20,400; (b) $30,600; (c) $33,000; (d) $39,600

39. Net after-tax cash flow from the disposal of the equipment at the end of 10 years would be: (a) $17,000; (b) $20,000; (c) $33,000; (d) $50,000

40. The net present value of the project would be: (a) ($66,911); (b) ($72,600); (c) ($96,906); (d) ($39,600)

→ **Compare your answers with those at the end of the chapter. Review any questions missed.**

PRACTICE TEST

PROBLEM 1

A capital investment project requires an investment of $200,000. It has an expected life of five years with annual cash flows of $50,000 received at the end of each year. Ignore income taxes.

Instructions:

1. Compute the payback period for the project.

PROBLEM 1 *(Continued)*

2. Determine the accounting rate of return for the project based on the initial capital investment.

3. Compute the internal rate of return for the project.

4. Compute the net present value of the project using a 6% discount rate.

PROBLEM 2

A capital investment project requires an investment of $50,000 and has an expected life of four years. Ignore income taxes. Annual cash flows at the end of each year are expected to be as follows:

Year	Amount
1	$15,000
2	20,000
3	25,000
4	15,000

Instructions:

1. Compute the payback period assuming that the cash flows occur evenly throughout the year.

2. Determine the accounting rate of return for the project based on the initial investment.

3. Compute the net present value of the project using a 10% discount rate. (Round amounts to dollars.)

PROBLEM 2 *(Continued)*

4. Compute the internal rate of return for the project.

PROBLEM 3

The McEvers Company is considering a capital investment project that requires an investment of $37,910. The project is expected to have annual cash inflows of $10,000 occurring at the end of each of the next five years. Ignore income taxes.

Instructions:

1. Determine the internal rate of return for the project.

PROBLEM 3 *(Continued)*

2. Determine the net present value of the project using discount rates of:

a. 8%

b. 10%

c. 12%

3. What are your observations about the effect the discount rate has upon the project's net present value?

PROBLEM 4

The Martin Company is evaluating two mutually exclusive projects with three-year lives. Each project requires an investment of $10,000. The projects have the following cash inflows received at the end of each year. Ignore income taxes.

Year	Project 1	Project 2
1	$ 2,000	$ 6,000
2	4,000	4,000
3	6,000	2,000
Total	$12,000	$12,000

Instructions:

1. Determine the net present value of each project using an 8% discount rate.

2. What can you conclude about the effect the timing of the cash flows has upon a project's net present value?

PROBLEM 5

Bingham, Inc., is considering two mutually exclusive projects.

Project 1 requires an investment of $100,000, while Project 2 requires an investment of $110,000.

Revenues and costs for each project are shown below:

	Project 1			
Year	1	2	3	4
Revenues	$40,000	$60,000	$70,000	$80,000
Variable costs	10,000	15,000	20,000	20,000
Fixed costs	5,000	5,000	6,000	8,000

	Project 2			
Year	1	2	3	4
Revenues	$60,000	$75,000	$51,000	$45,000
Variable costs	20,000	25,000	17,000	15,000
Fixed costs	7,000	7,000	7,000	8,000

The company estimates that at the end of the fourth year Project 1 would have a salvage value of $20,000 and Project 2 would have a salvage value of $10,000. Ignore income taxes.

Instructions:

Determine the net present value of each project using a 14% discount rate.

PROBLEM 5 *(Continued)*

Use this page to continue your answer.

PROBLEM 6

The Jensen Company is considering a project that requires an investment of $200,000. The project is expected to generate cash flows of $100,000 per year for six years. The cash flows would be received at the end of each year.

The asset is considered five-year property for MACRS depreciation purposes. The asset has no salvage value and would be disposed of on the first day of the seventh year. Assume the required rate of return is 8% and the income tax rate is 34%.

Instructions:

Determine the net present value of the asset. (Round amounts to dollars.)

PROBLEM 6 *(Continued)*

Use this space to continue your answer.

PROBLEM 7

W.A. Hartz & Co. is evaluating a project that requires an investment of $400,000. The property is considered five-year property for MACRS depreciation purposes; however, the company plans to dispose of the property at the end of the fourth year. Salvage value at that time is expected to be $50,000. Information about the cash flows associated with the project is as follows:

Revenues	$250,000 per year
Variable costs	40,000 per year
Fixed out-of-pocket costs	60,000 per year

Assume all the cash flows occur at the end of the year and assume the required rate of return is 12% and the tax rate is 34%.

Instructions:

1. Determine the net present value of the project. (Round amounts to dollars.)

PROBLEM 7 *(Continued)*

Use this page to continue your answer.

PROBLEM 7 *(Continued)*

2. Prepare a memorandum to management with your recommendation regarding whether Hartz should invest in the project.

MEMORANDUM

DATE:

TO:

FROM:

SUBJECT:

PROBLEM 8

Obermark, Inc., presently owns production equipment which it acquired two years ago at a cost of $100,000. The equipment was classified as seven-year property for tax purposes. The equipment is expected to last another five years with a salvage value of $15,000. Annual variable operating costs are $60,000, and fixed out-of-pocket costs are $20,000 per year.

New production equipment could be acquired now at a cost of $120,000. If the new equipment is acquired, the old equipment would be sold now for $70,000. Annual variable operating costs are $40,000, and fixed out-of-pocket costs are $20,000 per year. Salvage value of the new equipment at the end of five years is expected to be $25,000. The new equipment is classified as seven-year property for tax purposes.

Revenues are expected to be $200,000 per year. All operating costs are expected to occur at the end of the year. The cost of capital is 10%.

Assume the assets would be disposed of at the end of the fifth year and Obermark uses MACRS. The tax rate is 34%. Round amounts to dollars.

Instructions:

1. **a.** Compute the net present value of keeping the old equipment.

PROBLEM 8 *(Continued)*

Use this space to continue your answer.

b. Compute the net present value of replacing the old equipment with the new production equipment.

PROBLEM 8 ***(Continued)***

Use this page to continue your answer.

PROBLEM 8 *(Continued)*

2. Prepare a memorandum to management with your recommendation.

MEMORANDUM

DATE:

TO:

FROM:

SUBJECT:

PROBLEM 9

Magic, Inc., is evaluating whether it should use JIT techniques, including the use of manufacturing cells. It is estimated that new equipment costing $2 million would be required. The new equipment would be considered seven-year property for tax purposes, and straight-line depreciation would be used. (Ignore the half-year convention.) The existing manufacturing equipment is fully depreciated for tax purposes and has no salvage value.

JIT manufacturing is estimated to save $400,000 per year resulting from reduced costs for maintenance, inspection, and materials handling. The cost savings would occur over the next 20 years. The tax rate is 40% and the cost of capital is 12%.

PROBLEM 9 *(Continued)*

Instructions:

1. Using straight-line depreciation, calculate the net present value of the investment.

2. Prepare a memorandum to management with your recommendation regarding the new equipment. Include a discussion of any qualitative factors that influenced your recommendation.

MEMORANDUM

DATE:

TO:

FROM:

SUBJECT:

ANSWERS

KEY TERMS TEST

1. capital investment decisions
2. Compounding of interest
3. discounted cash flows
4. discount factor
5. Future value
6. independent projects
7. Net present value
8. Nondiscounting models
9. Required rate of return
10. accounting rate of return
11. annuity
12. cost of capital
13. Discounting
14. discounting model
15. discount rate
16. Internal rate of return
17. mutually exclusive projects
18. payback period
19. Present value
20. MACRS
21. half-year convention
22. postaudit
23. Sensitivity analysis

CHAPTER QUIZ

1. Discounting, Nondiscounting
2. 1. payback period
   2. accounting rate of return
3. 1. net present value
   2. internal rate of return
4. Original investment/Annual cash flow
5. (Average annual net cash inflows – Average annual depreciation)/Investment
6. Future value × Discount factor
7. Future value annuity × Annuity discount factor
8. NPV
9. discount rate
10. internal rate of return
11. Depreciation deduction × Tax rate
12. Asset cost × MACRS%
    Cost of asset/Class life
13. b
14. c
15. c and d
16. d
17. b
18. b ($10,000 × .681) = $6,810
19. d ($10,000 × 3.993) = $39,930
20. b ($500,000/$80,000) = 6.25 years
21. a ($80,000 – $25,000)/$500,000 = 11%
22. b ($80,000 × 7.606) – $500,000 = $108,480
23. d $500,000/$80,000 = 6.25; The present value annuity factor for 15 years and 14% is 6.142; therefore, the internal rate of return is approximately 14%.
24. a
25. b False Depreciation is *not* a cash flow. Depreciation can be deducted for tax purposes resulting in a tax savings and reducing the cash outflow for taxes.
26. b False A loss produces a tax savings, which is viewed the same as a cash inflow.
27. b False Because of the half-year convention, the depreciation deduction would be $15,000 for the first and the eighth year.
28. a True
29. b False After-tax cash inflows from operations would be $30,000 [$50,000 × (1 – .40)].
30. b False Cars and light trucks are classified as 5-year property.
31. a True
32. b False One half of the usual depreciation deduction is allowed in the year of disposal.
33. a True
34. b False Because of the half-year convention, 5-year property is depreciated over 6 years.
35. b False The net cash flow at disposal would be $23,400, calculated as follows:

	Calculations	Cash Flows
Selling price	$ 20,000	$20,000
Tax basis	30,000	
Loss on sale	$(10,000)	
Tax savings (34% × loss)		3,400
Net cash flow from disposal		$23,400

36. a ($400,000 × 14.29%) = $57,160
37. b ($400,000 × 14.29% × 34%) = $19,434
38. d ($90,000 – $30,000) × 66% = $39,600
39. c ($50,000 – $0 book value) = $50,000 gain
    $50,000 × 66% = $33,000 after-tax cash flow

40. c

	0	1	2	3	4	5	6	7	8	9	10
Investment	$(400,000)										
After-tax cash from operations		39,600	39,600	39,600	39,600	39,600	39,600	39,600	39,600	39,600	39,600
Tax savings MACRS:											
$400,000 × 14.29% × 34%		19,434									
$400,000 × 24.49% × 34%			33,306								
$400,000 × 17.49% × 34%				23,786							
$400,000 × 12.49% × 34%					16,986						
$400,000 × 8.93% × 34%						12,145					
$400,000 × 8.92% × 34%							12,131				
$400,000 × 8.93% × 34%								12,145			
$400,000 × 4.46% × 34%									6,066		
Cash flow from disposal											33,000
Totals		59,034	72,906	63,386	56,586	51,745	51,731	51,745	45,666	39,600	72,600
PV factors, 14%		× .877	× .769	× .675	× .592	× .519	× .456	× .400	× .351	× .308	× .270
Present values	303,094	51,773	56,065	42,786	33,499	26,856	23,589	20,698	16,029	12,197	19,602
Net present value	$ (96,906)										

PRACTICE TEST

PROBLEM 1

1. Payback period $= \dfrac{\text{Capital investment}}{\text{Annual cash flow}}$

$= \dfrac{\$200,000}{\$50,000}$

= 4 years

2. Accounting rate of return $= \dfrac{\text{Average annual incremental income}}{\text{Initial capital investment}}$

$= \dfrac{\text{Average annual net cash inflows} - \text{Average annual depreciation}}{\text{Initial capital investment}}$

$= \dfrac{\$50,000 - \$40,000^*}{\$200,000}$

= 5%

*Depreciation = $200,000/5 years = $40,000

3. Internal rate of return:

Use the following equation to solve for the present value factor:

Investment = Annual cash flows × Annuity discount factor
$200,000 = $50,000 × Annuity discount factor

Annuity discount factor = 4

Under 5 years in Exhibit 18B–2 on page 782 of the text, the annuity discount factor of 4 falls between 6% and 8%. The exact IRR can be determined using interpolation:

Discount factor, 6%	4.212	4.212
Discount factor—IRR	4.000	
Discount factor, 8%		3.993
	.212	.219

$$\text{IRR} = 6\% + \left[2\% \times \frac{.212}{.219} \right]$$

= 7.94%

4. Net present value using a 6% discount rate:

Year	Cash Flow Description	Cash Flow Amount	Discount Factor	Present Value
0	Investment	$(200,000)	1.000	$(200,000)
1–5	Cash inflows (annuity)	50,000	4.212	210,600
Net present value				$ 10,600

PROBLEM 2

1. If the cash flows occurred evenly throughout the year, payback would occur in 2.6 years:

Year	Projected Net Cash Inflows
1	$15,000
2	20,000
3	15,000 (.6 × $25,000)
	$50,000

2. $$\text{Average annual net cash inflows} = \frac{\$15{,}000 + \$20{,}000 + \$25{,}000 + \$15{,}000}{4} = \$18{,}750$$

$$\text{Average annual depreciation} = \frac{\$50{,}000}{4 \text{ years}} = \$12{,}500$$

$$\text{ARR} = \frac{\$18{,}750 - \$12{,}500}{\$50{,}000} = 12.5\%$$

3. Net present value:

Year	Cash Flow Description	Cash Flow Amount	Discount Factor	Present Value
0	Investment	$(50,000)	1.000	$(50,000)
1	Operations	15,000	.909	13,635
2	Operations	20,000	.826	16,520
3	Operations	25,000	.751	18,775
4	Operations	15,000	.683	10,245
Net present value				$ 9,175

4. Because the cash flows are uneven, the IRR method must be determined using trial and error. The IRR is the discount rate that results in a NPV of zero.
Since a positive NPV resulted when using 10% discount rate, the IRR must be greater than 10%.

Net present value using 18% discount rate:

Year	Cash Flow Description	Cash Flow Amount	Discount Factor	Present Value
0	Investment	$(50,000)	1.000	$(50,000)
1	Operations	15,000	.847	12,705
2	Operations	20,000	.718	14,360
3	Operations	25,000	.609	15,225
4	Operations	15,000	.516	7,740
Net present value				$ 30

Net present value using 20% discount rate:

Year	Cash Flow Description	Cash Flow Amount	Discount Factor	Present Value
0	Investment	$(50,000)	1.000	$(50,000)
1	Operations	15,000	.833	12,495
2	Operations	20,000	.694	13,880
3	Operations	25,000	.579	14,475
4	Operations	15,000	.482	7,230
Net present value				$ (1,920)

Interpolation:

Present value, 18%	$50,030	$50,030
Investment	50,000	
Present value, 20%		48,080
	$ 30	$ 1,950

$$IRR = 18\% + \left[2\% \times \frac{\$30}{\$1,950} \right]$$

$$= 18.03\%$$

PROBLEM 3

1. Use the following equation to solve for the annuity discount factor:

   Investment = Annual cash flows × Annuity discount factor
   $37,910 = $10,000 × Annuity discount factor

   Annuity discount factor = 3.791

   Under 5 years in Exhibit 18B–2 on page 782 of the text, the annuity discount factor of 3.791 correspond to 10%.

2. a. Net present value using an 8% discount factor:

Year	Cash Flow Description	Cash Flow Amount	Discount Factor	Present Value
0	Investment	$(37,910)	1.000	$(37,910)
1–5	Cash inflows (annuity)	10,000	3.993	39,930
Net present value				$ 2,020

   b. Net present value using a 10% discount factor:

Year	Cash Flow Description	Cash Flow Amount	Discount Factor	Present Value
0	Investment	$(37,910)	1.000	$(37,910)
1–5	Cash inflows (annuity)	10,000	3.791	37,910
Net present value				$ –0–

   c. Net present value using a 12% discount factor:

Year	Cash Flow Description	Cash Flow Amount	Discount Factor	Present Value
0	Investment	$(37,910)	1.000	$(37,910)
1–5	Cash inflows (annuity)	10,000	3.605	36,050
Net present value				$ (1,860)

3. There is an inverse relationship between the discount rate and the NPV. When the discount rate increased, the NPV decreased. Also note that the discount rate of 10% that resulted in an NPV of zero was the IRR calculated in Requirement 2.

PROBLEM 4

1. Net present value of Project 1:

Year	Cash Flow Description	Cash Flow Amount	Discount Factor	Present Value
0	Investment	$(10,000)	1.000	$(10,000)
1	Operations	2,000	.926	1,852
2	Operations	4,000	.857	3,428
3	Operations	6,000	.794	4,764
Net present value				$ 44

Net present value of Project 2:

Year	Cash Flow Description	Cash Flow Amount	Discount Factor	Present Value
0	Investment	$(10,000)	1.000	$(10,000)
1	Operations	6,000	.926	5,556
2	Operations	4,000	.857	3,428
3	Operations	2,000	.794	1,588
Net present value				$ 572

2. Since money has a time value, the sooner the money will be received, the greater the present value will be.

PROBLEM 5

Schedule of cash flows for Project 1:

Year	Revenues	Variable Costs	Fixed Costs	Salvage Value	Total Cash Flow
1	$40,000	$(10,000)	$(5,000)		$25,000
2	60,000	(15,000)	(5,000)		40,000
3	70,000	(20,000)	(6,000)		44,000
4	80,000	(20,000)	(8,000)	$20,000	72,000

Net present value of Project 1:

Year	Cash Flow Description	Cash Flow Amount	Discount Factor	Present Value
0	Investment	$(100,000)	1.000	$(100,000)
1	Operations	25,000	.877	21,925
2	Operations	40,000	.769	30,760
3	Operations	44,000	.675	29,700
4	Operations and Salvage value	72,000	.592	42,624
Net present value				$ 25,009

Schedule of cash flows for Project 2:

Year	Revenues	Variable Costs	Fixed Costs	Salvage Value	Total Cash Flow
1	$60,000	$(20,000)	$(7,000)		$33,000
2	75,000	(25,000)	(7,000)		43,000
3	51,000	(17,000)	(7,000)		27,000
4	45,000	(15,000)	(8,000)	$10,000	32,000

Net present value of Project 2:

Year	Cash Flow Description	Cash Flow Amount	Discount Factor	Present Value
0	Investment	$(110,000)	1.000	$(110,000)
1	Operations	33,000	.877	28,941
2	Operations	43,000	.769	33,067
3	Operations	27,000	.675	18,225
4	Operations and Salvage value	32,000	.592	18,944
Net present value				$ (10,823)

PROBLEM 6

Schedule of cash flows:

Year	After-tax Cash Inflow from Operations (1 – .34)($100,000)	Tax Savings from Depreciation[a]	Total Cash Flow
1	$66,000	$13,600	$79,600
2	66,000	21,760	87,760
3	66,000	13,056	79,056
4	66,000	7,834	73,834
5	66,000	7,834	73,834
6	66,000	3,917	69,917

[a]Tax savings from depreciation:

	Cost		Depreciation Percentage		Depreciation Deduction		Tax Rate		Tax Savings
Year 1	$200,000	×	20.00%	=	$40,000	×	34%	=	$13,600
Year 2	$200,000	×	32.00%	=	$64,000	×	34%	=	$21,760
Year 3	$200,000	×	19.20%	=	$38,400	×	34%	=	$13,056
Year 4	$200,000	×	11.52%	=	$23,040	×	34%	=	$7,834
Year 5	$200,000	×	11.52%	=	$23,040	×	34%	=	$7,834
Year 6	$200,000	×	5.76%	=	$11,520	×	34%	=	$3,917

Net present value:

Year	Cash Flow Description	Cash Flow Amount	Discount Factor	Present Value
0	Investment	$(200,000)	1.000	$(200,000)
1	Operations	79,600	.926	73,710
2	Operations	87,760	.857	75,210
3	Operations	79,056	.794	62,770
4	Operations	73,834	.735	54,268
5	Operations	73,834	.681	50,281
6	Operations	69,917	.630	44,048
Net present value				$ 160,287

PROBLEM 7

1. Schedule of cash flows:

Year	After-tax Cash Inflow from Operations (1 – .34)($250,000 – $40,000 – $60,000)	Tax Savings from Depreciation[a]	Disposal[b]	Total Cash Flow
1	$99,000	$27,200		$126,200
2	99,000	43,520		142,520
3	99,000	26,112		125,112
4	99,000	7,834	$64,334	171,168

[a]Tax savings from depreciation:

	Cost		Depreciation Percentage		Depreciation Deduction		Tax Rate		Tax Savings
Year 1	$400,000	×	20.00%	=	$80,000	×	34%	=	$27,200
Year 2	$400,000	×	32.00%	=	$128,000	×	34%	=	$43,520
Year 3	$400,000	×	19.20%	=	$76,800	×	34%	=	$26,112
Year 4	$400,000	×	11.52% × 1/2	=	$23,040*	×	34%	=	$7,834

*One half of the usual amount of depreciation can be deducted in the year of disposal.

[b]Net after-tax cash flow from the disposal is calculated as follows:

	Calculations	Cash Flows
Selling price	$ 50,000	$50,000
Tax basis*	92,160	
Loss on sale	$(42,160)	
Tax savings (34% × Loss)**		14,334
Net cash flow from disposal		$64,334

*($400,000 – $80,000 – $128,000 – $76,800 – $23,040 = $92,160)

**A loss can be offset against other income, thereby reducing the amount of tax the company must pay.

Net present value:

Year	Cash Flow Description	Cash Flow Amount	Discount Factor	Present Value
0	Investment	$(400,000)	1.000	$(400,000)
1	Operations	126,200	.893	112,697
2	Operations	142,520	.797	113,588
3	Operations	125,112	.712	89,080
4	Operations and Disposal	171,168	.636	108,863
Net present value				$ 24,228

2. A sample memo is shown below:

MEMORANDUM

DATE: *(insert current date here)*

TO: W.A. Hartz & Co. Management

FROM: Management Consulting, Inc.

SUBJECT: Evaluation of Capital Budgeting Project

This memo regards your request for an evaluation of the capital budgeting project under consideration. Based on the information given, the project is acceptable because the project's return is greater than the required return of 12 percent. This is indicated by a positive net present value. (See attached calculations.)

Other factors to consider when evaluating this capital budgeting project include:

- the reliability of the estimates used
- the quality of the product produced
- environmental concerns
- customer satisfaction with the product
- competition and the market for the product

If you have any questions regarding the capital budgeting analysis, please contact me. We hope that we can serve your consulting needs in the future.

PROBLEM 8

1. a. Net present value of keeping old equipment

Schedule of cash flows:

Year	After-tax Cash Inflow from Operations (1 – .34)($200,000 – $60,000 – $20,000)	Tax Savings from Depreciation[a]	Disposal[b]	Total Cash Flow
1	$79,200	$5,947		$85,147
2	79,200	4,247		83,447
3	79,200	3,036		82,236
4	79,200	3,033		82,233
5	79,200	1,518	$12,934	93,652

[a]Tax savings from depreciation:

	Cost		Depreciation Percentage		Depreciation Deduction		Tax Rate		Tax Savings
Year 1	$100,000	×	17.49%*	=	$17,490	×	34%	=	$5,947
Year 2	$100,000	×	12.49%	=	$12,490	×	34%	=	$4,247
Year 3	$100,000	×	8.93%	=	$8,930	×	34%	=	$3,036
Year 4	$100,000	×	8.92%	=	$8,920	×	34%	=	$3,033
Year 5	$100,000	×	8.93% × 1/2	=	$4,465	×	34%	=	$1,518

*The equipment was acquired 2 years ago, therefore in Year 1 of the analysis the MACRS percentage is 17.49%.

[b]Net after-tax cash flow from the disposal is calculated as follows:

	Calculations	Cash Flows
Selling price	$15,000	$15,000
Tax basis*	8,925	
Gain on sale	$ 6,075	
Taxes on gain (34% × Gain)		(2,066)
Net cash flow from disposal		$12,934

*Remaining amount not depreciated = [(1/2 × 8.93%) + 4.46%] × $100,000
= $8,925

Note that the original cost of the equipment incurred 2 years ago is not included because it is a sunk cost. Depreciation for the first two years is not shown in the previous table.

Net present value:

Year	Cash Flow Description	Cash Flow Amount	Discount Factor	Present Value
1	Operations	$85,147	.909	$ 77,399
2	Operations	83,447	.826	68,927
3	Operations	82,236	.751	61,759
4	Operations	82,233	.683	56,165
5	Operations and Disposal	93,652	.621	58,158
Net present value				$322,408

b. Net present value of replacing the old equipment with new production equipment

Schedule of cash flows:

Year	After-tax Cash Inflow from Operations (1 – .34)($200,000 – $40,000 – $20,000)	Tax Savings from Depreciation[a]	Disposal[b]	Total Cash Flow
1	$92,400	$5,830		$ 98,230
2	92,400	9,992		102,392
3	92,400	7,136		99,536
4	92,400	5,096		97,496
5	92,400	1,822	$27,424	121,646

[a]Tax savings from depreciation:

	Cost		Depreciation Percentage		Depreciation Deduction		Tax Rate		Tax Savings
Year 1	$120,000	×	14.29%	=	$17,148	×	34%	=	$5,830
Year 2	$120,000	×	24.49%	=	$29,388	×	34%	=	$9,992
Year 3	$120,000	×	17.49%	=	$20,988	×	34%	=	$7,136
Year 4	$120,000	×	12.49%	=	$14,988	×	34%	=	$5,096
Year 5	$120,000	×	8.93% × 1/2	=	$5,358	×	34%	=	$1,822

[b]Net after-tax cash flow from the disposal is calculated as follows:

	Calculations	Cash Flows
Selling price	$25,000	$25,000
Tax basis*	32,130	
Loss on sale	$ (7,130)	
Taxes savings (34% × Loss)		2,424
Net cash flow from disposal		$27,424

*($120,000 – $17,148 – $29,388 – $20,988 – $14,988 – $5,358)

Net present value:

Year	Cash Flow Description	Cash Flow Amount	Discount Factor	Present Value
0	Investment	$(120,000)	1.000	$(120,000)
0	Disposal of old equipment[c]	71,178	1.000	71,178
1	Operations	98,230	.909	89,291
2	Operations	102,392	.826	84,576
3	Operations	99,536	.751	74,752
4	Operations	97,496	.683	66,590
5	Operations and Disposal	121,646	.621	75,542
Net present value				$ 341,929

[c]Disposal of old equipment is calculated as follows:

	Calculations	Cash Flows
Selling price	$70,000	$70,000
Tax basis*	73,465	
Loss on sale	$ (3,465)	
Taxes on loss (34% × Loss)		1,178
Net cash flow from disposal		$71,178

*Tax basis = [$100,000 – ($100,000 × 14.29%) – ($100,000 × 24.49% × 1/2)]
= $100,000 – $14,290 – $12,245
= $73,465

Based upon the information given, the company should buy the new equipment because it has a higher NPV.

2. A sample memo is shown below:

MEMORANDUM

DATE: *(insert current date here)*
TO: Obermark, Inc. Management
FROM: Management Consulting, Inc.
SUBJECT: Evaluation of Production Equipment Replacement

This memo relates to your request regarding the evaluation of the replacement of production equipment. Based on the quantitative information given, I recommend that Obermark, Inc., purchase the new equipment because the new equipment results in a higher rate of return.

The net present value of keeping the current equipment is $322,408 and the net present value of replacing the current equipment is $341,929. Although both have positive net present values (indicating a return greater than the cost of capital of 10 percent), the new equipment has a *higher* return.

Qualitative factors to consider are the possibility the new equipment would produce a higher-quality or improved product, the ease of operation, and possible reluctance to replace equipment that is only two years old.

We appreciate the opportunity to assist you in evaluating this project and look forward to assisting you again in the future.

PROBLEM 9

1.

Investment	$(2,000,000)
Tax savings: Depreciation [($2,000,000/7) × 40% × 4.564]	521,600
After-tax cost savings ($400,000 × 60% × 7.469)	1,792,560
Net present value	$ 314,160

2. Your memorandum should contain the following information:

The quantitative analysis indicates that the project has a return in excess of the cost of capital of 12 percent. Therefore, from a financial viewpoint, the project should be accepted. Qualitative factors to consider include the possibility of the new equipment producing an improved or higher-quality product, greater production flexibility, and competitive advantages.

CHAPTER 19
Inventory Management

CHAPTER REVIEW

TRADITIONAL INVENTORY MANAGEMENT

Inventory Costs

- If inventory consists of goods purchased from an outside supplier, the two inventory-related costs are:
  - ordering costs, and
  - carrying costs.
- If inventory consists of goods produced internally, the two inventory-related costs are:
  - setup costs, and
  - carrying costs.
- **Ordering costs** are the costs of placing and receiving an order. Examples include the clerical costs of processing an order, the cost of insurance for shipment, and unloading costs.
- **Setup costs** are the costs of preparing equipment and facilities for production. Examples include wages of idled production workers, lost income from idled production facilities, and the costs of test runs (labor, materials, and overhead).
- **Carrying costs** are the costs of carrying inventory, such as storage and handling costs, the opportunity cost of funds invested in inventory, and insurance and taxes on the inventory.
- Since both ordering costs and setup costs are costs of acquiring inventory, they are treated in the same manner.
- **Stockout costs** are the costs associated with having insufficient amounts of inventory. Stockout costs include:
  - lost sales (both current and future)
  - costs of expediting (overtime or increased transportation costs)
  - costs of interrupted production

Traditional Reasons for Holding Inventory

- Traditional reasons for holding inventories are:
  - to balance ordering or setup costs and carrying costs
  - to satisfy customer demand (meet delivery dates)
  - to avoid shutting down manufacturing facilities due to machine failure, defective or unavailable parts, and/or late delivery of parts.
  - to buffer against unreliable production processes
  - to take advantage of discounts
  - to hedge against future price increases

Economic Order Quantity: The Traditional Inventory Model

- An inventory policy addresses two questions:
  - How much inventory should be ordered (or produced)?
  - When should the order be placed (or the setup performed)?

Order Quantity and Total Ordering and Carrying Costs

- The order quantity used should minimize the total cost of ordering and carrying inventory.

$$\text{Total cost} = \text{Ordering cost} + \text{Carrying cost}$$
$$= PD/Q + CQ/2$$

where P = the cost of placing and receiving an order (or the setup cost for a production run)
D = the known annual demand
Q = quantity (the number of units ordered each time an order is placed or the lot size for a production run)
C = the cost of carrying one unit of stock for one year

- The **economic order quantity** is the order quantity that minimizes the total cost.

Computing EOQ

- The economic order quantity is calculated as:

$$EOQ = \sqrt{2PD / C}$$

- The EOQ is the order size that results in ordering costs equaling carrying costs.
- The economic order quantity model can also be used to determine the most economical size of a production run. The only difference is that setup costs for starting a production run are substituted for ordering costs.

Reorder Point

- The **reorder point** is the point at which a new order should be placed (or a setup started).
- The reorder point equals the amount of inventory that will be used from the time the order is placed until it arrives.
- **Lead time** is the time required to receive an order once it is placed (or a setup is initiated). The reorder point (ROP) is calculated as follows:

$$\text{ROP} = \text{Rate of usage} \times \text{Lead time}$$

- **Safety stock** is extra inventory that serves as a cushion for preventing stockouts. Safety stock is calculated as follows:

$$\text{Safety stock} = (\text{Maximum usage} - \text{Average usage}) \times \text{Lead time}$$

- With safety stock, the reorder point becomes:

$$\text{ROP} = (\text{Average rate of usage} \times \text{Lead time}) + \text{Safety stock}$$

EOQ and Inventory Management

- The traditional approach to inventory management is called a *just-in-case system.*
- The traditional manufacturing environment uses mass production of a few standardized products that typically have a very high setup cost. The high setup cost encourages a large batch size and long production runs. Diversity is viewed as being costly and is avoided.

JIT INVENTORY MANAGEMENT

- Competitive pressures have led many firms to abandon the EOQ model in favor of a just-in-time (JIT) approach to manufacturing and purchasing. JIT offers increased cost efficiency and simultaneously has the flexibility to respond to customer demands for better quality and more variety.

Basic Features of JIT

- **JIT (just-in-time) manufacturing** is a demand-pull system. Products are produced only when demanded by customers.
- **JIT purchasing** occurs when parts and materials arrive just in time to be used in production.
- Two strategic objectives of JIT are:
  - to increase profits, and
  - to improve a firm's competitive position.
- JIT pursues continuous improvement by eliminating waste and nonvalue-added activities. Nonvalue-added activities are either unnecessary, or necessary but inefficient and improvable. Necessary activities that are performed efficiently are essential to the business and/or are of value to customers.
- JIT can:
  - reduce inventory levels because production is geared to demand
  - improve quality
  - increase productivity
  - reduce lead time
  - reduce setup time
  - lower manufacturing costs
  - increase production rates
- Differences between JIT and traditional manufacturing are summarized on page 382.
- Under JIT's manufacturing cell structure, all the processes necessary for the production of a single product are collected in one area.
- The costs of operating the manufacturing cell are all directly traceable to the product produced.
- JIT challenges the traditional reasons for holding inventory and uses other solutions to the problems.

Setup and Carrying Costs: The JIT Approach

- The traditional approach takes setup costs as given and then tries to minimize total carrying costs and setup costs.
- JIT attempts to reduce setup costs (or ordering costs) by:
  - reducing the time it takes to set up for production, and
  - reducing the number of orders through long-term contracting.
- If setup and ordering costs are insignificant, the only remaining cost to minimize is carrying cost, which is minimized by reducing inventories to insignificant levels.

Manufacturing Systems

	JIT	Traditional
System:	■ pull-through system based on demand	■ push-through system
Inventory effects:	■ suppliers deliver parts just in time to be used in production ■ uses a few suppliers with long-term contracts	■ higher levels of inventory than JIT ■ inventory used as a buffer because of delayed reaction time ■ greater number of suppliers with short-term contracts
Plant layout:	■ **manufacturing cells** consist of a set of machines that produce a particular product or product family ■ multiskilled labor where workers are trained to operate all machines within the cell ■ requires less space and reduces lead times	■ departmental structure with machines performing similar functions are located together in a department ■ specialized labor where workers operate a specific machine
Grouping of employees:	■ service departments providing support services, such as materials stores, are reassigned to work with manufacturing cells ■ cell workers perform more of support services, such as setup and preventive maintenance	■ service departments providing support services are centralized ■ a central stores location handles materials ■ a central purchasing department places all purchase orders for materials
Employee empowerment:	■ increased employee participation, which increases productivity and cost efficiency ■ input from employees is sought ■ managers act as facilitators to develop people and skills	■ less participation by employees in management of organization ■ managers act as supervisors
Total quality control:	■ poor quality cannot be tolerated without inventories ■ quest for defective-free products	■ **acceptable quality level (AQL)** permits defects to occur as long as they do not exceed a certain level
Traceability of overhead costs:	■ uses more direct tracing of overhead costs and less driver tracing and allocation ■ use of manufacturing cells results in more costs being directly traceable to products	■ relies more on driver tracing and allocation

LONG-TERM CONTRACTS, CONTINUOUS REPLENISHMENT, ELECTRONIC DATA INTERCHANGE, AND JIT II

- **Continuous replenishment** is a system in which a manufacturer assumes the inventory management function for the retailer, telling the retailer when and how much stock to reorder.
- **Electronic data interchange (EDI)**, an early form of e-commerce, allows suppliers access to a buyer's on-line database, permitting the supplier to deliver needed inventory just in time for use.
- JIT II purchasing carries the JIT partnership arrangement to an even higher level. JIT II involves the supplier's sales representative working on site at the customer's facility while being paid by the supplier. On site 100% of the time, the in-plant representative provides continuous supplier support. Such arrangements may include *evergreen contracts*, long-term contracts with no end date.

Due-Date Performance: The JIT Solution

- In the past, finished goods inventories have been used to ensure a firm's ability to meet a requested delivery date.
- JIT uses shorter lead times to meet requested delivery dates and to respond quickly to the demands of the market.
- JIT reduces lead time by:
  - reducing setup times
  - improving quality, and
  - using manufacturing cells to reduce travel distance between machines and inventory.
- Most companies experience at least a 90 percent reduction in lead times when they implement JIT.

Avoidance of Shutdown and Process Reliability: The JIT Approach

- Most shutdowns occur because of one of three reasons:
  - machine failure
  - defective material or subassembly
  - unavailability of material or subassembly
- The traditional solution to the above problems is to hold inventory.
- JIT solves the problems by emphasizing:
  - **total preventive maintenance** to reduce machine failures. Cell workers perform preventive maintenance during idle manufacturing time, thereby reducing downtime for unexpected repairs.
  - total quality control to reduce defective materials or subassemblies. The goal is zero defects.
  - the right kind of a relationship with suppliers to ensure the availability of material or subassemblies.

Total Quality Control

- The problem of defective parts is solved by striving for total quality control (zero defects).

The Kanban System

- The Kanban system is used to ensure that parts or materials are available when needed.

- The **Kanban system** is an information system that uses markers or cards to control production.
- The basic Kanban system uses three Kanban cards:
  - a **withdrawal Kanban**, which specifies the quantity that a subsequent process should withdraw from a preceding process
  - a **production Kanban**, which specifies the quantity that the preceding process should produce
  - a **vendor Kanban**, which indicates to the supplier the quantity of materials to deliver and the time of delivery
- The use of Kanbans ensures that the subsequent process withdraws the necessary quantity from the preceding process at the appropriate time. The Kanban system also controls the preceding process by allowing it to produce only the quantities withdrawn by the subsequent process. In this way, inventories are kept at a minimum, and the components arrive just in time to be used.

Discounts and Price Increases: JIT Purchasing versus Holding Inventories

- Traditionally, inventories are held so that a firm can take advantage of quantity discounts and hedge against future price increases.
- JIT uses long-term contracts with a few chosen suppliers who are selected based on price, quality, and reliability.
- Benefits of long-term contracts include:
  - they stipulate prices
  - they stipulate quality levels
  - they reduce the number of orders placed, thereby reducing ordering costs

JIT's Limitations

- Sharp reductions in inventory when implementing JIT may cause high levels of stress in workers.
- JIT may result in shortages and lost sales, as there is no inventory buffer.

THEORY OF CONSTRAINTS

- The theory of constraints (TOC) recognizes that the performance of any organization is limited by its **constraints** of limited resources and limited demand.
- TOC focuses on three objectives:
  - *Increasing throughput.* **Throughput** is the rate at which an organization generates money through sales.
  - *Minimizing inventory.* **Inventory** is the money spent in turning materials into throughput.
  - *Decreasing operating expenses.* **Operating expenses** are defined as the money spent in turning inventories into throughput.

TOC Steps

- The organization wants to produce the optimal product mix given the firm's constraints. The TOC inventory system is often called the **Drum-Buffer-Rope (DBR) System**. There are five steps to improve performance by managing constraints:
  1. Identify the organization's constraint(s).
     - **External constraints** are limiting factors from external sources (such as market demand).

- **Internal constraints** are limiting factors found within the firm (such as machine-time availability).
- **Loose constraints** are constraints whose limited resources are not fully used by a product mix.
- **Binding constraints** are constraints where all the resources available are fully utilized.
- Identify the one binding internal constraint. Determine the product mix to produce using the *contribution margin per unit of scarce resource* as the critical factor.
- Consider any external binding constraints on the product mix.

2. Exploit the binding constraint(s).
   - The major binding constraint is called the *drummer* (setting the drumbeat for the entire plant). The drummer constraint's production rate sets the production rate for the entire plant.
   - A **time buffer** is the inventory needed to keep the constrained resource (drummer) busy for a specified period of time. In scheduling, the operation immediately preceding the drummer constraint should produce the parts needed by the drummer resource for a specified period of time (inventory or *time buffer*).
   - **Ropes** tie the rate at which materials are released into the plant's first operation to the production rate of the drummer constraint. The drummer rate controls the rate at which the first operation produces.
3. Subordinate everything else to the decisions made in Step 2.
4. Elevate the binding constraint(s). Use a program of continuous improvement to reduce the limitations that the binding constraint(s) have on the organization's performance. For example, add a shift to the drummer constraint to create more machine time.
5. Repeat the process. Improve the drummer constraint until the new drummer constraint is identified. Then repeat the TOC process.

KEY TERMS TEST

Test your recall of the key terms as follows. Try to recall as many key terms as possible without assistance. If you need assistance, refer to the list of key terms at the end of this section.

1. ________ ________ is the time to receive an order once placed or the time to produce a product from start to finish.

2. ______________ ________ are the costs of placing and receiving an order.

3. __________ __________ is extra inventory that serves as a cushion for preventing stockouts.

4. ______________ ________ are costs of preparing equipment and facilities so that they can be used for production.

5. The point in time at which a new order (or setup) should be initiated is the ____________ _________.

6. ______________ ________ are the costs of holding inventory.

7. ______________ ________ ____________ or ________ is the amount that should be ordered (or produced) to minimize the total ordering (or setup) and carrying costs.

8. ______________ ________ are the costs of insufficient inventory.

9. An information system that controls production on a demand-pull basis through the use of cards or markers is a(n) ____________ ____________.

10. A card or marker that specifies the quantity that the preceding process should produce is a(n) _________________ ____________.

11. A card or marker that signals to a supplier the quantity of materials that need to be delivered and the time of delivery is a(n) _________________ ____________.

12. A marker or card that specifies the quantity that a subsequent process should withdraw from a preceding process is a(n) _________________ ____________.

13. _________ __________________ __________________ has a goal of zero machine failures.

14. _____________ is the money an organization spends in turning materials into throughput.

15. _____________ _____________ are the money an organization spends in turning inventories into throughput.

16. _______________ _______ ______________ or _______ is an inventory management method that allows suppliers access to a buyer's on-line database.

17. A system in which a manufacturer assumes the inventory management function for the retailer is called ______________ ___________________.

18. ________________ is the rate at which an organization generates money through sales.

19. A mathematical expression that expresses a resource limitation is a(n) ________________.

20. Constraints whose resources are fully utilized are ____________ ________________.

21. Constraints whose limited resources are not fully used by a product mix are ____________ ________________.

22. __________ ______________ are limiting factors imposed on the firm from external sources (such as market demand).

23. __________ ______________ are limiting factors found within the firm (such as machine time availability).

24. A(n) ________-________-________ __________ is the TOC inventory management system that relies on the drumbeat of the major constrained resource, time buffers, and ropes to determine inventory levels.

25. A(n) ______ __________ is the inventory needed to keep the constrained resource busy for a specified time interval.

26. _________ are actions taken to tie the rate at which material is released into the plant (at the first operation) to the production rate of the constrained resource.

27. ______________________ _________ consist of a set of machines that produce a particular product or product family.

28. ________ _____________________ is a demand-pull system that strives to eliminate waste by producing a product only when it is needed and in quantities demanded by customers.

29. ________ ____________________ is a purchasing method that requires suppliers to deliver parts and materials just in time to be used in production.

KEY TERMS:

binding constraints
carrying costs
constraints
continuous replenishment
Drum-Buffer-Rope System
economic order quantity (EOQ)
electronic data interchange (EDI)
external constraints
internal constraints
inventory
JIT manufacturing
JIT purchasing
Kanban system
lead time
loose constraints
manufacturing cells
operating expenses
ordering costs
production Kanban
reorder point
ropes
safety stock
setup costs
stockout costs
throughput
time buffer
total preventive maintenance
vendor Kanban
withdrawal Kanban

→ **Compare your answers with those at the end of the chapter. Review any key terms missed.**

CHAPTER QUIZ

Write your answers in the spaces provided.

1. If inventory consists of goods purchased from an outside supplier, the two inventory-related costs are:

   1. ______________________
   2. ______________________

2. If inventory consists of goods produced internally, the two inventory-related costs are:

   1. ______________________
   2. ______________________

3. Three examples of carrying costs are:

   1. ______________________
   2. ______________________
   3. ______________________

4. The economic order quantity is the order size that results in ______________ equaling ______________. It is the order quantity that minimizes total inventory costs.

5. The reorder point is the point at which a new order should be placed. The reorder point is calculated as:

   ROP = ______________ × ______________

6. Safety stock serves as a cushion for preventing ______________.

7. If safety stock is carried, the reorder point is calculated as:

   ROP = (______________ × ______________) + ______________

8. List three reasons why companies have traditionally held inventory:

   1. ______________________
   2. ______________________
   3. ______________________

9. When JIT is used, cell workers perform ______________ during idle time.

10. When JIT manufacturing is used, suppliers are selected based upon:

    1. ______________________
    2. ______________________
    3. ______________________

11. Benefits of using long-term contracts with suppliers include:

    1. ______________________
    2. ______________________
    3. ______________________

12. Complete the following:

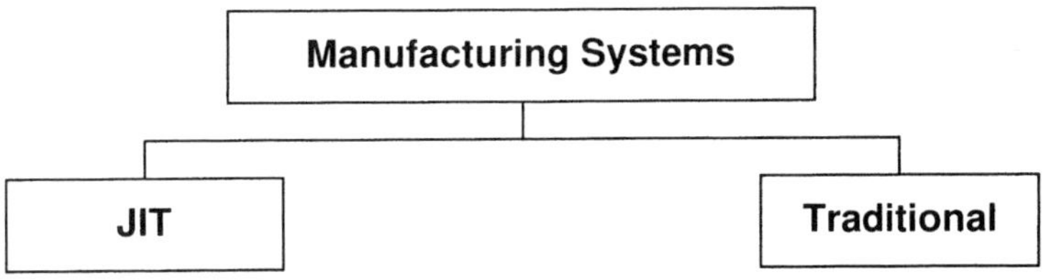

System:		
Inventory effects:		
Plant layout:		
Grouping of employees:		
Employee empowerment:		
Total quality control:		
Traceability of overhead costs:		

→ **Compare your answers with those at the end of the chapter. Review any questions missed.**

PRACTICE TEST

PROBLEM 1

Instructions:

Below are listed five reasons why companies have traditionally held inventory. Indicate the JIT solution for each of the reasons for holding inventory.

Traditional Approach	JIT Approach
1. Hold inventories to minimize total carrying costs and setup costs.	______________
2. Use inventories to insure the firm meets delivery dates and avoids stockouts.	______________
3. Hold inventory in case there is a shutdown due to machine failure.	______________
4. Hold inventory to avoid shutdowns due to defective parts.	______________
5. Hold inventory to take advantage of quantity discounts and hedge against future price increases.	______________

PROBLEM 2

The Till Company manufactures a special blend of tea. The company buys one of the spices used in the tea in 10-pound bags that cost $5 each. The company uses 50,000 of the bags per year, and usage occurs evenly throughout the year.

The average cost to carry a 10-pound bag in inventory per year is $1, and the cost to place an order is $12.

Instructions:

1. Determine the economic order quantity for the spice in terms of 10-pound bags.

2. If the company works 250 days per year, on the average how many bags of spice are used per working day?

3. If the lead time for an order is normally 5 working days, determine the reorder point.

4. If the company normally carries 50 bags as safety stock, determine the reorder point for the spice.

PROBLEM 3

Smith Manufacturing produces lawn mowers. In order to produce the frames for the mowers, special equipment must be set up. The setup cost per frame is $50. The cost of carrying frames in inventory is $4 per frame per year. The company produces 10,000 mowers per year.

Instructions:

1. Compute the number of frames that should be produced per setup in order to minimize total setup and carrying costs.

2. Compute the total setup and carrying costs associated with the economic order quantity.

PROBLEM 4

Craig Corporation produces two types of products, A and B. Product A has a unit contribution margin of $50, and Product B has a unit contribution margin of $100. Product A uses 1 hour of grinding time, and Product B uses 4 hours of grinding time. There are 200 hours of grinding time available per week. This is the only constrained resource.

Instructions:

1. **a.** Determine the optimal mix.

   b. What is the total contribution margin?

2. Assume that market conditions will allow the sale of only 100 units of each product.

   a. Determine the optimal mix.

   b. What is the total contribution margin?

ANSWERS

KEY TERMS TEST

1. Lead time
2. Ordering costs
3. Safety stock
4. Setup costs
5. reorder point
6. Carrying costs
7. Economic order quantity, EOQ
8. Stockout costs
9. Kanban system
10. production Kanban
11. vendor Kanban
12. withdrawal Kanban
13. Total preventive maintenance
14. Inventory
15. Operating expenses
16. Electronic data interchange, EDI
17. continuous replenishment
18. Throughput
19. constraint
20. binding constraints
21. loose constraints
22. External constraints
23. Internal constraints
24. Drum-Buffer-Rope System
25. time buffer
26. Ropes
27. Manufacturing cells
28. JIT manufacturing
29. JIT purchasing

CHAPTER QUIZ

1. 1. ordering costs
   2. carrying costs
2. 1. setup costs
   2. carrying costs
3. 1. storage and handling costs
   2. the opportunity cost of funds invested in inventory
   3. insurance and taxes on the inventory
4. ordering costs, carrying costs
5. Rate of usage × Lead time
6. stockouts
7. (Average rate of usage × Lead time) + Safety stock
8. 1. to balance ordering or setup costs and carrying costs
   2. to satisfy customer demand
   3. to avoid shutdowns

   (There are other possible correct answers.)
9. preventive maintenance
10. 1. price
    2. quality
    3. reliability
11. 1. They stipulate prices.
    2. They stipulate quality levels.
    3. They reduce the number of orders placed, thereby reducing ordering costs.
12. See page 382.

PRACTICE TEST

PROBLEM 1

1. Reduces setup costs and then minimizes inventory carrying costs.
2. Reduces lead time by reducing setup time and uses manufacturing cells to reduce distance between machines.
3. Uses total preventive maintenance to reduce downtime for unexpected repairs.
4. Uses total quality control and strives for zero defects.
5. Uses long-term contracts with a few suppliers to obtain price concessions and a reliable supply.

PROBLEM 2

1. $EOQ = \sqrt{2PD / C}$

   where EOQ = economic order quantity
   P = cost of placing and receiving an order
   D = annual demand in units
   C = annual cost of carrying one unit in stock for one year

   $EOQ = \sqrt{(2)(\$12)(50{,}000) / \$1}$
   $= 1{,}095$ bags

   The economic order quantity is 1,095 bags of spice.

2. Bags used per day = 50,000 bags used per year/250 working days
= 200 bags per working day

The Till Company would use an average of 200 bags of spice per working day.

3. Reorder point = Rate of usage × Lead time
= 200 bags × 5 working days
= 1,000 bags

4. Reorder point = (Average rate of usage × Lead time) + Safety stock
= (200 bags × 5 working days) + 50 bags
= 1,050 bags

Problem 3

1. $EOQ = \sqrt{(2)(\$50)(10{,}000) / \$4}$

$EOQ = 500$

In order to minimize costs, 500 frames should be produced per setup.

2. Total setup costs = ($50)(10,000/500)
= $1,000

Total carrying costs = ($4)(500/2)
= $1,000

The EOQ results in total setup costs equaling total carrying costs.

Problem 4

1. a. Contribution margin per scarce resource:
Product A: $50/1 hour = $50 per hour of grinding time
Product B: $100/4 hours = $25 per hour of grinding time
Optimal mix: 200 units of Product A

b. Total contribution margin:
200 hours grinding time/1 hour per unit of Product A = 200 units of Product A
200 units × $50 contribution margin per unit = $10,000

2. a. Optimal mix:
Product A: 100 units
Product B: 25 units
200 hours – (100 units × 1 hour) = 100 hours available
100 hours available/4 hours per unit = 25 units of Product B

b. Total contribution margin:

100 units of Product A × $50 =	$5,000
25 units of Product B × $25 =	625
	$5,625